Transcending Taboos

Transcending Taboos

A moral and psychological examination of cyberspace

Garry Young and Monica T. Whitty

Routledge
Taylor & Francis Group

LONDON AND NEW YORK

First published 2012
by Routledge
27 Church Road, Hove, East Sussex BN3 2FA

Simultaneously published in the USA and Canada
by Routledge
711 Third Avenue, New York NY 10017

*Routledge is an imprint of the Taylor and Francis Group, an informa
business*

British Library Cataloguing in Publication Data
A catalogue record for this book is available from the British Library

Library of Congress Cataloging in Publication Data
Young, Garry, 1966–
    Transcending taboos: a moral and psychological examination of
cyberspace / Garry Young, Monica Whitty.
        p. cm.
    Includes bibliographical references and index.
    ISBN 978–0–415–57933–9 (hardback) – ISBN 978–0–415–57936–0
(softcover)   1. Virtual reality–Moral and ethical aspects.   2. Cyberspace–
Moral and ethical aspects.   3. Virtual reality–Psychological aspects.
4. Cyberspace–Psychological aspects. I. Whitty, Monica T., 1969–
II. Title.
    HM851.Y57 2012
    170′.44028567–dc23

                                                            2011034394

ISBN: 978–0–415–57933–9 (hbk)
ISBN: 978–0–415–57936–0 (pbk)
ISBN: 978–0–203–12676–9 (ebk)

Typeset in Times
by RefineCatch Limited, Bungay, Suffolk
Cover design by Andrew Ward

MIX
Paper from
responsible sources
FSC
www.fsc.org   FSC® C004839

Printed and bound in Great Britain by
TJ International Ltd, Padstow, Cornwall

Contents

PART 3
Psychological parity and changes to the self

Acknowledgements

Some of the material in this book has been published previously by the authors in the following articles:

Whitty, M.T. (2003). Cyber-flirting: Playing at love on the Internet. *Theory and Psychology*, *13*, 339–357.

Whitty, M.T. and Carr, A.N. (2003). Cyberspace as potential space: Considering the web as a playground to cyber-flirt. *Human Relations*, *56*, 861–891.

Whitty, M.T. and Carr, A.N. (2005). Taking the good with the bad: Applying Klein's work to further our understandings of cyber-cheating. *Journal of Couple and Relationship Therapy*, *4*, 103–115.

Whitty, M.T., Young, G., and Goodings, L. (2011). What I won't do in pixels: Examining the limits of taboo violation in MMORPGs. *Computers in Human Behavior*, *27*, 268–275.

Young, G. (2010). Virtually real emotions and the paradox of fiction: Implications for the use of virtual environments in psychological research. *Philosophical Psychology*, *23*, 1–21.

Young, G. and Whitty, M.T. (2010). Games without frontiers: On the moral and psychological implications of violating taboos within multi-player virtual spaces. *Computers in Human Behavior*, *26*, 1228–1236.

Young, G. and Whitty, M.T. (2010). In search of the Cartesian self: An examination of disembodiment within 21st century communication. *Theory and Psychology*, *20*, 209–229.

Young, G. and Whitty, M.T. (2011). Progressive embodiment within cyberspace: Considering the psychological impact of the supermorphic persona. *Philosophical Psychology*, *24*, 537–560.

Young, G. and Whitty, M.T. (2011). Should gamespace be a taboo-free zone? Moral and psychological implications for single-player video games. *Theory and Psychology*, *21*, 802–820.

1 Introduction

The phrase *transcending taboos* is designed to capture the essential aim of this book, which is to examine not so much what a taboo is but how one copes with the appearance of recognized offline taboos within different virtual spaces, although our focus is ultimately multiplayer gamespace. Does one's attitude towards a given taboo transcend spaces, particularly between on- and offline worlds? And how does one manage or cope with what one experiences, or how one feels, when encountering putative taboo violation, especially within the context of a game or when otherwise at play? Moreover, what system should we use to police and ultimately decide the permissibility of offline taboos within cyberspace?

It is our contention that contemplating whether a particular virtual representation is or should be 'taboo' and therefore morally prohibited is to consider the wrong sort of question. Instead, a more pertinent measure of permissibility is not whether *x* is right or wrong, or good or bad, but whether, psychologically, we can cope with what is being represented or enacted within a given virtual space. Permissibility should therefore be informed by a greater understanding of the *psychological* impact of encountering taboos online, rather than the morality of the virtual act itself.

The purpose of this book is to present evidence and argument in support of this claim. We accept, however, that, in an attempt to do this, the book raises a number of questions, not all of which are answered to the extent that we would like or are indeed answerable at present. This is largely owing to the paucity of research relating directly to the issue of taboos within cyberspace. Whilst recognizing this fact, we nevertheless consider what *is* discussed, and therefore the arguments and evidence that are presented, to be useful in informing future empirical research by providing a clearer conceptual framework out of which we hope will emerge testable hypotheses.

PART 1: SHOULD CYBERSPACE BE A SPACE WHERE, VIRTUALLY, ANYTHING IS PERMISSIBLE?

In Part 1 we consider the issue of permissibility within cyberspace: what kinds of representation, expression and interaction should be allowed and, conversely, what (if any) should not. Of course, we recognize and reiterate throughout the book that cyberspace is not a homogeneous space. In fact, this forms the main theme of Chapter 2, which considers the contingent relation that exists between a given space and what that space affords in terms of representation and interaction. Permissibility is inherently evaluative and so one may feel entitled to question whether what is deemed permissible within a given space should be based on judgements that stem from a moral (even legal) system that is contingent on a different space (e.g. our offline world). To illustrate: it is relatively commonplace within virtual space to represent oneself in ways that differ more or less from one's physical appearance, including gender. Should this be permitted? Some may consider such an act to be harmless, even playful; others might question the individual's motives for doing this. Equally, in certain spaces, one can represent oneself as a serial killer and/or rapist, and engage in these (virtual) activities. This would not be permissible offline and the degree to which it should be permissible online is contentious. Virtual killing/murder is much more common than virtual rape, for example, with the former seemingly more acceptable than the latter: but why is this? Should we in fact distinguish between virtual activities that are equally prohibited offline, permitting one but not the other? Might each be judged as equally harmless or playful? Should they be?

In Chapter 3, we consider the role of disgust as a measure of moral wisdom or moral fallibility. Disgust is often elicited in the presence of taboos; so it is within the context of symbolic or virtual taboos that we evaluate the appropriateness of disgust as a measure of what should be permissible or not within cyberspace. In Chapter 4, we discuss the relation between disgust and obscenity, and consider different definitions of obscenity (specifically those of the United States [US] and the United Kingdom [UK]). We also consider obscenity across different virtual spaces and question whether a virtual image, which is not itself a representation of anything offline, could be (or indeed should be) classified as obscene.

In Chapter 5, we engage with what we call the *passive voyeur* – the Internet spectator who views images of real-life events (photographs, video recordings) online. We speculate over the extent to which the voyeur is in fact passive, and ultimately the permissibility of their actions – questioning whether one could ever view images judged to be taboo offline within a virtual space free from moral condemnation. As part of our discussion, we consider whether images with a purely virtual genesis might constitute just such a permissible image of a taboo event. If this is the case, then any expression of disgust towards such an image might be construed as an example of moral fallibility. However, for such an emotional response (disgust) to be deemed genuine, we must first overcome the challenge presented by the *paradox of fiction* – the claim that a genuine emotional response cannot be elicited from a character/event known to be fictitious (or virtual).

In Chapter 6, we present the paradox of fiction, and consider its applicability to virtual space. We also present arguments supporting the view that emotional responses elicited within a virtual environment, despite the threat posed by the paradox of fiction, are indeed genuine. We therefore provide a valid basis for the question: If interactions with fictitious characters/events can elicit genuine emotions then how might one cope with the sort of emotion elicited by taboo activity within cyberspace? This is a question that we attempt to answer in the chapters that follow. In addition, characters/events with a purely virtual genesis are most commonly found in video games or role-playing spaces like *Second Life*. It can be argued that these spaces are essentially playful spaces. In fact, one might wish to extend this claim to the majority of cyberspace – holding that it is essentially a virtual playground.

This view is taken up in Chapter 7, where we introduce theories of play and consider the psychological ramifications of engaging in play that involves, potentially, symbolic taboo activities (STAs). In fact, in Chapters 8 and 9, we discuss STAs in relation to single- and multiplayer gamespace, using examples of actual and hypothetical video and online games (hereafter, simply 'video games' unless otherwise stated). We return to the issue of permissibility within these spaces of altered contingencies, and ask: If it is permissible to engage in STAs such as murder and torture, even cannibalism, then why should it not be equally permissible to engage in STAs that feature rape, paedophilia, necrophilia or even incest? After all, it is just a game!

In sum, throughout Part 1, we provide evidence and arguments to support the view that in spaces with altered contingencies, where representations and actions within those spaces have a strictly virtual genesis, moral prohibition or permissibility, if they are to occur, must stem from a moral system born of those spaces, constitutive of the same altered contingencies. As such, moral questions that stem from a system of morality born of our offline world, that concern the permissibility of certain virtual acts, are the wrong sorts of questions to be asking. Instead, we should look to that which transcends the online and offline space – namely, the individual. How is he or she able to cope, psychologically, with the potentially greater moral freedoms afforded within cyberspace? To help address this question, we must examine the nature and authenticity of representations of selves and experiences of embodiment within cyberspace.

PART 2: THE NATURE AND AUTHENTICITY OF SELVES WITHIN CYBERSPACE

Part 2 is concerned with the different ways in which one may present and experience oneself within cyberspace. In Chapter 10, we consider early claims by Internet theorists that cyberspace afforded the realization of a kind of Cartesian ideal whereby one was able to experience one's self as disembodied. A closer examination of interactions within cyberspace reveals, however, that we typically express ourselves as embodied in one form or other; and although we may escape the physical body within cyberspace, embodiment *per se* remains a feature of who we are and how we present and experience ourselves.

In Chapter 11, we move away from the idea of disembodiment and consider different theories of the embodied self as applied to virtual environments. Here, we again utilize the notion of altered contingencies and examine more closely the array of possible selves afforded by cyberspace, and how these might be considered as more or less authentic representations of one's self by others as well as oneself. In Chapter 12, we develop the idea of embodiment further and introduce the notion of *progressive embodiment*. How might our representation and experience of self progress as a product of the altered contingencies of a given space, and how might this require us to reconfigure our understanding of authenticity of selfhood within or across different spaces? Answers to these questions impact on our sense of psychological parity, we contend, as we try to maintain a sense of self across different spaces with potentially different representations and experiences of the embodied selfhood, or even as we attempt to compartmentalize different selves in relation to these different spaces.

PART 3: PSYCHOLOGICAL PARITY AND CHANGES TO THE SELF

Part 3 begins in Chapter 13 with an overview of research that has looked at the consequences of playing violent video games, often relating to behavioural changes – most commonly, aggression – but also changes in affect and cognition. Chapter 13 also includes leading theories/models proffered to explain aggression, which have been applied to those who play violent video games. In Chapter 14, we consider a more fundamental process that might explain why some players of violent games are affected more than others, behaviourally, cognitively or in terms of changes in affect. This process we call *psychological parity*. Chapters 14 and 15 consider the importance of identification with one's virtual self to the question of psychological parity and how one copes with the potential differences in one's embodied appearance, or how one acts in these different spaces, especially when engaged in or witnessing STAs. In addition, we draw on empirical evidence detailing gamers' views on STAs before, finally, in Chapter 16, proffering informed considerations and hopefully some direction for future research, which looks at the effect of changes brought about by the process of maintaining psychological parity across spaces and across different representations of self.

Part 1

Should cyberspace be a space where, virtually, anything is permissible?

2 Virtual immediacy

Altered contingencies, altered possibilities

It might be said of cyberspace that it is a space constrained only by the limits of technology and imagination; and although this constraint is permanent, it is nevertheless fluid. Consequently, within these acknowledged parameters, cyberspace really does appear to be a space where, virtually, anything is possible. Such a claim is far from hyperbolic, but neither is it literally true; for there are, of course, some obvious exceptions. Even in cyberspace, it is necessarily the case that I am not at the same time all black and all white; neither can I be a married bachelor, or own a four-sided triangle. Two plus two must still equal four, and if all virtual men are mortal and virtual and Socrates is a man, then he too must be mortal.

Logical contradictions that exist in our offline world must be adhered to within cyberspace; if they are not, then they should (necessarily) be as incomprehensible in virtual space as they are within the space we typically occupy. On the other hand, where a relation is contingent, there exists the possibility for change: for things to be other than they are. This is the scope of cyberspace. It is perfectly feasible, for example, in a given space for virtual telephones to have wings – the ultimate mobile phone! In this space, I might even present myself as a member of the opposite sex, or as more or less able-bodied than I actually am, or even as a half-man/half-beast hybrid. Alternatively, I may simply choose to present myself as myself. It is also possible, and not uncommon, to travel in virtual worlds almost instantaneously. One moment I am located in one part of my virtual world, the next I have travelled a vast virtual distance to some other part (e.g. *Entropia Universe*). Having arrived at my new destination, it may be that I can just as easily adopt the role of superhero as supervillain, and engage in acts of saintliness or depravity, or perhaps something in between.

ALTERED CONTINGENCIES AND VIRTUAL IMMEDIACY

In this chapter, we present the case for cyberspace as a space of altered contingencies – that is, as a space where things can be other than they are in our offline world because the contingent relations that exist in a given virtual space have been altered (i.e. the rules and costumes of a space that govern how we interact, or even the nature of the environment and our embodiment within it, are all potentially different). To illustrate, take the online game *City of Heroes* (http://eu.cityofheroes.com/en/). In this space, one is invited to be a superhero or supervillain and, if the words of the game's homepage are to be believed, protect 'all that is good and just' or 'leave a trail of fear and chaos everywhere'. Equally, as a would-be player, I am asked to consider whether I am 'the brutish type wanting to be in the middle of the action', or prefer 'to fire deadly attacks ... from afar' or whether 'slicing and dicing' is something I consider 'a good time'. Alternatively, in a different space, more of a *sandbox* environment, where one is less constrained by the rules of a game (e.g. *Second Life*), one may wish to appear as a 'furry' (an anthropomorphic feline, canine, lupine, animal hybrid) or, borrowing an example from Boellstorff (2008) of two heterosexual men, decide to maintain an online relationship as the other's lesbian lover.

What these examples illustrate is that, within cyberspace, not only does there exist the possibility for altered contingencies – for things to be other than they are offline (which is not in and of itself unique to cyberspace) – but also for this change in environment, embodiment and governance to be potentially, perhaps even typically, more far-reaching and more immediate than seems possible offline: a phenomenon we call *virtual immediacy*.

Virtual immediacy captures not only the scope of cyberspace in terms of the immediacy of the ontological transformation from offline to online world, but also transformations across the different virtual worlds within cyberspace itself. (Later in this chapter, we will define how we intend to use the term 'cyberspace', as well as related terms such as 'virtual reality' and 'virtual environment'.) Moreover, accompanying the immediacy of these (virtual) transformations in environment, embodiment and governance is the possibility of *experiential* change that is likewise much more immediate and far-reaching than that typically found offline. My experience of my virtually embodied self may be as someone with enhanced physical prowess, for example, or special skills, perhaps even with heightened charisma and sex appeal. These characteristics are not something I necessarily need to develop over time (although in certain spaces this may be the case); rather, with relative ease, and a little knowledge of how to customize my avatar (or whatever means of presentation I choose to employ), I can have a presence in cyberspace with almost immediate effect. It is also possible (even likely) that how I choose to present myself will reflect some aspect of the altered contingencies constitutive of a given space (in Chapter 12 we discuss this possibility in terms of the potential for 'progressive embodiment'). Of course, divergent 'spaces' existed long before the advent of virtual technology and continue to exist today; indeed, in these non-virtual spaces one can also be different selves (Gergen, 1991). This we accept. What the term 'virtual immediacy' aims to convey is the speed of accessibility we have to these many divergent spaces, which, when coupled with the altered contingencies afforded by the virtual, provide the *potential* for a shift in environment, embodiment, governance (including personal attitude and moral code) and experience of some magnitude.

In effect, through virtual immediacy and the altered contingencies of a given space, to borrow from Manovich (2001), cyberspace functions much like a portal into another world where every computer user has the potential to become like Carroll's *Alice*. Or, to paraphrase Castronova (2006): within the virtual worlds of cyberspace, like nowhere on Earth, one has the freedom to be whomever or whatever one wishes to be. Thus, if you do not like a particular aspect of the cyberworld you are in, you can either change the contingency relation to suit what you do like, or find another virtual space in which this contingency already holds. One advantage of cyberspace over our offline world, then, is that a change to the contingency relation is more immediately obtainable. A view shared by Turkle (1995, p. 185) when describing multi-user dungeons or domains (MUDs), an earlier form of text-based role-playing game:

> MUDs can be places where people blossom or places where they get stuck, caught in self-contained worlds where things are simpler than in real life, and where, if all else fails, you can retire your character and simply start a new life with another.

Of course, as already alluded to, altered contingencies do not have to be restricted to role-playing games. Whitty and Carr (Whitty, 2003a; Whitty and Carr, 2003; 2006a) argue that cyberspace offers a multitude of safe spaces for the shy and socially anxious to explore who they are, as well as spaces where those who are unsure of their sexual preferences can explore various aspects of their sexuality. They note, for example, that some individuals intentionally take on different personas in cyberspace (e.g. gender switching) in order to be able to express hidden 'truths' about themselves. Whitty (2002) suggests that one of the benefits of gender switching for men is that it can enable them to disclose emotional aspects of themselves that, in other spaces, they may feel socially prohibited from doing. In fact, research has shown that self-disclosure in general increases when engaged in computer-mediated communication compared to face-to-face dialogue (Bargh, *et al.*, 2002; Henderson and Gilding, 2004; Joinson, 2001; Schouten *et al.*, 2007, 2009; Tidwell and Walther, 2002; see also Suler's, 2004, study on the *online disinhibition effect*).

Yet who we are within cyberspace is but one aspect of this possibility for change (this virtual immediacy). As acknowledged above (with passing reference to altered rules, costumes and governance), the way we represent others and the actions we carry out or permit to occur to ourselves and to others are also based on altered contingencies. Whitty and Gavin (2001, p. 629), in their study on chat rooms, found that white lies, 'paradoxically, opened a space for a deeper level of engagement with others'. This is illustrated in the following two interview extracts:

> *You can never be sure that anyone you talk to on the Net is telling the truth so there's very little trust. That can work both ways because you're free to be whatever you like, which means you're not intimidated by what people think.*
> (17-year-old male)

> *You also lose the ability to be able to judge people's honesty effectively. It's a lot easier to do that in person, um, but there's a certain advantage to it. You lose your inhibitions, your insecurities. You can talk a lot more easily to people. It's a bit of an even cut of pros and cons.* (29-year-old male)
>
> (Whitty and Gavin, 2001, p. 629)

Whitty and Gavin argue that because of the altered contingencies of this space, lying about how one physically appears (something that is very difficult to manipulate face to face) can allow an individual to experience what it feels like to be physically attractive. Take, for example, the person in the following extract who created a new attractive persona for himself in a chat room:

> *They all think I'm a six foot tall tanned lifesaver. I tell them certain things that are true, but other things are bull****. I mean, I can get away with it so why not? What they don't know won't hurt them. I will admit that I am pretty sly when it comes to smooth talking certain ladies on the Net and if it means lying to get to second base then go for it.* (22-year-old male)
>
> (Whitty and Carr, 2001, p. 629)

Our moral attitudes, which typically accompany and often police our own behaviour or how we judge the behaviour of others, are themselves a product of a contingency relation (see Chapter 3). Just as cyberspace affords the potential for a whole host of altered contingencies (of interactions and representations), so it likewise provides spaces in which we can adopt a whole host of moral attitudes. Some of these might permit us to engage in offline taboo activities whilst in a particular virtual space – i.e. the albeit cartoonish video game *Cannibal Warrior* (http://www.pulptoon.com/warrior/) in which one can play the role of an 'Amazon warrior' who, we are told, must 'battle dangerous foes' and capture girls in order to 'serve them up for dinner' (see Chapter 8). Or, away from the gaming world, one may wish to visit shock sites like *ogrish.com* (or *realogrish* as it is now) and view captured moments of uncensored reality (see Chapter 4). More recently, a site has emerged – *Chatroulette* – where it is possible to randomly connect to other site users at the touch of a button. Users may communicate by text, audio or, more likely, webcam connection. The traffic was originally uncensored and, in the words of Slattery (2010, p. 1), became 'infamous for genital exposure'.[1]

MORAL AMBIGUITY ACCOMPANYING THE POSSIBILITY FOR CHANGE

The point of these examples is to illustrate that different spaces afford different representations of self and others, and different interactions: such is the scope of cyberspace proliferated through the phenomenon of virtual immediacy. The altered contingencies and moral ambiguities of cyberspace are alluded to by Ducheneaut (2010) when discussing multiplayer online environments, particularly games (environments that will similarly be a focus of much discussion within this book). As Ducheneaut (2010, p. 144) notes:

> [O]nline games are not just carbon copies of the real world. They are societies in their own right, capable of evolving their own norms and cultures. Some (but not all) of these indigenous cultures will be influenced by the way the software is architected, which permits certain actions and prevents others. When using online worlds to understand human behavior, it is important to define and isolate these 'game laws' as much as possible if any generalizability is to be achieved. But of course, one could always simply consider the worlds to be interesting 'sui generis', and simply study them as fully-fledged social worlds in their own right, without immediately attempting any parallel with offline environments.

One of the aims of this book, then, is to consider the means by which we evaluate the possibility for change afforded by cyberspace. One approach is to conduct a moral inquiry whereby we ask whether a system of morality that is structured around the contingencies of this world is able to transcend domains when, in countless spaces in countless virtual worlds, these contingencies are different, or is it that each world is *sui generis*? To help address this question, we will examine the extent to which our moral values transcend offline and online worlds (a descriptive account) and the extent to which they should be permitted to do so (a normative account). The moral values of interest to this book are those surrounding taboos. Discussion will therefore focus on whether taboos are context dependent, so as to match the contingent nature of the interactions available within a given space – one possible outcome being to render certain virtual spaces *taboo-free zones* – at least in terms of any adherence to offline taboos. Alternatively, it may be that our attitudes towards taboos necessarily transcend worlds because, along with our wider sense of morality, they guide those actions, attitudes and values which themselves transcend worlds. What these actions, attitudes and values are, and why they are (if indeed they are) able to make this transition, will also be discussed.

What we hope to show in Part 1, however, through a detailed discussion of these issues, is that when evaluating the possibility for change afforded by cyberspace, questions regarding the morality of a given virtual action or representation are the wrong sorts of questions to ask. Instead, a more fruitful line of inquiry is to consider the impact of cyberspace, including the moral freedoms afforded by certain virtual spaces, on the *psychology* of the individual (see Parts 2 and 3). In order to justify this claim, we need to show why an evaluation of the changes afforded by cyberspace is better informed by a greater understanding of the psychology involved in the transition across spaces than by the application of a system of morality imported from one (offline) world into another. This is ultimately the goal of this book.

To help illustrate some of these issues, consider the much-discussed and somewhat infamous example of virtual rape (the 'Mr Bungle affair'), which occurred in 1992 in LambdaMOO (see Dibbel, 1993, and also Turkle, 1995, for a more detailed account). The rape occurred within the context of one of the original text-based multiplayer role-playing games (MUDs). In this space, individuals took on the role of a character and moved about interconnected rooms. Numerous people were connected at the same time. The rooms and objects in LambdaMOO were created by the users themselves. As the story goes, Mr Bungle was a character that Turkle (1995, p. 251) describes as 'an oleaginous, Bisquick-faced clown dressed in cum-stained harlequin garb and girdled with a mistletoe-and hemlock belt whose buckle bore the inscription "KISS ME UNDER THIS BITCH" '. This player masqueraded as another player's character by using a MUD programming technique often referred to as a 'voodoo doll'. The Mr Bungle character used the voodoo doll to force another character to perform sexual acts on him. Even when he was ejected from the room, he was able to continue his 'sexual assaults' by getting one character to swallow their own pubic hair and making another attack herself sexually with a knife. The act caused much upset for the community, with one of the characters who was 'assaulted' calling out for 'civility' and 'virtual castration', whilst others maintained that it was only a game and therefore rape should be allowed.

We will have more to say on this incident and related examples in later chapters. What it highlights in relation to this chapter, however, is the moral ambiguity, or certainly the potential for moral ambiguity, surrounding different virtual spaces, as well as the fact that although there appears to be a normative element implicit within these spaces, not all agree on what this is or, indeed, should be. For some members of the LambdaMOO community, for example, virtual rape *should* be allowed; for others, it *should not*. Either way, this involves a normative judgement. The normative element evident within our own inquiry therefore requires a re-working of an earlier assertion. It is not our aim to consider whether cyberspace is a space where, virtually, anything is possible; rather, we are interested in the question: Should cyberspace be a space where, virtually, anything is *permissible*?

The focus throughout this book is on online taboos – what we refer to as *symbolic taboo activities* (STAs) – and the effect that STAs have on individuals who either engage in or witness them. The altered contingencies within virtual spaces also raise questions about the authenticity of self within and across these spaces and, ultimately, the psychological impact of STAs and/or altered representations of self on the individual. Is virtual immediacy and the potential freedoms afforded the self psychologically healthy? Consideration of this question will be postponed until Parts 2 and 3. In Part 1, we concern ourselves with whether cyberspace should be a space where, virtually, anything is permissible, and the extent to which *moral* judgements are appropriate when deciding on the permissibility of actions/representations within cyberspace.

DEFINING CYBERSPACE

What should be evident from the discussion so far is that we are not treating cyberspace as a unitary space. We recognize that cyberspace contains disparate spaces, which have the potential to be as far removed from each other as they are from our offline world, or as close. We also recognize that the term 'cyberspace' is open to interpretation; and the diversity of its meaning is matched only by the technology used in its creation. Furthermore, we accept that the line between what is virtual and what is real is somewhat nebulous and that a *strict* dichotomy between offline and online 'worlds' or the real and the virtual is at best ill-informed and controversial, and at worst simply false (see Lehdonvirta, 2010, for a recent discussion on this issue). When discussing the virtual world of *Cybercity*, for example, Carter (2005, p. 160) notes how it is 'both embedded in, and an integral part of, its inhabitants' daily lives'; so much so that, for many, it 'is often just another place to meet friends. . . . In this respect, cyberspace is no longer distinct and separate from the real world' (p. 164). Whilst accepting this fact, we neverthe-less recognize that some working definition of cyberspace is required before we proceed further, and some contrast made between it and the diversity of spaces that we commonly refer to as the 'real' or 'offline' world. After all, the interac-tions that occur within these different spaces may be, or at least have the potential to be, quite different, even if a strict dichotomy cannot be, or should not be, enforced. In the final part of this chapter, then, we outline what we mean by cyber-space and how we intend terms such as 'virtual reality', 'virtual environment' and the 'Internet' to relate to it.

It was, of course, William Gibson who first coined the term 'cyberspace' in his futuristic novel, *Neuromancer* (Gibson, 1984). Since then, there has been much debate over how this medium should be defined and conceptualized. Whitty (2003a, p. 343), for example, has argued that 'cyberspace is the space generated by software within a computer that produces a virtual reality'. An alternative view, she suggests, is that it existed before the origins of the Internet, in the form of telephone calls or even the telegraph (Standage, 1998). Stratton (1997, p. 29) has suggested that cyberspace should be understood essentially 'as the space produced by human communication when it is mediated by technology in such a way that the body is absent'. In fact, a broad definition of cyberspace encompasses not only computer-generated virtual space, but also the spaces created by works of fiction, or even by such everyday communication as text messaging and the telephone (see Whitty and Carr, 2006a, for an in-depth discussion). As Feather-stone and Burrows (1995, p. 5) note:

> [C]yberspace is best considered as a generic term which refers to a cluster of different technologies, some familiar, some only recently available, some being developed and some still fictional, all of which have in common the ability to simulate environments within which humans can interact.

In addition, often synonymous with cyberspace are terms such as '*virtual reality*' and '*virtual environment*', each of which is used interchangeably in much of the thinking and literature on the subject. Schroeder (2006, p. 439), for example, describes a virtual environment as providing users 'with the sensory experience of being in a place other than the one [they] are physically in, and being able to interact with that place'. Here, the *environment within which humans can interact,* which is a characteristic of Featherstone and Burrows' (1995) definition, is refined to include the *sensory* experience of *being in a place other than their physical location*. A further useful distinction is made by Parés and Parés (2006), who distinguish between virtual environments (VEs), which they define as static structures, and virtual reality (VR), which constitutes the structures of VEs put into action. The two are interrelated in so far as 'VR is a real time experience a user can have of a VE' (Parés and Parés, 2006, p. 528).

Throughout this book, cyberspace will be used synonymously with VE, both of which are taken to represent the medium through which the subject is able to experience an *embodied interactive* VR, which constitutes a sensory experience of being somewhere other than where they are physically located (however, see Chapter 10 for a discussion on the possibility of experiential *disembodiment* within cyberspace). In addition, on occasion we will distinguish between immersive and non-immersive VEs. An immersive environment is that which 'surrounds the body, often engulfing the senses' (Biocca, 1997, p. 11), and is achieved through the use of 'immersive technology' such as stereoscopic helmets, data gloves and even body suits – devices that 'are designed to establish a certain kind of interaction with the human body, focusing especially on its external sensory and motoric apparatus' (Lisewski, 2006, p. 202). In contrast, non-immersive environments typically include such relatively commonplace interactive spaces as dating sites, social networking sites and discussion boards, as well as online role-playing games (although we do acknowledge that, with the increase of accessibility and portability, even these spaces have a more immersive feel; something that will no doubt increase in the future). The fictional objects used to elicit a VR experience may on occasion represent actual objects that exist in the 'real' world (an actual location or person, for example) but need not. Finally, the term 'Internet' will be used synonymously with 'cyberspace' unless otherwise stated.

To conclude, the purpose of this chapter was to introduce the phenomenon of virtual immediacy and the idea of cyberspace as constitutive of a diversity of spaces with altered contingency relations. The possibilities afforded by these altered contingencies impact on the way we choose to present ourselves and represent others in this space, as well as the manner of our interactions. Altered contingencies also afford altered morality, with the possibility of spaces that are, at their most extreme, taboo-free zones in so far as they potentially permit the occurrence of anything that is considered taboo offline (the aforementioned STAs). As noted earlier, it is our contention that the permissibility of actions and/or representations should be based on psychology rather than morality. In Part 1, then, we begin in earnest the groundwork to support this claim. As the activities we are interested in relate to STAs, our measure of permissibility will commence with an exploration of our sense of disgust. Thus, in Chapter 3 we introduce the issue of moral disgust and consider whether it is an appropriate measure of morality within the context of cyberspace, and therefore across the divergent spaces available on the Internet. In short, should a disgust response to virtual images and events representing offline taboos be taken as a sign of moral wisdom or moral fallibility?

3 Disgust

A measure of moral wisdom or moral fallibility?

In this chapter we examine the relationship between disgust and taboos. We consider whether feeling disgust, in the context of cyberspace and STAs, should be used as a measure of moral wisdom, such that what is found to be 'disgusting' or to elicit a disgust response is correctly deemed to be bad or wrong, or whether the association between disgust and wrongness is in fact evidence of moral fallibility and hence symptomatic of a system of morality that has been imported from one space into another with a completely different (potentially incompatible) set of contingency relations.

THE RELATIONSHIP BETWEEN TABOOS AND DISGUST

According to Freud (1950 [1913]), the word 'taboo' is ambivalent in so far as it has two divergent meanings. On the one hand, it denotes that which is sacred or consecrated; on the other, that which is forbidden or unclean. Taboos are also emotionally ambivalent, Freud tells us, involving both the desire for x (where x is a taboo activity or item) and the desire to avoid x (to detest x, in fact). Putting this ambivalence aside, if indeed it exists beyond a psychoanalytic interpretation, it is the latter meaning that is of interest to us here – namely taboos as prohibitive, *qua* forbidden and unclean – along with their negative emotional association often manifest as disgust.

Gutierrez and Giner-Sorolla (2007, p. 853) define taboos as a violation of norms that are 'expected to provoke inflexible, disgust-related responses'; adding that, in Western society, violations typically centre on *taboos of the body*, particularly with regard to sexual practice or other ways in which the body might be 'used' (e.g. gastronomically). Borg *et al.* (2008) likewise argue for an intimate relation between taboos and disgust, claiming that the same phylogenetically old mechanisms of aversion, used to steer us away from potential pathogens and other noxious substances, have been 'co-opted' (2008, p. 1529): initially as a means of avoiding inappropriate sexual encounters (e.g. incest), and then, more generally, as a way of guarding against other moral transgressions. In essence, our phylogenetically older concerns about physical contamination have extended outwards 'to include concerns over the purity of the individual's character and social conduct'

(Horberg *et al.*, 2009, p. 964). Through the advent of higher cortical processing, our original disgust response has become more highly developed and elaborative, so as to include social and moral concerns (Toronchuck and Ellis, 2007). In support of this view, Borg *et al.* (2008) report that the three categories of disgust response (pathogen-related, sexual and moral) trigger separate but overlapping patterns of brain activity.[1]

According to Rozin *et al.* (Rozin and Fallon, 1987; Rozin *et al.*, 1999), our visceral response to potential contaminates (e.g. faeces and vomit) constitutes *core disgust*. Core disgust emerges early in childhood, and is followed by further response categories such as *animal-reminder* (which may be sex or health related, or based or personal hygiene – e.g. an aversion to incest, gaping wounds or defecating in the street) and *interpersonal* and *sociomoral* (e.g. avoiding a diseased or immoral person, or an intolerance of lying, cheating or inequality). Stevenson *et al.* (2010) offer support for at least some of these categories. In a recent study, they identified developmental patterns of disgust-response in children exposed to core, animal-reminder and sociomoral elicitors. However, they suggest that Rozin *et al.*'s original taxonomy should be more broadly construed as either concrete elicitors (core and animal) or abstract elicitors (interpersonal and sociomoral). The evolution of our repertoire of disgust elicitors – from the simple revulsion of more concrete pathogens and noxious substances to the relatively complex prohibition of abstract socially based taboos – is explained by Oaten *et al.* (2009) as a means of managing disease-related threats. Through socialization and moralization, Oaten *et al.* suggest, we have adapted the disgust response of our primitive ancestors to act as a mechanism for social compliance, by functioning as a means of disease avoidance through the moral and legal prohibition of certain sexual acts (for example) with certain other people, or certain proclivities for bodily excretions.

A recent debate, however, has concerned the extent to which the language of disgust (i.e. 'that's disgusting', or 'sickening' or 'vile') should be interpreted metaphorically when directed towards moral violations (Bloom, 2004; Nabi, 2002). Royzman and Sabini (2001), for example, note that when stating 'Person x is disgusting', we are declaring not only our moral disapproval but also the intensity of our negative feeling towards that person, which is conveyed rhetorically by our use of the word 'disgusting'. It would seem that, universally, we 'borrow from the lexicon of disgust when describing moral transgressions' (Jones and Fitness, 2008, p. 613); although as Royzman and Sabini (2001) caution, it is more likely that the underlying negative feeling captured by the term 'disgusting' is that of anger, hatred or contempt, rather than disgust *per se*. Nevertheless, Danovitch and Bloom (2009, p. 111; emphasis added) note how 'children come to find entities like feces and vomit . . . disgusting, and . . . are able to describe them as such, and . . . adults direct the *language* of disgust to what they see as moral violations'.

It may be the case, then, that what we judge to be disgusting is largely a product of social conditioning. Such a view is endorsed by Knapp (2003, p. 262), who maintains that those objects and events that trigger disgust are not inherently disgusting; rather, associations are 'acquired through a socially mediated learning process'. As evidence for this, Knapp cites the different stages of disgust development demonstrated by children and the lack of a disgust response in documented cases of feral children. Further support is found in the study by Stevenson *et al.* (2001), who report a correlation between the child's reactivity to sociomoral elicitors and parental responsiveness to these same elicitors. Knapp (2003, p. 263) goes on to concede, however, that such a predominantly social process 'does not preclude the contribution of innate structures'. Knapp talks of potential disgust triggers (PDTs), which we are disposed to be disgusted by, and contrasts these with actual disgust triggers (ADTs), which we *learn* to be disgusted by. The contingent relation between PDTs and ADTs (i.e. the means by which a PDT becomes an ADT) is mediated by social conditioning. By way of a caveat, then, although it may be that the language of disgust is often used as a rhetorical device, one cannot discount the possibility that these learned associations are capable of eliciting the same kinds of visceral response originally used (solely) to dispel our interest in noxious substances. Royzman *et al.* (2008) concur, and challenge the idea that the disgust associated with moral violation is merely rhetorical. Instead, they argue that in the case of some moral transgressions, our reference to disgust should be taken literally – what they call the *moral dyspepsia hypothesis*. As they explain:

> [A]n appraisal of certain proscribed acts (perhaps those with sexual overtones) as immoral may, in and of itself, trigger genuine gastrointestinal discomfort, not unlike that brought on by the consumption of foul-tasting foods or the smelling of fetid odors.
>
> (Royzman *et al.*, 2008, p. 100)

In support of this hypothesis, Royzman *et al.* found that descriptions of morally prohibited acts (such as incest) produced oral inhibition, comprising of 'nausea, gagging, and diminished appetite' (p. 100). It would appear that, in some cases, our responses to moral transgressions are visceral, eliciting what Kekes (1992) calls *deep disgust*, whereby '[t]o say that we are sickened by them is not a metaphor; we are nauseated' (p. 433). Kekes includes, among the taboos that elicit this level of disgust, cases of extreme torture. Moreover, Kekes informs us, to *not* exhibit deep disgust at the sight of such profound revulsion, suggests repression or pathology, or perhaps brutalization.

DISGUST AS MORAL WISDOM OR MORAL INFALLIBILITY

In addition to deep disgust, violations of taboos typically elicit a condemning moral attitude. In fact, Kass (2002) argues that adhering to our sense of repugnance constitutes a kind of *moral wisdom* (see also Wonderly, 2008). Prinz (2006) regards such professed 'wisdom' as evidence of Hume's (1978 [1739]) sentimentalism – the view that judgements about what is morally right or wrong are grounded on a sentiment of disapproval. Disgust, then, indicates where the boundaries of social constraint lie (Miller, 1998): for a fundamental aspect of our moral identity is rooted in the revulsion we feel towards those who transgress taboos. Revulsion, it would seem, plays a key role in constraining necessity. As Kekes (1992, p. 439) explains:

> The rules whose violations constitute moral taboos regulate universal aspects of human lives: consumption, elimination, protection of security, and so on. The rules regulate the performance of these natural activities by setting standards of appropriateness regarding such matters as their place, time, manner, privacy or publicity, frequency, significance, and so on. . . . We do not thereby eliminate necessity; rather, we control it by imposing form on it. . . . These civilising rules occupy the gap between what we must and what we can do. . . .

The constraint imposed on us by our sense of disgust can, however, lead to what Haidt *et al.* (1993) refer to as *moral dumbfounding*: the view that a taboo is still morally indefensible even if no subsequent harm (to anyone) ensues. (It is viewed to be morally dumbfounding because it overrides the more liberal position, which states that one is free to act in any way one wishes so long as it does not cause harm to oneself or others.) For this reason, Nussbaum (2004) argues that disgust is inappropriate as a basis for moral prohibition, and therefore as a means of rendering an act criminal (for further discussion, see Arneson, 2007; Feinberg, 1988).

The failure of the disgust response to abate even in the face of evidence of no harm is well illustrated by the cockroach-in-the-juice study (Rozin and Nemeroff, 1990) (although in this example it occurs in relation to contamination rather than moral dumbfounding *per se*). Here, a completely sterilized, dead cockroach is placed temporarily in a glass of the study participants' favourite juice. Participants still show an aversion to drinking the juice even though there is no possibility of contamination. In addition, Angyal (1941) notes how an otherwise neutral object can remain repulsive simply through contact with a disgusting item, even if that item is no longer present. 'One would have great resistance to eating from a container once used to keep stools, urine, or sputum', he tells us (p. 396). Such an object elicits a kind of residual contamination, or is perhaps what Porzig-Drummond *et al.* (2009, p. 1006) refer to as 'invisibly dirty' or even 'ideationally contaminated'.

Beyond issues of contamination, however, disgust still remains an important arbiter in matters of taboo. To illustrate, Gutierrez and Giner-Sorolla (2007) discuss two fictitious examples. The first involves two consenting adults who happen to be brother and sister (and knowingly so). They decide to engage in a one-off act of love-making (a similar example is discussed by Haidt and Hersh, 2001). Contraception is used, and neither party regrets what they did. Afterwards, each is able to engage in meaningful relationships with other people, and their brother–sister bond is not damaged. What occurred also remains forever private. The second example involves necrophilia. In this scenario, sex occurs with other group members who willingly agree to donate their bodies after death for this purpose. As with the first example, the group and their practice remain forever private. When the incest and necrophilia scenarios were presented to participants, Gutierrez and Giner-Sorolla (2007) discovered that even when it was explicitly stated that no harm occurred to anyone (not even to the relatives of the brother and sister or the dead person – because they remained completely unaware of each respective event), the participants nevertheless inferred that harm must have occurred, even if not to those engaged in the activity, then to others. The inference of harm was often accompanied by a sense of anger or outrage, and used to justify the ensuing moral condemnation. However, when it was made clear that a claim to harm was not justified – because it was reiterated that no harm to anyone had occurred – disgust at the 'violation' remained, even if the anger abated.

As a general principle, it is necessary for our survival that we eat, rather than not eat, procreate, rather than not, and kill rather than be killed. Yet even when adhering to this necessity, there still remains a degree of flexibility and therefore choice over what we eat, have sex with and kill. Taboos restrict this flexibility by placing a moral constraint on our freedom, thereby stifling our 'right' to choose without transgression. Violating a taboo, even if the consequences are purportedly harmless (as noted by Gutierrez and Giner-Sorolla, 2007), remains *symbolically* potent. Such hypothetical transgressions might appear or claim to be innocuous, but they breach a code of values implemented and enforced within a given society often through majority consent. To flaunt these values, even symbolically, is to provoke the severest moral condemnation.

Within a given society, there exists what Horberg *et al.* (2009) refer to as a *purity domain*. Taboos police this domain and use disgust as a heightened means of demarcation. As a consequence, those experiencing disgust will make stronger moral judgements about those who engage in behaviours that are perceived to violate the *purity domain*. Perhaps at its most extreme, Taylor (2007) conjectures, disgust may be an important instigator in the generation of prejudice and general antipathy towards those construed as the out-group – who are likely held to be in some way contaminated (see below). Psychosocial factors regarding perceived in-group and out-group members can in turn influence the perception of disgust. To illustrate, Raman and Gelman (2008) reported that children tend to find the thought of someone they dislike sneezing on them more disgusting than being sneezed on by a friend. Case *et al.* (2006) found that mothers regard their own baby's faecal smell as less disgusting than the faeces of other babies.

In consideration, then, disgust may have evolved as a mechanism for the avoidance of potentially harmful toxins, particularly relating to food but, according to Prinz (2007), it is equally the case that our moral judgements, particularly where taboos are concerned (we contend), are grounded on emotional (disgust-related) responses. As a means of illustrating this point, Prinz asks us to consider why raping a toddler who will never remember the event is wrong. When answering his own question, he considers that to say that it is just wrong is not to fail to have a reason, or to be unable to articulate it. '[W]e are not obviating reason', he declares; rather, 'we are explicitly giving one' (p. 31). Saying it is wrong *is* the reason; it is *just wrong*.[2] Haidt (2001, p. 830) holds a similar position, supported by empirical evidence: 'that moral emotions and intuitions drive moral reasoning', just as Hume (1978 [1739]) proposed.

As was shown by participant responses to the Gutierrez and Giner-Sorolla (2007) scenarios, even in the absence of clear reasoning for why it should be wrong, the negative sentiment – the sense of disgust – remained. Articulated reasons, then, do not form the basis for disgust (according to Prinz, 2007); rather, they are *post hoc* additions that help us justify the moral judgements we make, which are, fundamentally, sentiment based. In the absence of reason, the sentiment remains, and can even prove reason enough for the moral judgement. Consequently, disgust 'is well suited for use as an emotion of social rejection' (Schnall *et al.*, 2008, p. 1097); for as Jones and Fitness (2008, p. 613) note: 'the action tendency motivated by disgust is to distance oneself from the disgust elicitor'.

This is a view echoed by Sternberg (2003) when outlining his triangular theory of the structure of hate, which he posits as a contributing cause of extreme inter-group hostilities. Disgust causes the negation of intimacy through the process of distancing oneself from the disgust elicitor, who is also the target of hate. Schnall *et al.* (2008) offer a word of caution, however, by noting that although people often use rapid affective appraisal as a useful heuristic, such a 'rule of thumb' can nevertheless be error prone. Lichtenstein *et al.* (2007), for example, claim that taboo violations tend to elicit a stronger negative effect when scenarios do not require extensive cognitive processing – that is, when we do not need to think about the situation too much in order to make a judgement. With this in mind, perhaps we have reason to be cautious, and to conclude that disgust should not be overly relied on, at least not to the extent suggested by Kass (2002), as a measure of moral wisdom.

So far, we have argued that the disgust response has developed from an initial reaction to potentially harmful food-related items to something that can be elicited by perceived moral violation. In cases of morally prohibited action, our sense of disgust is more than metaphoric; it can be literal, producing a nauseous, visceral response to the perceived moral transgression. Moreover, at least in terms of moral disgust, we endorse the view adopted by Knapp (2003), and echoed here by Gert (2005, p. 346), that 'a given human will not find anything disgusting without the right sort of social conditioning'. We are taught what to revile, and certainly this view finds support from research on the cultural relativity of certain moral taboos (Prinz, 2007). What is considered appropriate behaviour varies across cultures: be it related to sexuality or even something as relatively mundane as the consumption of food. In England, for example, it is acceptable to kiss in public, yet frowned upon to eat dogs. Such a relativist stance holds that what is deemed taboo, and therefore what elicits moral disgust, is contingently related to a given time and place. To illustrate, Rozin and Singh (1999) report the changing reaction to cigarettes and cigarette smokers in America. Yet it is also a fact that there seem to occur, *in our time*, universal taboos of a kind that elicit the sort of deep disgust described by Kekes (1992). Eating faeces would be one, we contend (see Elwood and Olatunji, 2008). Consuming live animals would appear to be another although there are exceptions, such as eating live oysters, or the Japanese method of *ikizukuri* – meaning 'prepared alive' (referring to fish) – which is a controversial form of cuisine, even in Japan. Perhaps, today, consuming live *mammals* would be a more accurate exception-free category. Incest, child abuse and necrophilia are others, as is murder (although what constitutes incest, child abuse or murder may vary across cultures). Yet, might it be that these seeming universal taboos are themselves contingently related to the offline space we occupy?

Prinz (2007, p. 167), whilst defending a form of moral relativism based around Hume's (1978 [1739]) sentimentalism, presents what he calls '*constructive sentimentalism*'. This is the view that moral judgements stem from sentiment – feelings, disapprobation or approbation (see Greene *et al.*, 2001; Nichols and Mallon, 2005) – but, importantly, these sentiments form the basis for rules that have their own objective status within the socially constructed space they occupy: 'Things that we construct or build come from us, but, once there, they are real entities that we perceive' (Prinz, 2007, p. 168). Prinz's position is compatible, we contend, with the neosentimentalism proffered by Gibbard (1990), who, in building on an earlier point, argues that wrongful acts are judged to be so, not simply because one has a negative feeling towards the act but because such a feeling is appropriate. The addition of this normative element – that the negative feeling of guilt (for example) is not simply something we happen to feel but what we should feel – means, for Nichols (2008, p. 258; emphasis in original), that 'even if one has lost any disposition to feel guilt about a certain action, one can still think that feeling guilty is *warranted*'. Nichols goes on to argue that the emotions we feel in relation to a given action have helped shape our cultural norms, by determining which are sustained and which are lost. His *affective resonance hypothesis* essentially states that: 'Norms that prohibit actions to which we are predisposed to be emotionally averse will enjoy enhanced cultural fitness over other norms' (p. 269).

For the new generation of sentimentalists like Prinz and Nichols, whether an action is deemed good or bad, or right or wrong, is in no small part dependent on the emotion we feel towards that action. However, these theorists have built on more traditional Humean sentimentalism by arguing for a degree of objectification within a given space. Thus, if at a given time I experience a sense of disapprobation towards an individual's actions, this does not *as a general rule* – based as it is on how I feel *right now* – make my disapproval grounds for the judgement that what this person is doing is bad; nor does it make my disapproval a good thing, unless that disapproval is warranted.

Prinz's constructive sentimentalism, which we would argue is compatible with Nichols' affective resonance hypothesis, allows for a socially agreed (and therefore objectified) system of morality to operate that is relative to, and therefore contingent on, a given space with a given cultural history and evolution. It may be that seeming universal taboos are a product of constructive sentimentalism, and that their seeming universality is merely an artefact of certain similarities (universalities) in our biologically and even socially evolved sentiment, shaped in accordance with Nichols' affective resonance hypothesis. Or it may be, in contrast to constructive sentimentalism, that there exist universal taboos (at least, universal today), irrespective of any adherence to sentimentalism (e.g. child sexual abuse or rape in general). Resolving this issue does not concern us here, for either position is compatible with the arguments forwarded throughout this book. This is because it is our view that even if there existed universal moral taboos, they would be contingently related to the *universal* space we occupy. We say this whilst recognizing cultural diversity and relativity: for, traditionally, even socially constructed spaces share certain contingent properties (and so are universal in this respect) – they are spaces in which we interact as physically (biologically) embodied beings. So, irrespective of whether morality is relative to a given culture with no privileged moral position outside of that culture or whether moral absolutes exist, either position is contingent, we contend, on ourselves as physically embodied agents. But what about spaces in which we are embodied, but not *physically* embodied?

SYMBOLIC AND VIRTUAL TABOOS

As noted in Chapter 2, with the advent of cyberspace, there now exists the potential for virtual immediacy – the possibility for new interactive spaces, and the construction of new social realities and new forms of embodiment. In such brave new worlds, is the enforcement of *offline* taboos a necessary requirement for *online* social cohesion? Does online social cohesion require its own taboos, which may not be the same as those enforced offline? If so, might these taboos be necessarily context specific; or must our offline socially constructed or putatively universal taboos necessarily transcend worlds – making the latter truly universal and the former socially transcendent? In short, could a *social* space exist that is devoid of offline taboos, where such traditional taboo-based morality has no foothold, or must deep disgust constrain even our most virtual interactions because we import these taboos into whichever space we enter?

In relation to these questions, recall how moral dumbfounding can lead to a reaction of disgust even in scenarios where no harm is caused to anyone. Recall also how Kass (2002) conceives of such disgust (or repugnance) as a form of moral wisdom. Yet it was claimed that such associations are contingently related (based as they are on a particular form of social conditioning or learning), and that we should not place our trust in the wisdom of moral repugnance. As a further point of relevance, consider Damasio's (1994) *somatic marker hypothesis*.

According to Damasio, somatic markers are sensations – either visceral or non-visceral – that facilitate efficient decision making by reducing the number of viable choices available to us. Negative feelings towards a particular option will quickly eliminate that option from the choices available. Conversely, a strong positive feeling may encourage or prioritize the selection of a particular course of action or judgement. Somatic markers are contingently related to external events and are therefore a product of our education and socialization within a given culture. This process (of education and socialization) typically includes 'social conventions and ethical rules' (Damasio, 1994, p. 179) (recall the neosentimentalism of Prinz and

Nichols), and amounts to, amongst other things, the development of associations between particular stimuli and particular somatic states: for at the neuronal level, Damasio informs us, 'somatic markers depend on learning within a system that can connect certain categories of entity or event with the enactment of a body state, pleasant or unpleasant' (p. 180). The habituation of bodily responses (somatic markers) to external moral and social conventions is such that merely *thinking* about breaking these conventions can trigger a physiological response. As Damasio (1994, p. 180; emphasis added) notes:

> When the choice of option X . . . leads to a bad outcome Y, . . . [r]e-exposure of the organism to option X, or the *thought* about outcome Y, will now have the power to re-enact the painful body state and thus serve as an automated reminder of bad consequences to come.

And again: 'Whether the body states are real or *vicarious* ("*as if*"), the corresponding neural pattern can be made conscious and constitute a feeling' (p. 185; emphasis added).

A similar point is made by Fitzgerald *et al.* (2004) when stating that excitation of the neural pathways underlying our response to disgust-eliciting objects/events can occur even in the absence of external triggers. If the mere thought of taboos is sufficient to elicit deep disgust, then it seems reasonable to conjecture that any *virtual* display of taboos – what we are calling symbolic taboo activities (STAs) – will likewise elicit a visceral response. However, if this is the case, should we not interpret this as further evidence for the fallibility of repugnance as moral wisdom? The examples of moral dumbfounding provided by Gutierrez and Giner-Sorolla (2007) (involving hypothetical cases of purportedly harmless incest and necrophilia) suggest that even symbolic transgression provokes strong moral condemnation. With some justification, one might extrapolate from these to cyberspace, and conclude that such transgressions might be similarly received if enacted virtually. We might feel a strong aversion to such actions, but would we (in virtual space) be warranted to do so?

The problem we presently face is that little is known about whether behaviours considered to be illegal offline, relationship transgressions or even deeply immoral, are viewed in the same way in a variety of other spaces online. As has been previously noted, cyberspace is not a homogeneous space. Some spaces set out to be more playful and less real than others (i.e. less representative of offline reality). Game sites, for example, often involve individuals role-playing characters in a game. In this space, engaging in cybersex with another who is not one's (offline) partner may not be considered a relationship transgression (Whitty, 2010). The rules and understandings of what behaviour is deemed permissible in 'role-playing spaces' – where individuals do not interact as themselves – could plausibly be quite different from those spaces where the contingency relation matches more closely the offline world, and therefore one's offline identity. Unfortunately, to date, research is less clear on whether such activity is commonly judged as infidelity in *all* spaces online (Whitty, 2003b, 2010; Whitty and Carr,

2006a). However, it is important to note that research has found that in many spaces online, engaging in emotional or sexual acts with a person other than one's partner is deemed to be just as upsetting and equally likely to be deemed acts of betrayal as the equivalent acts carried out face to face (see Whitty, 2008c).

The importance of understanding and therefore contextualizing the space in which STAs potentially occur is demonstrated by Hemenover and Schimmack (2007). Here, participants were presented with film clips depicting 'disgusting humour'. Hemenover and Schimmack reported that in this space, when asked to take the perspective of the observer, the viewing participants were able to express concurrent feelings of disgust and amusement: a state that Rozin (1990) refers to as *benign masochism*. Perhaps the expression of such mixed feelings and even the behaviour itself is likely to be tolerated much more in this space than in, say, a space in which the same behaviour is played out for real.

Acts of infidelity (or even disgusting humour) hardly constitute prototypical taboo violations, or elicit the levels of deep disgust noted by Kekes (1992). Yet the same underlying ambiguity surrounding virtual interactions that may or may not constitute infidelity also clouds questions regarding what should or should not be permissible within virtual space, particularly when one is concerned with an action that amounts to a taboo violation offline. Two overarching questions that concern Part 1 of this book, then, are first: Do attitudes towards taboos that are affected by offline contingency relations hold sway over actions that occur within cyberspace (a space where these same contingency relations may not, and certainly need not, exist)? Any response to this question will be essentially descriptive. In addition, a more normative position can be adopted in response to the second question: *Should* attitudes towards taboos that are affected by offline contingency relations hold sway over actions that occur within cyberspace (a space where these same contingency relations may not, and certainly need not, exist)?

By way of a first assault on these questions, in Chapter 5 we will consider perhaps the most passive form of virtual engagement, the Internet spectator. Before that, however, it is necessary to discuss the issue of obscenity, its relation to disgust and morality, and the extent to which STAs might be judged as obscene.

4   Obscenity

A measure of offence or depravity?

In Chapter 3, we saw how a sense of disgust prevailed even in cases where it was claimed that no harm had occurred, and how this was taken by some as evidence of the moral fallibility of disgust. Might the same moral fallibility be applied to the obscene, or must that which is obscene *be* morally harmful? The question of whether virtual obscenity exists is perhaps dependent on how one defines 'obscenity'. And what of the moral corruption associated implicitly or explicitly with different obscenity laws: is this warranted in cases of STAs? In this chapter, we discuss obscenity law as it currently stands in the UK and US, and consider the extent to which STAs satisfy the necessary and sufficient conditions for a classification of 'legally obscene' in either country. We also consider whether STAs that are or might be judged legally obscene are necessarily morally harmful.

THE RELATIONSHIP BETWEEN DISGUST AND OBSCENITY

According to Kieran (2002, p. 32), to judge that something is obscene 'seems intimately tied to rather strong negative affective responses that explain the vehemence of condemnation'. So much so that a feeling of disgust often accompanies the judgement that *x* is obscene, for example, even though the co-occurrence of disgust appears neither sufficient nor necessary for such a verdict. It is not sufficient because one may be disgusted at the sight of photographs graphically depicting medical procedures and/or ailments (for example), but would refrain from calling their display obscene in the context of a medical journal used to inform students about procedure and diagnoses; unlike the scenario in which they are used to solicit delight at deformity and the mockery of those so afflicted (Kieran, 2002). Neither is disgust necessary: for I may judge the publication of images of adult sexual intercourse to be obscene without finding the images themselves disgusting – if they were published in a children's schoolbook, for example, rather than a *Guide to Lovemaking*. Similarly, an image of Myra Hindley (a convicted child killer) is not in and of itself obscene – when, for example, it is found in a family album or even in a police file containing her personal details – nor does it typically elicit a strong disgust response; but when created from the handprints of children by artist Marcus Harvey (in his work entitled *Myra*; see

Figure 4.1), the portrait provoked heavy criticism when exhibited in the *Sensations* exhibition at London's Royal Academy in 1997 and prompted accusations of obscenity (see Young, 2000). Thus, one cannot adopt disgust as a marker of the obscene; neither, White (2004) argues, can one determine what is obscene through content alone.

Figure 4.1 Myra by Marcus Harvey, 1995, acrylic on canvas, 156 × 126 in. (396.2 × 320 cm)
Credit: Photograph: Stephen White. Courtesy of White Cube.

Context seems more important to whether something is judged to be obscene than to whether it is capable of eliciting a disgust response. It is just as likely that one would produce a disgust response when wading through liquid excrement in an old sewer – where one would expect to find such a product – as when entering a disused apartment block where one would not; or when one has to cannibalize the corpses of the victims of an air disaster in order to survive until rescue arrives, compared to cannibalizing in order to satisfy non-essential gastronomic pleasures. In contrast, and as the Myra Hindley example illustrates, what constitutes an obscenity is often context dependent. Consequently, *showing* graphic CCTV footage of a man caught having sexual intercourse with a goat, as evidence for the prosecution, would not be considered obscene by many people, whereas broadcasting it as part of a television entertainment programme entitled *People Do the Strangest Things* would (see Taylor, 2002, for the news story that inspired this example). Similarly, according to Jay (2009, p. 89), using obscene language in the context of a conversation with friends can have positive social effects, including 'promoting social cohesion' (see also Želvys, 1990).

In Chapter 3, we described how disgust is a reflexive response; an automatic reaction to an object/event originally shaped by our evolutionary past to avoid such things as noxious substances, but whose underlying mechanisms have more recently been co-opted to form part of our social and moral conditioning. Because of this, disgust is held by some to be a measure of moral worth, yet by others is said to be vulnerable to a charge of moral dumbfounding. Disgust in the presence of x is often accompanied by a negative attitude towards x; and for those who consider disgust to be an expression of moral wisdom, it is reason enough for the claim that x is morally wrong or bad. The continued presence of this negative attitude even when, in the case of extreme taboo violation, it is established that no harm ensues is used by some to illustrate moral dumbfounding – in effect, that our disgust response is fallible and should not be used to inform moral decisions (recall the hypothetical examples of brother–sister incest and necrophilia in Chapter 3).

A charge of obscenity is independent of our disgust response (as we have established); yet being disgusted by x is often antecedent to a proclamation that x is obscene, at least where x is a taboo violation. In layperson's terms (we will consider legal definitions below), being disgusted by x is reason enough for me to claim that x is obscene, which is just another way for me to say that x is morally wrong. Yet morally prohibited behaviours are not morally prohibited *because* they elicit a disgust response; rather, through 'successful' conditioning, they elicit a disgust response because they are morally prohibited to begin with. One might say that disgust simply reminds us of that fact (although not infallibly so, it has been argued).

OBSCENITY AS A LEGAL TERM

Obscenity should be understood as a legal term, not a moral one, whose referent changes periodically and geographically. As White (2006, p. 31) explains:

To be obscene, as the law defines such a status, is to belong to a legal class of things, which varies over time and space. This is because attitudes and views about what is appropriate and offensive change over time in communities.

So, just as that which elicits disgust – at least in terms of a sociomoral context – can vary across cultures and throughout history, so that which is deemed obscene appears to be correspondingly relative. Likewise, just as our negative attitude and sense of disgust seem to prevail towards the disgust-eliciting taboo (even in the absence of harm), equally resistant to revision (when the same absence of harm is established) is our reaction towards the obscene. As Kieran (2002, pp. 32–33; emphasis in original) notes:

> [M]ost people would still have a strong affective reaction to and condemn that which is judged to be obscene even if they were aware that, *ex hypothesi*, it had been conclusively proved that there could be no significant causal influence upon the attitudes, dispositions and behaviours of those who indulge in it.

It would seem, then, that although obscenity is, strictly speaking, a purely legal term, independent of morality, the connection between obscenity and morality is hardly tenuous and, if anything, appears intuitive, implied and somewhat conventional. Yet if disgust as a measure of moral worth is fallible, is it not possible that our reluctance to separate obscenity from moral harm is equally dumbfounding?

The current standard by which obscenity is measured in the US – often referred to as the *community standard test* – is taken from *Miller v California* (413 U.S. 15) in 1973, and is comprised of the following three components or tests, which, if met, classify the object/event as legally obscene:

- whether 'the average person, applying contemporary community standards' would find that the work, taken as a whole, appeals to the prurient interest;
- whether the work depicts or describes, in a patently offensive way, sexual conduct specifically defined by the applicable state law;
- whether the work, taken as a whole, lacks serious literary, artistic, political or scientific value (see Feinberg, 1988, for a detailed discussion).

By this standard, a juror would determine something to be legally obscene if they are of the opinion that the average person within the community would consider the object/event to be an offensive expression of sexual conduct that appeals to those with an inordinate and shameful interest in sex, which 'experts' judge to be of no serious value. The community standard test thereby permits local, rather than national, standards of tolerance (and presumably intolerance) and acceptability (unacceptability) to apply; to the extent that individuals 'subordinate their own personal standards to those of the average adult resident in the community' (Scott, 1991, p. 29). But as White (2004) points out, the US measure of obscenity tells us more about the person looking on than the thing itself. On its own, being of no serious value hardly signifies the obscene, only the insipid. Importantly, then, it must *cause offence*. However, as Dillon (1982, p. 260) notes, it is not clear whether it is 'we who project obscene qualities on otherwise neutral material', thereby being the architects of our own offence, or whether it is in 'the nature of the material to present itself as obscene to any unbiased observer', who then might claim to be justifiably offended. For White (2004), there is nothing about the object/event itself that constitutes evidence of obscenity; the only evidence is our reaction to it. Thus, Scott (1991, p. 129; emphasis in original) declares: 'what is obscene is not known until a judge or jury finds, beyond reasonable doubt, that the material violates community standards by applying the *Miller* test'.

The difficulty with relying on one's interpretation of local community stand- ards is well illustrated by Dixon and Linz (1997) when discussing the lyrical content of rap group 2 Live Crew's album, *As Nasty As They Wanna Be*. In 1990, a US federal court judge ruled that the album was legally obscene. Because of this ruling, the group was then prosecuted for continuing to perform the material live (even to an adult-only audience). However, jurors in the second trial are reported to have found the lyrics humorous when read aloud, even comical, rather than obscene. Consequently, Manning (1988, p. 194) warns us of the dangers of adopting an *offence principle* as a marker of the obscene, in so far as it 'locates the assessment of obscenity in the eye of the beholder', thereby making the line demarcating the obscene from the erotic, or even pornographic, objectively imperceptible (Linsley, 1998).

The emphasis on offence within US federal rulings on obscenity is clearly illus- trated in the 2001 case *American Amusement Machine Association v Kendrick*.[1] When discussing whether the obscenity test should be applied to the content of violent video games, the presiding judge (Judge Posner) reasoned thus:

> [T]he main reason for the proscription of obscenity 'is not that it is harmful, but that it is offensive.' Obscenity is regulated because people find it 'disgusting, embarrassing, degrading, disturbing, outrageous, and insulting,' not because it is 'believed to inflict . . . harm.'
>
> (cited in Stone, 2007, p. 1858)

Calvert (2002) likewise concludes that Judge Posner's understanding of the primary rationale for the regulation of obscenity is that it is offensive. However, and in contrast to the obscenity test, in the case of violent video games, regulation relates not to the *offence* caused but to the likelihood of *ensuing harm*, and not just to the player but also to those who they might encounter. Unlike offence, then, which has a subjective quality, harm seems more objective, based on 'some set of observables' (White, 2006, p. 119).

Perhaps in recognition of this difference, and certainly in contrast to the US measure, in the UK, the Obscene Publications Act 1959 determines something to be obscene:

> [I]f its effect or . . . the effect of any one of its items is, if taken as a whole, such as to tend to deprave and corrupt persons who are likely, having regard

to all the relevant circumstances, to read, see or hear the matter contained or embodied in it.

(Section 1:1)

Here, rather than the measure of obscenity being rooted in some form of offence principle reflecting community standards, classification is based on whether the material is likely to deprave or corrupt those who have access to it. In other words, what is considered obscene is couched in social pathology such that there would be a tendency towards 'moral and physical harm caused to vulnerable persons by exposure to obscene writings and images' (Hunter *et al.*, 1993, p. 138). In addition, and again showing a departure from mere offence towards social pathology, one's reaction to an obscenity must be more than disgust, even when this involves phys- ical revulsion and/or behavioural aversion: one must become (or be in danger of becoming) morally corrupted. Section 1 of the Obscene Publications Act 1959 thus tries to distinguish between what merely offends communal standards of accepta- bility and what is socially harmful.[2] Perhaps with this in mind, Stone (2007), in relation to the US obscenity test, argues that although offensiveness may well be part of the *definition* of what it means to be legally obscene, this should not rule out the possibility, even the likelihood, that regulation is enforced because obscenity causes or is believed to cause harm.[3]

OBSCENITY AND MORAL HARM

What sort of harm are we talking about? Kieran (2002, p. 41) defines obscene representations as those that solicit from us cognitive-affective responses towards objects/events that are morally prohibited, to the extent that we are commended 'to delight in them'. What we are prescribed to delight in, Kieran informs us, are morally prohibited sexual acts; or the infliction of pain or suffering or even death on another, either by one's own hand or vicariously. To commend us to delight in that which is already demarcated as morally prohibited, even taboo, is not only taken to be a measure of the obscene, *and* the implied intention of the creator of the material, but also a consequence of it for us, at least if the exposure to the obscene material is prolonged. Thus, it may be argued that obscenity is morally wrong because it morally corrupts; and by 'morally corrupts' we mean that it not only *commends* us to delight in the morally prohibited but also, and importantly, *causes* us to do so. The association of obscenity with moral corruption is further implied by Koppelman (2005, p. 1637), when commenting on US legislation:

> Material can be obscene even if it has no likelihood of inciting anyone to unlawful conduct, and even if no unwilling viewer is ever likely to see and thereby be offended by it. Obscenity law aims at preventing the formation of certain thoughts – typically, erotic ones – in the minds of willing viewers.

Even in the absence of illegal activity, and even in the absence of offence, Koppelman claims that something can still be deemed obscene if it leads to the formation of certain thoughts – most likely about morally prohibited acts or the desire to engage in or witness such acts – even in the minds of the willing. Obscenity is therefore judged to be detrimental to our psychological well-being, even if 'psychological well-being' is restricted to cognitive-affective states, thereby excluding behaviour. In part at least, the aim of obscenity legislation is to prevent the formation of such cognitive-affective states, perhaps because there is an implicit assumption that their formation will lead to, or greatly increase the risk of, violating morally proscribed, most likely illegal, behaviours.

On the surface, legal definitions of obscenity – from both the US and the UK – omit direct reference to morality, and of course not all that is immoral is obscene (as defined); yet contained within the UK definition is an evaluative stance: that the effect of obscenity is depravity and corruption and, as a corollary, this is taken to be a bad thing (it is socially pathological). Thus, obscenity is defined within the UK Obscene Publications Act 1959 by its effect, and its effect is implicitly taken to be a moral matter. The test of obscenity used in the US is also evaluative with implicit moral concerns, in so far as that which is obscene must be of no *serious value* (evaluative comment); it must be taken to be patently *offensive* (again, evaluative) and be of *prurient* interest. Prurient refers to *shameful* (explicitly morally evaluative) or *inordinate* (again, evaluative) sexual arousal; sometimes it is taken to mean *morbid, unhealthy* or *extraordinary* sexual urges (implicitly morally evaluative).

It may be that the object of one's sexual interest (animal, child or the dead, for example) is what makes one's interest shameful; or what it means to have extraordinary sexual urges may be deemed extraordinary because it is not ordinarily the case that we are sexually interested in animals, children or dead people. In fact, prurient appeal can be directed towards any clearly defined deviant sexual group, irrespective of whether it matches the sexual interests of the general public (Cenite, 2004). 'Moral harm [therefore] requires more than a certain kind of text [or image]. It also requires a certain kind of reader' (Koppelman, 2005, p. 1679). Yet one's sexual preferences are not typically a matter *for* the general public. As Cenite (2004, p. 37) notes, they are effectively a 'personal and private matter'. But as pointed out by Koppelman (2005), material can be obscene even if it has no likelihood of inciting anyone to unlawful conduct, and even if no unwilling viewer is ever likely to see and thereby be offended by it.

VIRTUAL OBSCENITY

Suppose that one's prurient interest or one's delight is not in what the representation represents but in the representation itself. It seems to be implicitly understood within discussion on obscenity that a representation is judged to be obscene because of what it is a representation *of*, and the extent to which the representation (because of what it represents) is intended within a given context to solicit certain cognitive-affective states such as prurient sexual interest or a delight in the pain and suffering of actual others represented by the images or within the dialogue (etc.). To reiterate: this prurient interest, or what the obscene commends us to delight in, is not taken to be directed towards the representation itself, but what it represents – in other words, *actual* animals, children or dead people. Of course, it is likely to be the case that what the representation is of is an actual animal, child or dead person (say, in the form of a photograph or video recording), perhaps involved in some morally prohibited act.[4] We condemn the manufacture, distribution and use of such material (see Chapter 5 for a detailed discussion on this). It may also be the case that adults (either alone or with other adults), engaged in acts that are deemed obscene, may have been exploited, or may be otherwise vulnerable (although not necessarily). We accept this possibility, but do not intend to discuss it further here (rather, see Chapter 5). Instead, we wish to consider whether representing morally prohibited acts in a VE in which the images have been generated virtually, without recourse to actual persons or things, should be classified as obscene. Now, it may seem immediately apparent that being virtual – *qua* fictional – does not in itself prevent at least the accusation of obscenity, irrespective of any successful prosecution: one has only to think of D.H. Lawrence's *Lady Chatterley's Lover*, banned in the UK until 1960. Nevertheless, as noted in previous chapters, the virtual immediacy inherent within cyberspace raises important questions concerning different contingency relations within different virtual spaces, and the impact that these altered contingencies could have on our moral judgement and, importantly, our psychological well-being when engaged in STAs.

Our ensuing discussion will therefore focus on two central issues: first, whether virtual representations can be obscene, particularly if the focus of one's cognitive-affective states is directed towards the representation itself and not what it is a representation of (see Chapter 5 for a discussion on the viewing of real-life footage); second, what the psychological ramification might be when one's change in cognitive-affective states is solicited by and directed towards the virtual representation itself.

In 2002, the US Supreme Court ruled that whilst 'it remains illegal to make, show or possess sexually explicit pictures of children . . . [there is] no compelling reason to prohibit the manufacture or exhibition of pictures which merely *appear* to be of children' (cited in Levy, 2002, p. 319; emphasis in original).[5] Included in this freedom from prohibition, Levy notes, is virtual child pornography. Unlike actual child pornography, no real children are involved in the production of these computer-generated images, so no actual children are harmed in their manufacture, regardless of what is depicted occurring. Importantly, these images must be completely virtual in nature; it is not permitted to produce distorted or morphed images of actual children. However, in the UK, the Coroners and Justice Act 2009 has made illegal the possession of such virtual (or pseudo) images. Such prohibition has been in place in Holland since 2002, and recently, in Japan, a similar ruling has been proposed but not yet passed.[6] The outlawing of 'sexually related' images of virtual children in certain countries is enforced irrespective of any judgement of obscenity. Nevertheless, it is worth considering whether such images could be judged obscene based on either US or UK tests/definitions of obscenity. Such discussion is, we contend, more than an academic exercise, as will become apparent as we progress.

If we adopt the offence principle, which forms a large part of the US test for obscenity, it is not difficult to concede that the vast majority of people would find virtual recreations – even pencil or ink drawings – of children being sexually abused (or involved in other STAs) deeply offensive. Even sexualized images of children touted as art are controversial – and their artistic merit debated. In 2009, for example, the Tate Modern in London was embroiled in controversy when it decided to exhibit a piece by artist Richard Prince entitled *Spiritual America* (see Adler, 1996). The artwork is a photograph of a photograph (a representation of a representation) of actress Brooke Shields, aged 10. She is depicted naked with oiled skin and heavy make-up, staring directly at the camera in what has been described as a provocative pose. The photograph was displayed away from the other exhibits, behind a closed door, with a warning that some may find the artwork 'challenging' (Singh, 2009).[7] Might the piece have prurient appeal? Children's campaigner Michele Elliot claimed that the image would act as nothing more than a magnet for paedophiles (cited in Singh, 2009). Certainly one could argue, perhaps with some justification, that it would elicit sexual arousal from this particular group of sexual deviants. But perhaps there is also concern over the fact that it may be interpreted by the onlooker as condoning the sexualization of a 10-year-old child and thereby soliciting from a more general audience the sexual appeal of children.

Is there a danger, then, that such an image might deprave or morally corrupt its viewer, or a certain subset of viewers? Such a possibility would be, or course, a clear indicator of the obscene based on the UK definition – although this may be countered (rightly or wrongly) if the object/event is judged to have artistic merit (see Section 4 of the Obscene Publications Act 1959). Discussion on the possibility of moral corruption will be postponed until later in this chapter. In the meantime, let us consider what it is about a representation that enables it to solicit prurient appeal.

The power of the representation to solicit a given response can be taken to be a measure of the representation's ability to represent. In other words, if the image closely matches what the image is an image of, then one's response to the image should be similar to how one would respond to the presence of the actual object/event (see Chapter 6 for a more detailed discussion on emotions elicited from fictional representations). Thus, the argument goes, if one is aroused by images of children being sexually abused, or of images of sex with animals or dead people, then one would be equally aroused at the sight of their actual occurrence. Moreover, it is because one is aroused by the actual sight of such things that their accurate representation elicits the same response. Such an argument has a certain intuitive appeal when used against those who possess images (and therefore representations) of actual abuse: for in order to obtain these images (these representations), actual abuse had to have occurred, if not by the viewer then by someone else. Nevertheless, there are those who claim to be interested only in looking at images – so-called *armchair paedophiles* (Ellen, 2009) – not in engaging in the actual abuse itself. We will have more to say about such 'onlookers' in Chapter 5. In the meantime, what if the images are manufactured such that they do not involve or indeed require actual abuse to occur – namely virtually generated images? The would-be armchair paedophile would have some justification in claiming that looking at these images, if it is a crime (as it is in the UK) is a victimless one; although one might fear the possibility of such an individual escalating his (or her) viewing habits to include images that are of actual abuse, or even to taking part in the abuse itself (see Bourke and Hernandez, 2009). Again, we will discuss this further in Chapter 5. Here, we are concerned with the question of obscenity. If such activity – STAs that might include looking at virtually generated images of child abuse, bestiality or necrophilia – were restricted to just looking or only *virtual* interaction, should such images or STAs be classified as obscene?

As far as the issue of obscenity is concerned, presumably what is involved in the manufacture of these images is irrelevant: for at the risk of labouring the point, it is what the image *represents* that is the basis for the obscenity charge – because it either offends or is deemed to have the potential to cause moral harm – not what was involved in actually creating the image.[8] But what if the image I possess does not represent anything that actually exists? The French philosopher Baudrillard (1983) refers to this as *simulacra*, which he takes to mean a copy or a representation of a thing that has no original. In keeping with Baudrillard's simulacra, suppose I possess a virtual image of a humanoid creature that interacts virtually with another humanoid creature, neither of which is meant to represent an actual creature, and certainly not our own species in any shape or form, including children, dead people or known animals. Let us say that all the virtual images I possess are of this kind; none represents an *actual* object/event. As such, they are not representations at all – at least not as we have been using the term. Nevertheless, they are constituted so that they share certain component features with actual objects and are capable of engaging in acts that resemble actual events – be they sexual or otherwise. Let us allow, for example, that one creature is small with large round eyes and a child-like voice; while the other is taller and bulkier and bullies the smaller creature, making it engage in activities that bear a certain resemblance to sexual acts of an oral nature. Or perhaps my virtual playmates are similar in stature to the Na'vi – the indigenous people of *Pandora*, as depicted in James Cameron's *Avatar* – only I make them appear much younger. A parallel to this is already available, of course, in the form of Japanese ultra-violent and/or sexually explicit *Manga* and *Hentai* cartoons, although the resemblance of these cartoon images to people, including children, is arguably much closer. However, the degree to which my virtual images might or should be classified as *legally* obscene is a matter for conjecture and the complexities of the law, and is not something that we intend to pursue further here. Instead, we would like to discuss in more detail the relationship between obscenity (however it is legally defined), morality and psychological harm.

As already noted, as a result of legislation passed in 2009, it is now illegal in the UK to possess virtual, sexually related images of children, yet not in the US. Clearly, this includes virtual representations of child sexual abuse. As things stand, the legal status of these images is unambiguous, even if different in each respective country; but what about their moral status? Is the possession of these images, or even engaging in virtual paedophilia with either computer-generated virtual children or online role-playing adults in the guise of child avatars, morally problematic? It could be argued that online engagement of this kind is harmless (certainly if one means by this, victimless) because no children are *involved* let alone actually harmed. However, taking our guidance from the UK definition of obscenity, or even what seems to be implied by the US test, we might wish to argue that engagement of this kind is morally problematic because it is morally harmful, either to oneself or to others, or both.

By judging x to be morally harmful, the implication seems to be that it will cause the individual engaged in virtual activity x to think and/or feel and/or behave in ways that are morally prohibited offline, *when offline*. Does that mean that x is morally wrong only because of its potential (inevitable?) consequences, or is it wrong in and of itself? If it is not wrong in and of itself, then does engaging in x only *become* wrong *if* one starts to think and/or feel and/or behave in ways that are morally prohibited offline, when offline? If so, does this mean that for those who do not express equivalent thoughts, feelings and behaviours offline, engaging in virtual activity x is not morally wrong? Moreover, if the morality of engaging in virtual activity x is independent of the morality of engaging in x offline then what 'mechanisms of consequence' (causal factors) underlie the viewing of virtual activity x such that, for some, x does not lead to duplication offline whereas for others it does? If we can divorce the morality of the virtual activity from the activity as it occurs offline, then the pertinent question becomes not what is right or wrong in these virtual spaces, or good or bad, but what we can cope with psychologically to enable us to transcend spaces with differing moral freedoms.

Our recommendation that we examine the underlying psychological mechanisms at work in these spaces is not to deny that there are not moral issues related to the virtual enactment of actions morally prohibited offline; rather, it is to assert that an understanding of how we cope, psychologically, with certain potential moral freedoms expressed through STAs will help inform future moral judgements. Of course, one might wish to argue that engaging in virtual child abuse is wrong in and of itself, irrespective of any consequential harm. However, and as noted in Chapter 2, such an argument may be vulnerable to the charge of importing a moral system into virtual space that is constituted from the contingencies of our offline world (see Chapter 8 for further discussion).

These issues will be discussed in more detail throughout the chapters to follow. A question we have not yet addressed, however – which some may feel is an obvious question – is: Why would anyone *want* to engage in virtual child abuse, rape or bestiality, or even necrophilia? We will begin to examine this question in Chapter 7 and return to it in subsequent chapters. Before then, however, in the next chapter we explore further the notion of altered contingency and, with it, a number of different virtual spaces in which one can engage in offline taboo activities. We begin by looking at what might arguably be called the most passive form of taboo engagement: that associated with the Internet *spectator*.

5   The passive voyeur

Where's the harm in looking?

Without doubt, the Internet has provided users with unprecedented access to the sum of human affairs. A wealth of knowledge and opinion, fact and propaganda, is but a web address away. The highs and lows of human invention and creativity display themselves seemingly on an equal footing. In an attempt to access this information, the user may adopt what they believe to be the role of 'mere spectator', almost nonchalantly observing the spectacle unfold; their only involvement (they may believe), other than logging on, is selecting what to view.

In this chapter, we discuss the role of the Internet spectator and explore some of the spaces they may enter during their time in cyberspace. Is our spectator really able to observe the ebb and flow of this digitized traffic passively from a vantage point of altered contingencies, where taboo activities may be viewed in a space beyond the realm of offline moral accountability? Moreover, should they be? The moral accountability of our Internet spectator will therefore be judged not only in terms of the degree of passivity *actually* involved in their voyeurism but, equally, their reasons for selecting the material viewed. This reasoning will also be examined in relation to other non-Internet spaces where one can (allegedly) engage in a kind of voyeurism (e.g. the *Body Worlds* exhibit and *dark tourism*), as well as spaces that contain material with a purely virtual genesis (e.g. video games). To what extent is our voyeur passive, and how does this impact on their moral accountability when observing the 'goings on' within a space with altered contingencies? As is the theme throughout this book, the material we predominately concern ourselves with is taboo violation.

'VOYEUR' IN ITS BROADER CONTEXT

In considering the extent to which the Internet spectator acts as a kind of passive *voyeur*, it is important to be clear on what we mean by the term 'voyeur'. We use the term not in its strict clinical sense to mean 'the act of becoming sexually aroused by watching some form of nudity or sexual activity of unsuspecting, unconsenting individuals' (Adams, 2000, p. 216), but in a more general way to describe someone who merely seeks to observe without interaction (although we accept that this may include practices in keeping with the clinical definition). By way of justification for our use of the term, Metzl (2004) notes how 'voyeurism' is used within American culture in a much broader sense than its original clinical definition intended. Moreover, rather than being the pastime of a pathological fringe, Rye and Meaney (2007) report that a sample of undergraduate Canadian university students (predominantly women studying human sexuality) admitted that they would be willing to surreptitiously watch an attractive person undress if they were confident of not being caught. In fact, voyeuristic-style television shows (often referred to as *Reality TV*) are increasing in popularity (Baruh, 2009, 2010), and include such programmes as *Temptation Island*, *Survivor* and *Big Brother*, and even Internet-based sites such as *voyeurlounge.com*. We even recall how, back in the mid-1990s, webcam pioneer Jennifer Ringley gained international fame when, as a college student, she placed a webcam in her room and started a website called 'Jennicam'. Similarly, in 2000, Mitch Maddox legally changed his name to DotComGuy and had his house in Dallas monitored with webcams 24/7. He was intent on living for one year in his house without leaving it, ordering everything he needed from the Internet.

With the advent of increasingly sophisticated viewing and recording equipment, the voyeur is able to observe a multitude of activities, some darker and more intrusive than others. Our focus here, however, is on the voyeur in arguably their least intrusive role – as an Internet user who wishes to observe the world (or at least some specific aspect of it) as presented on the multitude of sites that purport to offer uncensored reality. An extreme example of this is the site *SeeMeRot.com* where, allegedly, one can view corpses rotting in their caskets courtesy of live coffin cams (the authenticity of this site is debated, however). The uncensored reality purported on these sites may take the form of a live webcam feed or may amount to pre-recorded footage. Either way, within the privacy and comfort of their home, our alleged passive voyeur may consider that they are observing these 'snapshots' of life from a vantage point beyond the realm of moral obligation. After all, and particularly in relation to pre-recorded images, the material is already out there. The horse has already bolted. What harm is there in watching it run around?

Strictly speaking, the act of intentionally viewing such material constitutes more than a mere passive role. Andrejevic (2004) warns us that we are all interactive consumers. Google knows where we have been and uses this information. In the digital age, we are not required to even comment on what we have watched in order to be interactive with that content. In fact, Andrejevic (2007, p. 239) states that 'in an era of distributed surveillance, the amplification of panoptic monitoring relies on the internalized discipline not just of the watched, but also of the watchers'. By this, he means that individuals do not just expect to watch others but also put themselves 'out there' to be watched – for example by creating webpages of themselves (like Facebook, etc.). As Miller (1988) famously remarked: 'Big Brother is you, watching'.

Whilst recognizing and accepting the points above concerning our more active role as Internet viewers, it has nevertheless been argued that cyberspace is *perceived* by the user as a private space, even though in many ways it is a very public space (e.g. Whitty and Joinson, 2009). This sense of privacy might likewise create a greater *feeling* of passivity. As such, we would like to suggest that the passive voyeur may still *feel* as if they are viewing this material passively: simply observing the drama unfold. The passivity they feel, then, relates to their psychological investment in, or involvement with, the material being viewed (a point we shall return to).

THE INDEFENSIBLE VOYEUR

Of course, being a 'mere spectator' or passive voyeur is less morally defensible if the act itself leads to the promulgation of the material being watched. By creating a demand that needs to be satisfied, particularly when that demand is for something illegal, the passive voyeur is complicit in the creation of a global niche market. (As an aside: when we say 'creating a demand', we do not mean to suggest that the demand did not exist prior to the onset of the world-wide-web; but even if the demand already existed, one can still be complicit in its expansion, availability and consumption by an Internet audience.) The connection between supply and demand can be made explicitly if the voyeur's access to the material requires an exchange of monies; in which case, the passivity of the voyeur becomes harder to justify. Yet it may be that the site does not require payment from our voyeur directly. Financial rewards may be gleaned from those who target advertisements at patrons of the site, even if the advertisements direct the patrons to other sites where they do have to pay. But suppose the voyeur never buys the 'products' advertised on the site, and so never exchanges monies. In which case, our voyeur may feel that they are not directly culpable, and therefore immune to moral condemnation (let us ignore the fact that, typically, by simply clicking on the site one earns the host money). Nevertheless, the motivation for those who advertise on the site stems from the expectation that an audience exists. As such, it seems reasonable to argue that the exchange of monies between site owners and advertisers is motivated by the presence on the site of the increasingly *less passive* voyeur who is thereby complicit in the proliferation of the material presented.

With regard to offline taboos, the Internet user who intentionally views images of child pornography, bestiality or even images of live animals being crushed underfoot (known as 'crushing') is not the perpetrator of a 'victimless' crime. In such cases, the voyeur is not passive (for reasons stated above), nor are they observing from a vantage point beyond the realm of moral obligation. Therefore, our alleged passive voyeur can justly be accused of occupying the role of accomplice in the marketing of child pornography, acts of bestiality or 'crushing', however far removed they may *feel* from the manufacturing process itself. In such cases, the user's moral accountability transcends domains because the source of the material the voyeur is engaged with (however passively they may consider this engagement to be) originates offline. When the manufacturing of images occurs within a space occupied also by a system of morality that typically condemns such activity, it is difficult to separate the product from the process even when these images are imported from the offline world into the virtual realm. If one imports the product one must also import the moral condemnation – including the legal declaration of obscenity – that is typically directed not only at the process by which this product is created but also its publication and consumption.

Does this mean that whenever taboo images – including those judged to be obscene – are imported from offline, the viewer can never truly position him/ herself within cyberspace as a passive observer, free from moral obligation? In considering this question, the discussion to follow will predominately focus on sites that contain pre-recorded materials (including still photographs) that many would deem taboo (perhaps even obscene), but which were not originally produced for consumption by an Internet audience, although this is certainly the purpose of the sites presented below, and therefore the motivation for their genesis. To clarify, then, the majority of the material presented was not created for general viewing, on the Internet or anywhere else, but the sites that present this material were created for the purpose of disseminating this material (material that is already available and therefore 'out there') to a wider (Internet) audience. Having said that, the site *nowthatsfuckedup.com* used to receive footage sent by US troops of 'mangled body parts' (Zornick, 2005, p. 1) taken during the conflict in Iraq in exchange for unlimited access to the site's pornographic material (the site has since been shut down by the Polk County Sheriff's Office, Florida, US).

SHOCK SITES AND THE DEFENSIBLE(?) VOYEUR

Much of this section will involve discussing the site *ogrish.com* – or as it is now known, *realogrish.com* – whose homepage makes the claim that the viewer's 'life and thoughts are about to change'. (We will continue to use the old name, *ogrish. com* for convenience.) In addition, mention will be made of other shock sites such as *encyclopediadramatica.com* and *bangedup.com*, which, like *ogrish.com*, aim to present uncensored snapshots of reality.

According to Tait (2008, p. 92), *ogrish.com* was originally 'an underground gore fetish site' whose tagline read 'Can you handle life?'. Once past the front page – consisting of an image of a pair of bloody hands – one could select from a variety of other graphic images of terrorist executions, the carnage of war (Iraq in particular), crime scenes, suicides, accidents and even medical procedures. The uploaded material, it is fair to say, depicts, in rather gruesome detail, the fate of individuals – largely victims of one sort or another. It is uncensored and readily available to those who choose to look; but unlike the earlier examples of Internet child pornography, bestiality and 'crushing', these images are generally not manufactured for the Internet user. Our voyeur is not complicit in their genesis. Nevertheless, the site has come under criticism – being accused of packaging 'gore porn' or 'death porn' (Tait, 2008, p. 93).

In response to this accusation, Tait notes how the site has more recently sought legitimacy by distancing itself from any association with 'gore', replacing the term with the now preferred 'uncensored media'. Likewise, the tagline 'Can you handle life?', which, for Tait, implied a kind of machismo challenge, was replaced by 'Uncover reality', suggestive of a search for knowledge. The apparent transformation in the site's status – from alleged provider of 'body horror' (as Tait calls it) to the guardian of an uncensored, unsanitized reality – has created something of a moral ambiguity. The site's legitimating stance is that of bearing witness to the realities of life, conflict and, in particular, death: free from moral condemnation. Its mantra might well be: 'We have the right to know'. Such a view is supported by the testimony of a US soldier (alias 'shottyintheboddy') who admitted sending combat images to the site *nowthatsfuckedup.com*. His reason for doing so was to give 'civilians a more accurate view of his life in Iraq' (Zornick, 2005, p. 1; see also Ross, 2010). Our passive voyeur is therefore left to judge for themselves – if they wish to judge at all – the morality of what they see (after all, even the images sent by the US soldier are *his* edited view of reality). But are we not likewise entitled to judge the morality of what the voyeur does – that is, their act of bearing witness *in this way*?

Irrespective of any move towards the alleged legitimacy of uncensored reality, and away from the gore fest that is now claimed to be incidental to the goal of the site, there are those who still find appeal in the fact that they are looking at images of bodies 'rendered monstrous by violence' (Tait, 2008, p. 108). It is these individuals who are of interest to us here. One user, for example, via the site forum, described how he was shocked at the sight of his first beheading, but after 30 minutes was 'hunting for more' (p. 101). Another openly declared that an image of a person being killed 'entertains me – that's all the justification I need' (p. 102). The images that appear on *ogrish.com* and other shock sites are, for many, disgusting – even for regular visitors. The shock site *bangedup.com*, for example, boasts that the viewer is about to see 'some really sick shit'. Our passive voyeur may be genuinely shocked by what they see, to the point of producing the kinds of physical, disgust-related responses outlined in Chapter 3. Perhaps such a reaction provides evidence for the argument that disgust in this context is and should be a marker for moral wisdom. The body horror one is disgusted by is real horror, as is noted on *ogrish.com*'s homepage: 'Our aim is to show you what goes on around the world and the fatal endings that people have'. Such examples are not hypothetical cases, in which no harm occurs; nor are they images of *virtual* body horror. What the images capture actually occurred. Therefore, disgust as an arbiter of moral wisdom seems appropriate, we argue, because such a response is elicited not simply by what the image symbolically represents, but by what has actually occurred to this person. We accept, however, that the moral line can be nebulous. On other shock sites, in which images may be of a person eating excrement or of individuals vomiting into one another's mouths (e.g. *encyclopediadramatica.com* and *sickestsites.com*), it could be argued that if no harm to anyone occurs (even in light of questionable hygienic and therefore health-related behaviour), then the use of disgust as a marker of moral worth could be challenged (even if one wished to uphold the legal claim to obscenity). One may be left to wonder, however, the extent to which those involved in these acts had been coerced, or were pathological or otherwise vulnerable to exploitation. And even if, for argument's sake, there was no coercion or pathology involved, one may still be concerned over the possibility that viewing these images would lead some if not all to become depraved and morally corrupted (as is the noted concern of the UK Obscene Publications Act 1959; see Chapter 4). There is also the potential for psychological harm not anticipated by the consumer of excrement, or other taboo violators – namely shame; even if not for the act itself, then as a result of its dissemination across the Internet.

That issue aside (for now), in the case of *ogrish.com*, many viewers who are initially shocked by what they see – disgusted even – continue (immediately or a short time later) to search for images that further shock and disgust them (recall the forum member from Tait's article, who was shocked at the sight of his first beheading, but quickly began searching for similar images). Perhaps this is an example of the concurrent feelings of disgust and some other emotion or sensation similar to that reported by Hemenover and Schimmack (2007) (see Chapter 3; recall that, in their study, participants were both disgusted and amused by what they saw). Suppose that our passive voyeur is both disgusted and, say, excited by what they see: To what extent are they still *passive*? They may not be complicit in the act of rendering monstrous, for as one user pointed out, we are 'not participating in the death by looking' (Tait, 2008, p. 102). To reiterate, the violence did not occur for the benefit of an Internet audience; but our alleged passive voyeur's changing physiological and emotional state would seem to make them far from nonchalant: it would be incorrect to call them a disinterested party.

Such visitors to the site are not bearing witness to the images presented out of a sense of indignation brought on by the sort of sanitized and censored news coverage we are (allegedly) typically exposed to; rather, they are motivated by (what is for them) entertainment value. Therefore, *in this context*, one might wish to argue that the images presented should be considered legally obscene: for if one is to bear witness to such scenes of body horror, then should not the act of bearing witness require that we take up the mantle of moral arbiter, thereby re-contextualizing the images and the motivation for viewing? Indeed, as Tait (2008, p. 99) points out (when discussing the views of Chouliaraki, 2006), 'the role of the news-maker is to perform moral labour that enables the viewer to take an ethical stance in relation to the suffering of others'. Unz *et al.* (2008) likewise report that those who take an interest in the news typically experience more intense 'moral' emotions, such as anger and disgust, or even contempt when the violence is perceived to be intentional. Such findings, they conclude, go against the 'cliché of news as unemotionally informing the audience' (2008, p. 148). Members of *ogrish.com*, by comparison (at least, if forum discussion is anything to go by), prefer to 'speculate over the cause and nature of death or injuries' (Tait, 2008, p. 100) – they seem more akin to what Unz *et al.* classified in their study as '*entertainment seekers*' – those who see news coverage more as a means of entertainment. So, do these entertainment seekers hold a morally defensible position?

The contrast between the positions of moral arbiter and entertainment seeker, we contend, concerns the instrumental nature of the images on display. To illustrate, Rudinow (1979, p. 176) notes an asymmetry within the act of voyeurism:

The voyeur seeks a spectacle, the revelation of the object of his interest, that something or someone should be open to inspection and contemplation; but no reciprocal revelation or openness is conceded, for the voyeur requires at the same time to remain hidden.

Thus, through the act of voyeurism one may find something to contemplate – the cause of the individual's death, perhaps – but this does not typically require that someone contemplate in return the motivation for the voyeur's interest, or even the value in it. In fact, Rudinow (1979, p. 176) further argues that, in maintaining an asymmetrical relationship with the object of voyeuristic interest, 'it cannot be touched, and one cannot be touched by it'. Now, it may be that Rudinow is talking literally about not being able to touch or be touched by the object. Nevertheless, one could also argue that the asymmetry identified by Rudinow also makes it less likely that one feels compelled to bear witness to the acts represented on sites like *ogrish.com*. If one is not 'touched' (*qua* moved to the point of moral outrage) by what one sees then perhaps one's role is transformed from *witness with a moral voice* to *audience with a non-moral agenda* – that is, to be entertained.

It is our contention that on sites like *ogrish.com*, the act of bearing witness is incomplete – perhaps distorted – to the point where it is likely that viewers are or become more interested in the forensic details than in taking a moral stance. In short, if used to invite the voyeur to engage in a moral reckoning, then the images presented on sites like *ogrish.com* are a means to that end. In the role of moral informant, the display of body horror is not gratuitous, and has some value. By comparison, as a vacuous clip bereft of context, the body horror served up on *ogrish.com* functions as an end in itself. If we are to judge these clips, *so presented*, as gratuitous and morally vacuous, then should we not likewise judge the viewing of them in this way as morally wrong?

Although not complicit in its manufacture, and therefore not an accomplice in the same way that the viewer of Internet child pornography is said to be, the alleged passive voyeur is nevertheless viewing material generated offline in a way that appears (at least for some, maybe even many) to serve no other purpose than ghoulish entertainment. But why should viewing this material for its entertainment value elicit moral condemnation? Perhaps it is because it is judged to be symptomatic of a lack of respect for the victim, or because it demonstrates a disregard for the hurt felt by the victim's family/friends/colleagues. Perhaps it may even lead some to fear further moral corruption on the part of the voyeur: a slippery slope or downward spiral effect leading to the depravity and moral corruption that the UK legislation on obscenity seeks to protect us from.

OTHER FORMS OF ALLEGED VOYEURISM

Parallels regarding the moral ambiguity of *ogrish.com* can be drawn with Gunther von Hagens' *Body Worlds* exhibition (first shown in Japan in 1996 and, according to the official website – http://www.bodyworlds.com/en.html – continuing to be exhibited in various countries throughout the world). *Body Worlds* exhibits donated bodies in varying degrees of anatomical completeness through a process of *plastination* (a polymer that preserves tissue). Moore and Brown (2007, p. 232) report that initial reactions to the exhibition were ambivalent and on occasion openly hostile, being described by some as 'shock art' or 'Dr Frankenstein's exhibition'. They also recount the words of Herschovitch (2003), who at the time declared that the exhibit spoke to 'an unsatiated, voyeuristic public fascinated with body, immortality and death' (2007, p. 828). (For an older exhibition that parallels aspects of *Body Worlds*, see King's Capuchins' Catacombs of Palermo, at http://motomom.tripod.com/index-3.html and also http://www. sacred-destinations.com/italy/palermo-capuchin-catacombs). According to Moore and Brown, concerns over the exhibition have tended to centre on the 'nebulous line between reverence for the dead and dehumanization of life' (p. 238) and, more broadly, between education and art. Those who view the exhibition as educational, and as a celebration of the human form, denounce the idea that it dehumanizes those who have donated their bodies. Moore and Brown seem to side with this more favourable view, arguing that plastination affords the average person an opportunity to experience something few outside of the medical profession would typically see. Thus, one is able to bear witness to the marvels of the human body. For, as Moore and Brown note, 'The poses are designed in part to show the mechanical capacities of the human body in performing various everyday acts as well as athletic feats, displaying the complex of muscles, nerves, vessels and organs involved in these actions' (p. 232). In addition, one is able to cast an eye over these 'wonders' without succumbing to the sense of revulsion that often has to be overcome during more traditional dissections.

Again, then, we are presented with the argument that being invited to bear witness to, in this case, the realities and marvels of the human body (as opposed to 'the fatal endings that people have' – recall *ogrish.com*'s homepage) placates the charge of dehumanization or even ghoulishness, and with it the force of the moral condemnation. Dissenters would perhaps challenge the primacy of the educational element within the *Body Worlds* exhibition, however, holding instead that, primarily, *Body Worlds* is a collection of works of art or, perhaps at its crudest level, novelty entertainment. This latter criticism makes *Body Worlds* vulnerable to the charge of satisfying a more macabre voyeurism, much as Herschovitch (2003) remonstrated. However, against this charge (and drawing on the findings of Leiberich *et al.*, 2006), Moore and Brown conclude that public feedback indicates that voyeuristic motivations are low, surpassed by a more widespread acknowledgement of the exhibition's educational worth. And so the debate continues.

The *Body Worlds* exhibit has sometimes been included within a broader phenomenon first referred to by Lennon and Foley (1996) as *dark tourism* – which involves visiting 'sites associated with death, suffering and the seemingly macabre' (Stone, 2006, p. 146). Among its destinations, dark tourism includes locations of natural disaster or conflict (such as New Orleans in the aftermath of hurricane Katrina, former battlefields such as the Somme or Waterloo) and even crash sites (Lockerbie in Scotland, for example) or other locations of death (Auschwitz-Birkenau or the killing fields of Cambodia). Motivations for visiting such places no doubt vary, as do the moral views concerning the appropriateness of a dark tourism industry. Debate centres primarily on whether one's motive is 'morbid curiosity or a malicious indulgence in another person's suffering' (Stone, 2006, p. 148) or whether one's actions 'lend moral meaning to sites of death and the macabre' (p. 150). Thus, a more morally favourable stance might hold that rather than supplying experiences intended to satisfy a fascination with death, 'dark tourism sites must engender a degree of empathy between the sightseer and the past victim' (p. 152). Stone and Sharpley (2008) acknowledge, however, that not all may be so edified or even seek edification through being a 'dark tourist'. Nevertheless, a more morally acceptable position seems to be procured by those who seek to bear witness to what has happened at these locations and engage in empathic concern and/or moral contemplation.

BEYOND THE LONE SPECTATOR

Thus far, we may be guilty of giving the impression that the Internet voyeur is (or has to be) a lone spectator (unlike those who visit *Body Worlds* or dark tourism sites, for example). However, many Internet sites that disseminate the kinds of images discussed above are social spaces with their own forums in which the user can discuss what they are witnessing, as is evident from the examples used by Tait (2008) (taken from the *ogrish.com* forum). As such, it may be that within these spaces the audience is invited to interact, and even encouraged to adopt a moral stance by the site's creator(s). It may even be that members of the site themselves *self*-regulate the space and the moral stance adopted. Just such an act of (alleged) self-regulation was reported by Kaigo and Watanabe (2007). Kaigo and Watanabe analysed the content of a Japanese Internet bulletin board forum – *Channel 2* – renowned for its dissemination of risqué and taboo content (at least, risqué and taboo by Japanese standards), at a time when execution images of a Japanese hostage taken during the Iraq conflict in 2004 were posted onto the site. They reported how the images 'triggered feelings of shock' amongst the users of the site, which led to 'a strong impetus toward moderation in the forum' (2007, p. 1264).

The same striving for consensus, and establishing of norms of behaviour, was discussed by Rye and Meaney (2007) in relation to groups of offline voyeurs – one group was made up of men who observed the goings on within offices using rooftop telescopes, the other was a group of couples observing each other's sexual activity (taken from Forsyth, 1996). Rye and Meaney (2007, p. 49) noted how 'both groups showed a disdain for "solo voyeurs" . . ., suggesting a need for social approval. A form of meta-normalization was seen here: The seeking of approval was itself a component of social validation'.

It would appear that just as the norms of acceptable viewing were established within the Channel 2 forum, so too the voyeur groups established their own norms of appropriate practice, and as a consequence disapproved of the lone voyeur who does not seek or seemingly require any form of 'social' validation. In addition, Kaigo and Watanabe (2007) acknowledge that not all the images that appear on Channel 2 are self-regulated in the way that the execution images were. They also accept as reasonable the suggestion that, with regard to the execution images, self-regulation occurred as a result of (amongst other things) 'feelings of identification among the users because the victim was Japanese' (p. 1264). Nevertheless, the question is not whether self-regulation occurs, or whether one is invited to adopt a particular stance, or bear witness to the images one views in a particular way, but whether one should be required to do this. Should one not be permitted to be 'simply entertained' by what is out there? Equally, should one's enjoyment need social validation by others who share that space? (*'It's ok to like it, because we like it too.'*) In relation to the first question (that of being entertained), the concern that *Body Worlds* (for example) dehumanizes those who have donated their bodies, or that *ogrish.com* demonstrates a lack of respect for the victims/families (etc.), could of course be removed (at least in terms of any specific and direct connection to actual persons) if the source of the alleged 'entertainment' was generated from within cyberspace itself.

In virtual space, the creation of anatomically accurate exhibitions of the human form or virtual body horror – execution, murder and torture (etc.) – could be achieved in the absence of any actual human element. However, one might wish to inquire: Who would visit a virtual version of *ogrish.com*? After all, what sort of reality would our voyeur be trying to 'handle'? Perhaps the motivation would be entertainment, pure and simple; and perhaps in some respects a purely entertainment-based version of *ogrish.com* has been with us for some time in the guise of literary and cinema fiction (for example) – particularly, but not exclusively, horror – or more recently by way of ultra-violent computer games. This being the case, the question of whether the images depicted within a virtual version of *ogrish.com* or more traditional works of fiction, or even violent computer games, are disrespectful to victims (of war/torture, etc.) in general is applicable. Just such an objection was forwarded by Dr Patel (2006) of the Medical Foundation for the Care of Victims of Torture when stating that video game depictions of torture serve only to trivialize the act; consequently, we risk normalizing violence prohibited by law (however, see Zagal, 2009, for a discussion on ethical video games). Waddington (2007, p. 127) likewise holds that ultra-violent virtual simulations are in danger of 'devaluing wrongness' – a process that will increase as it becomes harder to differentiate virtual from non-virtual violence.

BEARING WITNESS THROUGH OTHER MEDIA

Yet depictions of violence and even taboo violation are hardly restricted to modern video games. As noted already, literature and more recently cinema have explored and, at times, graphically presented them to their respective audiences. The 2008 film *Delta* (directed by Kornél Mundruczó), for example, concerns the topic of incest. Lynne Stopkewich's 1996 film, *Kissed*, centres around Sandra and her obsession with death: an obsession that develops into necrophilia. The 2005 film *Hard Candy* (directed by David Slade) tackles the issue of Internet grooming and paedophilia. Rape has been the subject matter of a number of films, although perhaps none more graphically and brutally represent it than *Irreversible* (directed by Gaspar Noé, 2002). Critiques of such films are not unaware of the sensitive nature of the subject matter portrayed, and often their reviews reveal a similar weighing up of moral stance/real-world authenticity against the possibility that the depiction is simply gratuitous or even obscene (extreme examples of the latter are arguably the Japanese Guinea Pig film series, including *Devil's Experiment* and *Flowers of Flesh and Blood*). Patterson (2009, p. 1), for example, declares, when reviewing *Delta*, that we may even be asked to consider whether 'incest isn't almost heroic – at least, that is, when a beautiful, amatory pair of half-siblings is compared with an evil rapist of a father'. This suggests that the director is inviting us to judge what we see within a wider context and/or against a backdrop of further taboo violation.

In *Irreversible*, the brutal rape scene has been the centre of much debate among reviewers. Mitchell (2003, p. 1), for example, states: 'It's no doubt that he [Gaspar Noé] wanted to make a film that navigates the fine line between noxious and obnoxious' and in doing so has presented us with one of the 'most gruesomely detailed rapes' ever to be witnessed on the screen. The camera takes in the scene 'without looking away – that's left up to you'. In a similar vein, McAllister (2006) asks whether the violence depicted in *Irreversible* was necessary or gratuitous. In response, he states: 'I would argue that these scenes are so horrifically convincing that they become virtually impossible to watch, and this is the effect that violence should have' (p. 1). Such fictional portrayals are not without risk, Koppelman (2005) reflects, but can be morally valuable precisely because they help to dispel the notion that evil is somehow outside of us.

Such cinematic examples represent but a tiny sample of the material that is already available to us. The extent to which violent images are, in their own brutal way, either edifying or gratuitous continues to be debated and is perhaps something that needs to be judged on a case-by-case basis; it is also something that needs to be placed within a wider context. It is therefore not so much that the situations *per se* that the film director chooses to depict are a target for our approval or disapproval; rather, it is how the director chooses to present them, which is concomitant with the way we are invited to view them, that is (or should be) of concern (Nussbaum, 1992; Poole, 1982).[1] This is made no more apparent than in some of the critical reviews of Mel Gibson's 2004 film, *The Passion of the Christ*. The importance of context is a theme that runs through many of the reviewers' comments, and is summed up in the words of film critic Kenneth Turan (2004, p. 1):

> The problem with 'The Passion's' violence is not merely how difficult it is to take, it's that its sadistic intensity obliterates everything else about the film. Worse than that, it fosters a one-dimensional view of Jesus, reducing his entire life and world-transforming teachings to his sufferings . . ..

Such sentiment echoes our objection to the viewing of the images on *ogrish.com* (and other shock sites), which are typically isolated from the wider context in which they occurred and therefore bereft of sufficient content to enable the viewer (if they wish to do so) to bear witness to the body horror in an informed way, or make a moral judgement beyond an acknowledgement of the horror of what is witnessed in isolation on the site. In fact, Champoux (2006) argues for the utility of film clips in informing classroom discussion and illustrating ethical theory in an educational environment – although admittedly these did not include violent scenes. Nevertheless, the principle remains the same if directed towards a mature audience, which is perhaps one of the intentions of the film director.

The topic of traditional fiction will be taken up again in Chapter 8, when compared with the sorts of images of violence available within single-player video games. As well as imagery and representation, video games also allow for a level of interaction not possible in the more traditional fictions. Thus, when earlier asked to consider why anyone would want to visit a virtual version of *ogrish.com*, perhaps an important incentive available within video games is the possibility of virtual interaction with the material/representations: for in addition to passively viewing virtual (*qua* fictional) characters interacting – as is typical with film audiences – computer-mediated spaces also afford a degree of agency not possible via more traditional fictions. Whatever remnants of passivity are associated with our voyeur, these can be largely dispelled by the much more extensive engagements and control given over to them in the virtual worlds of gamespace. Equally extended are the sorts of activities one might feel disgusted about. For as Kingsepp (2007, p. 370) notes:

> [I]n the world created by digital games, we can find almost anything according to taste, and nothing, not even the most bizarre, is impossible. On the contrary, everything is not only possible, it is also there, just waiting to be found . . ..

In single-player video games, the user (player) is permitted some autonomy within the gamespace, even to the extent that interactions can (and often do) occur that are incidental to the goal of the game. In *Grand Theft Auto: San Andreas*, for example, a player can take a break from the game's main storyline and gameplay in order to wreak havoc. These interactions may be considered gratuitous, and in a literal (gameplay) sense this may be true; but should they be judged as impermissible because of this? Alternatively, what if violating offline moral taboos is *an integral part of the gameplay*. In this respect, the actions are not gratuitous but, even so, should they be morally prohibited?

Single-player games also lack the need for social validation by others who share the gamespace because typically none do. By their very nature, single-player games are lone pursuits. Differences between single- and multiplayer games will be discussed in Chapters 8 and 9, as will the second of the two questions raised earlier, which is more applicable to multiplayer games – namely should one's enjoyment need social validation by others who share that space?

Before any of this can be discussed, however, if we are to evaluate the appropriateness of disgust as a measure of moral wisdom within VEs, we need to consider the extent to which emotions (of which disgust is one) can be elicited from within these virtual spaces. It was argued in Chapter 3 that if the physiological changes that occur in relation to disgust can be triggered by the mere thought of a taboo violation, then it seems reasonable to conjecture that any virtual display of taboo violation will likewise elicit a *genuine* disgust response. However, for this to be the case, we must overcome what is known as the *paradox of fiction*.

6 Virtually real emotions

Addressing the paradox of fiction

In Chapter 3, we discussed Damasio's (1994) somatic marker hypothesis, which posits that the mere thought of a taboo violation is sufficient to elicit a visceral response characteristic of disgust. We then conjectured that if simply thinking about such prohibited acts is capable of triggering a disgust response then it is a relatively small step to the claim that any *virtual* display of taboo violation should have a similar effect. However, before such a claim can be supported, we must overcome the *paradox of fiction*. Essentially, the paradox centres on the question of whether it is possible to express genuine emotion towards a character (or event) known to be fictitious. Over the years, many embroiled in this debate have argued that it is not, claiming instead that the putative emotional response is somehow 'not the same'; others disagree, considering the paradox itself to be fictitious – a pseudo-problem.

In this chapter we examine the paradox of fiction in an attempt to show that it is a pseudo-paradox. This is a necessary antecedent to any serious discussion on the emotional impact of STAs: for if it can be argued that disgust or any other emotion elicited by fictional characters/objects/events (fear, loathing, lust, etc.) is in fact not a real emotion, then the question of whether disgust can be used as a measure of moral wisdom becomes redundant. Therefore, with regard to the enactment of STAs on or by characters with a purely virtual genesis, before the issue of the moral wisdom or moral fallibility of virtually elicited disgust can even begin to be considered, it needs to be established that such an emotion is in fact genuine. Furthermore, if disgust is shown to be a pseudo-emotion then any investigation into the impact of STAs on the psychological well-being of individuals is compromised, at least with regard to the possibility of detrimental *emotional* consequences. Of course, it may seem obvious to some that we *do* experience real emotions when engaged with fiction. This intuition, we accept, is a powerful one. Nevertheless, it is important to establish why there is at least an alleged paradox of fiction before going on to show why this claim is false. Doing so, we contend, provides a securer platform on which to build a case for considering the permissibility (or not) of STA based on psychological impact rather than morality *per se*.

THE USE OF VR WITHIN PSYCHOLOGY

VR technology is employed more and more in the study of a wide range of psychological phenomena (Sanchez-Vives and Slater, 2005; Takatalo *et al.*, 2008). As Hoffman wrote over a decade ago: 'Virtual reality . . . has the potential to become a powerful scientific research tool for psychologists' (1998, p. 195). Even a cursory glance at some of the more recent publications in psychology suggests that this potential is well on the way to being realized. What appears to be motivating much, if not all, of these research examples is the general belief that a given study's findings can be generalized beyond the virtual realm. If the paradox of fiction holds, however, then the generalizability of these findings must be questioned: for how can we take the alleged pseudo-emotional responses of participants in VEs to be a valid measure of the sorts of emotional responses that would be elicited by people offline? The generalizability of these findings is not of direct concern here, however, at least not in terms of validating psychological studies in VEs (for further discussion, see Young, 2010). What is of concern is Fineman *et al.*'s (2007, p. 556) word of caution: that a direct comparison between virtual and non-virtual worlds is 'ontologically questionable'. This cautionary note forms the basis for the paradox of fiction; a paradox that needs to be resolved if the debate over disgust as a measure of moral wisdom within VEs is to have any gravitas (it is also relevant to the discussion on play in the next chapter).

THE PARADOX OF FICTION

In 1975 Radford asked us to consider how it could be that we are moved by the fate of the fictional character Anna Karenina. Shortly after, Walton (1978, p. 5), using a fictitious example, questioned the validity of the claim made by horror-movie-goer Charles: 'that he was "terrified" of the slime' as it moved across the screen, appearing to head in his direction. Was Charles *really* terrified? Are we *really* moved by the fate of Anna?

The (alleged) paradox of fiction is created by the fact that (a) it is somewhat commonplace for us to exhibit (what appear to be) emotions – fear, pity, anger, elation, etc. – towards fictional characters, and yet (b) it is understood that these characters do not exist. Thus, Walton (1978), in asking whether Charles was afraid of the slime, recognizes that the answer should inform a larger question concerning the relationship between fictional and real worlds – namely: Is the fictional world remote, and if so to what extent can this 'distance' or its 'barrier' be traversed?

Despite accepting the existence of certain ostensive similarities between Charles and someone exhibiting real emotion, Walton is nevertheless unwilling to concede that Charles's response to the slime is evidence of genuine fear. Importantly, although Charles exhibits physiological changes whenever the slime appears – increased tension in the muscles and adrenalin flow, a quickening of the pulse, even a behavioural change (clutching the chair) – he does not hold the belief that he is in any danger. As a consequence, Charles is not *really* afraid. Instead, when confronted by the on-screen slime, Charles experiences 'quasi-fear' (1978, p. 13). As he gets 'caught up' (p. 6) in the unfolding drama, in addition to the various physiological changes that occur, Charles adopts the *make-believe* belief that the slime is dangerous: not really dangerous, just make-believedly so (see also Novitz, 1980). Likewise, if one is moved by the fate of Anna Karenina, one is only make-believe moved; just as one is only make-believe saddened by the death of Forrest Gump's wife, Jenny, or by the death of Simba's father in *The Lion King*. In short, according to Walton, as a result of certain physiological changes, and the awareness of his make-believe beliefs about the slime, Charles can be said to have entered into a *distinctive* psychological state – that of being *quasi-afraid*, exhibiting *quasi-fear*. What he has not entered into, importantly, is an actual psychological state of fear. He is not really afraid.

In contrast, Radford (1975), after much discussion on how it is that we can be moved by the fate of fictional characters like Anna Karenina, concludes that being so moved, although 'natural' (p. 78), nevertheless demonstrates inconsistency and incoherence. Radford accepts that one can be *genuinely* frightened by certain episodes within a horror film, or *truly* moved by the fate of a fictional character (Radford, 1977), and consequently would accept that Charles is genuinely afraid of the slime. However, Charles's corresponding lack of belief that the slime is dangerous means that the fear he exhibits is in fact incoherent. Unlike Walton, Radford rejects the view that a lack of belief that something is dangerous relegates the emotion to a quasi-state. The existence of such a belief is not a necessary condition for the occurrence of a *genuine* emotional state of fear (for example); rather, 'such a belief is a necessary condition of our being unpuzzlingly, rationally, or coherently frightened' (1977, p. 210).

Walton, of course, is not troubled by claims of incoherence because, for him, Charles and those similarly caught up in the fiction exhibit quasi-emotions that are not vulnerable to such a charge. After all, it is perfectly compatible with the notion of make-believe that such a belief should be incoherent with other beliefs that are not make-believe. However, not everyone is satisfied by Radford's and Walton's respective attempts at resolving the 'paradox'. Mannison (1985, p. 73), for example, considers that Radford's conclusion 'insults us'. Consequently, over the past thirty years or so, numerous articles have been generated proposing various alternative solutions. Of particular interest to this chapter is Hartz's (1999) proposal. According to Hartz, at the centre of the paradox is the cognitive theory of emotion; or at least a particular take on it – what he calls *Generic Cognitivism*. Specifically, it is the view that 'every emotion must be caused by an appropriate belief' (1999, p. 559).

THE PARADOX AND COGNITIVISM

For the cognitivist, emotional states are intentional in so far as they are directed towards an object or event. I am afraid *of* the venomous snake crossing my path (for example). But they also involve an appraisal of the object (Arnold, 1960; Deigh, 1994; Lazarus, 1991; Solomon, 1988, 2004). I am afraid of the snake crossing my path because I believe it to be dangerous; and I believe it to be dangerous because I judge it to have certain properties I attribute to 'being dangerous' (Brock, 2007).

The importance of an appropriate belief, particularly in the form of an appraisal, is noted by Speisman *et al.* (1964, p. 367; an early example of the cognitivist tradition):

> [A] stimulus must be regarded by the person as a threat to his welfare in order for the stress response to be produced. Thus, the same stimulus may be either a stressor or not, depending upon the nature of the cognitive appraisal the person makes regarding [its] significance for him.

According to Speisman *et al.* (1964), not only must the stress response be elicited by an appropriate appraisal – say, that of a threat to one's welfare – but, equally, it can cease or not occur at all if the appraisal changes or is different to begin with. To elicit a genuine stress response, then (or indeed a genuine emotional response of any kind), underlying the appropriateness of the belief (*qua* appraisal) must be a more fundamental requirement – *existential commitment* (see also Wilkinson, 2000). In other words, one must believe in the existence of the intentional object to begin with (see Säätelä, 1994). But because we lack existential commitment with regard to the characters and events of fiction, yet are often emotionally responsive to them, a seeming conflict arises. Many who have written about the paradox try to resolve it in a similar way to either Radford or Walton, and, importantly, in a way that does not violate the cognitivist approach. Suits (2006, p. 372) describes their collective position as responding 'emotionally to the story, but not quite in the way we would respond if we really believed the story's events were taking place'.

This collective position is compatible with the view that these 'emotional' states are inconsistent and incoherent, or are really just quasi-emotions. Unfortunately, if this is the collective position (the majority response), it suggests that there is little point in positioning disgust as a measure of moral wisdom in VEs, or even arguing that it demonstrates moral fallibility. Similarly, we might challenge the idea that a representation (at least *qua* representation) can elicit genuine prurient appeal, as required by the US definition of obscenity (see Chapter 4); we may even contest the ability of such virtual representation to cause moral depravity and/or moral corruption – at least if such altered states are indicative of some form of genuine cognitive-*affective* change in us. In contrast to the collective position, then, and in an attempt to preserve the legitimacy of the debate over the role of disgust as an arbiter of our moral attitude, we will now discuss ways of resolving the paradox that do not leave virtually elicited emotions vulnerable to the charge of being ontologically distinct.

We have seen how Hartz (1999) places Cognitivism at the centre of the paradox of fiction. He does, however, further develop this argument by stating more precisely that it is not Generic Cognitivism *per se* that produces the paradox but a stricter version of it. This he calls *Rational Cognitivism*: the view that 'every emotion must be caused by an appropriate belief that is consistent with every other belief one holds at the time' (p. 559). It is therefore the lack of consistency or congruence between belief and emotion (a fundamental requirement of Rational Cognitivism) that creates the conflict. To illustrate: *because* Charles believes (knows) that the slime does not exist, it *logically follows* from this that he does not believe it is dangerous – something he attests to. So far, so good – the principle of Rational Cognitivism is upheld. Any further claim to the effect that Charles is afraid of the slime violates this principle: for in order to be afraid of the slime, he must believe it to be dangerous (which he does not); and in order to believe it to be dangerous, he must believe that it exists (which he does not). In the case of Charles, then, Rational Cognitivism requires either that he hold different beliefs from those claimed or that he is not really afraid of the slime.

Hartz, interestingly, provides us with a third possibility. Charles's assertion that the slime is not dangerous should not be 'taken as sufficient [evidence] to show that he does *not also* believe, in some more rudimentary way, that the slime *is* dangerous' (p. 560). Rational Cognitivism demands that Charles, on holding the belief that the slime does not exist, necessarily believes that it is not dangerous. This is indeed what he claims. Yet his reaction to its presence suggests otherwise. Generic Rationalism, in contrast, requires only that the emotion be caused by an appropriate belief, not necessarily one that is also rationally related to the subject's other beliefs. We take Hartz to be interpreting 'appropriate', here, as *caused by a belief about the slime*, as opposed to being caused by a belief about something else. The more rudimentary belief that Hartz mentions is essentially an unconscious belief. Hartz argues that, unlike Radford and Walton, by adopting a functional view of beliefs, he is not committed to the idea that they are necessarily mental states one must be aware of. Therefore, whenever the on-screen slime appears, it is 'automatically and involuntarily' (p. 563) assessed by Charles as a threat. A belief is subsequently formed that the slime is dangerous, but this 'is not consciously entertained' (p. 563). Consequently, it is possible for this unconscious belief to be 'inconsistent with what Charles explicitly avows' (p. 563) – that the slime is *not* dangerous – or with other beliefs, such as the belief that it does not exist.

DISSOLVING THE PARADOX

The paradox of fiction dissolves if (a) we adhere to the view that it is simply a product of the rationality constraint imposed on emotional states by Rational Cognitivism and (b) 'blind emotion-causing mechanisms in the brain [refuse] to abide by pre-conceived rational structures' (p. 577). Hartz does use the word 'refuse' when discussing these mechanisms. However, we prefer to think of them occurring *irrespective* of any preconceived rational structures. We suspect that Hartz would not object to this.

In addition, Kreitman (2006, p. 614) claims that emotional responses to fiction can only occur if a number of preconditions are in place, which then enable the 'affect-laden, prereflective knowledge of the [individual] ... to be brought into play'. Kreitman does, however, recognize that there is a potential gulf between fictional and real worlds (as was noted earlier), which feeds the seeming paradox, but resolves this by maintaining that, although the characteristics and constructs applied to works of fiction are arranged in novel ways, they are nevertheless derived from, and are therefore compounds of, actual experience. In short, fiction presents us with an 'unreal entity with real characteristics' (p. 616). (See also Shapiro and colleagues' work on the *perceived realism* of media characters, narratives, etc. – Shapiro *et al.*, 2010; Shapiro and McDonald, 1992; and Shapiro *et al.*, 2006; Busselle and Bilandzic, 2008.) Interestingly, Mannison (1985, p. 74) notes that Radford fails to discuss 'the common belief', which seems compatible with Kreitman's position, that a fictional character is someone we can identify with. This is a point we will return to in Chapters 14 and 15.

The commitment Kreitman (2006) demands of fictional objects is not, therefore, existential, but rather a commitment to authenticity. Real-world authenticity is measured by the number of attributes of a certain kind possessed by the object of fiction. He illustrates the connection (to real-world authenticity) by using the example of a shark (specifically, here, we are referring to the Great White). In real life, this creature is a formidable killing machine that possesses a number of dangerous, death-inducing attributes – size, speed, agility and, of course, large razor-sharp teeth. For Kreitman (2006, p. 617; emphasis in original), if such attributes are present, even in a novel way, with coherence and vivacity, then 'the compound image ... *must* be frightening, since the perception of these various properties is affect-laden'. We suggest that a good example of such attributes presented in a novel way is the creature in Ridley Scott's film, *Alien*.

By adding Hartz's view that the affect-laden-ness of our response to fictional objects can stem from unconscious beliefs about them (something Kreitman appears agnostic about), we are presented with a plausible account of why Charles is afraid of the slime: not quasi-afraid, or incoherently afraid, but genuinely afraid; and, likewise, why we can be genuinely moved by the fate of Anna Karenina. To further support our position, what is needed is an account of emotions that is compatible with our amalgamation of Hartz's and Kreitman's respective views. A position that will explain how emotional responses can occur automatically and unconsciously, in the presence of objects we have no existential commitment towards, and even in contrast to the content of other sincerely held beliefs about the object.

EMOTIONS AS COMPLEX OCCURRENCES

Griffiths (1990, 1997), whilst drawing on the work of Ekman (1980), argues for the existence of affect programs to explain why some emotional responses are:

- pan-cultural;
- involuntary and unconsciously initiated;
- in stark contrast to our consciously held beliefs.[1]

Affect programs are neural programs that store 'a predetermined set of responses which are activated in a co-ordinated fashion in rapid response to some external stimuli' (Griffiths, 1990, p. 182). Activation produces wide-ranging autonomic and physiological/behavioural change: musculoskeletal, hormonal; even facial and vocal. Moreover (and again in keeping with Ekman), Griffiths argues for the existence of some form of modular appraisal system capable of evaluating stimuli and triggering particular affect programs. Not only does such appraisal occur automatically; importantly, it functions independently of those cognitive systems that organize our beliefs along more consciously controlled and hence rational lines.

This time drawing from Fodor (1983), Griffiths (1990, p. 185) advocates an appraisal component that is *informationally encapsulated*: meaning that it is ' "separate" from the rest of the mind'. In the absence of any sharing of information between the informationally encapsulated appraisal module and these other, more consciously constituted, systems, '[i]t is possible for a modular system to respond as if a certain state of affairs obtains although the organism as a whole believes that that state of affairs does not obtain' (ibid.). A rapid response that errs on the side of caution is believed to have had survival benefits – it is better to flee and then realize that one was mistaken than hang around too long deliberating and end up injured or dead.

The appraisal system is compatible with Hartz's (1999) argument for the involvement of unconscious beliefs that are (or can be) incongruent with other more publicly aired and sincerely held beliefs. As was discussed earlier, the belief that the snake crossing my path is dangerous stems from my appraisal of the situation: I believe the snake to be dangerous because I judge it to have certain properties – properties I attribute to 'being dangerous'. Perhaps the assumption is that this appraisal/judgement is a conscious one. However, Solomon (2004, p. 77), a staunch advocate of 'emotions as judgements', concedes that a judgement need not be 'deliberative, articulate or fully conscious'.

The automatic appraisal mechanisms can also draw on memories of prior emotionally eliciting objects/events to inform which affect program to trigger. Should the currently perceived object/event be similar to that which previously elicited a fear response (for example), then it is likely that such a response will be triggered automatically now, irrespective of any additional conscious belief that, *this time*, it is safe. Again, we would argue that this is compatible with Kreitman's (2006) claim that what elicits the emotional response in cases of fiction is the pre-reflective knowledge we have of the characteristics of the fictional object – its authenticity. It is this authenticity that we respond to; it is this that gives it its affect-laden-ness: for 'the attributes of the fictional character are not themselves fictional; rather, they are drawn from experience, and hence may possess emotional potency' (Kreitman, 2006, p. 616). So even if the virtual image is not a representation of something actual – as exemplified by the *Alien* example – it nonetheless has authentic components that are capable of eliciting changes in our affective response to it (see Gerrig, 1993; Oatley, 1999b). In the case of the examples introduced in Chapter 4 – the young Na'vi or the small creatures with large eyes and a child-like voice – this may be sufficient to elicit prurient appeal.

What is interesting about the Ekman/Griffiths account is the complexity of the emotion. So far, the emotion has involved an appraisal (directed towards an object/event), which then automatically triggers an affect program response. This response involves physiological change. However, and importantly, as well as initiating memories (thoughts and images), the appraisal process can also (and does) trigger coping strategies. These can be context dependent and/or culturally specific. Thus, when exhibiting fear, a coping strategy may be to close one's eyes and turn one's head away, or even scream. These might be acceptable when watching a horror film (although perhaps the former more so than the latter); however, if hiding from a menacing and dangerous individual when alone and isolated, perhaps clasping one's hand over one's mouth is preferable. Either way, the coping strategy is not caused by the emotion; rather, it is a *component* of it.

Appraisal, affect programs and psychological and physiological/behavioural adjustment are each a component of the emotion. For Ekman and Griffiths, then, emotions are *complex occurrences*. Typically, these occurrences involve an appraisal that is congruent with one's conscious beliefs. I am afraid because I am hanging from a high ledge by my fingertips – a precarious position to be in – or because I know that the snake crossing my path is highly venomous and therefore extremely dangerous. On the other hand, because appraisal occurs independently of our conscious beliefs, it can be incongruent with them. This independence is able to account for the paradox of fiction; it is able to explain why Charles cowers at the sight of the slime despite his assertion that it is not dangerous. Charles is afraid of the slime in so far as he enters into an emotional state of fear whenever it appears. This state is produced by his unconscious appraisal of the perceived object, or, rather, the characteristics it possesses, which triggers an affect program response. But his emotional state also includes his cowering rather than his running for the exit.

Using Ekman and Griffiths' approach, the fact that Charles does not leave the cinema is not evidence of a lack of genuine fear (or evidence for Walton's quasi-fear); rather, it is simply a characteristic of that particular emotional state in that particular context. This, of course, suggests that each individual occurrence within a particular category of emotion – in this case fear – is different. Different, yes: but still with sufficient similarities not to be considered incommensurate. These similarities are based on physiological responses, cultural norms with regard to behavioural expression and coping strategies, and the context one finds oneself in. Differences likewise depend on context and variations in norms across cultures. How we choose to categorize these emotions, the variations that occur across cultures and whether there is a degree of arbitrariness in the taxonomy are all interesting questions; but they are not questions that deal *directly* with the existence of the emotional state *per se*. Consequently, they will not be addressed here.

Might it be, then, that Radford is correct in discriminating between an emotion that is incoherently manifest – triggered by fiction – and an emotion that, in being congruent with one's consciously held beliefs, is unpuzzling, rational and coherent? No, we do not believe so. To claim that fictionally elicited emotions are incoherent is (a) to fail to understand the mechanisms involved in triggering emotion and (b) to ignore the context in which the emotion is expressed. An emotion that includes, as a *component* rather than a consequence, peeking through the gaps between one's fingers as they cover one's face, is an emotion that is coherent with the context in which it is elicited.

When watching the horror film, Charles's emotional state is not incoherent; neither is it quasi-emotional. One might want to claim that it is an expression of 'fictional-fear' or even 'horror-fear' (see Carroll, 1990; Gaut, 1993; Laetz, 2008; Levine, 2001), but saying this is not relegating the fear to something less than genuine fear; instead, it is to contextualise it.[2] Horror-fear is a genuine emotional state that is expressed in a manner consistent with context (see Bartsch *et al.*, 2010). The person who runs away from a tiger does so because they are afraid, as is the person paralysed with fear. Is each person in exactly the same emotional state? Some components are the same, some are different. Our concern is not whether each should be categorized as simply 'fear' (rather than, say, 'energized fear' and 'paralysed fear'), but, instead, that each be recognized as a *genuine* emotional state.

EXTENDING ONE'S EMOTIONAL REPERTOIRE

Interestingly, what has also been noted by writers on the paradox of fiction is the fact that, even if *genuine* emotion is expressed, not all emotions seem capable of being expressed towards objects of fiction. This seems less so in cases of emotions elicited in interactive VEs.

There appear to be some emotional states, expressed in the virtual world, that are unattainable by those engaged in more traditional fictional pursuits. When reading about (or even watching) the exploits of Jean Valjean (the protagonist in Victor Hugo's novel, *Les Misérables*), for example, I may become angered by certain events, or saddened by some subsequent misfortune; but it is unlikely that I will feel guilt or remorse, no matter how unwarranted the tribulation that befalls him (this assumes an absence of pathology on my part, of course). More generally, I cannot take pride in some achievement, nor do I feel ashamed of some injustice, or jealousy towards some individual (Brock, 2007). A fairly uncontroversial reply is to state that such emotions are unavailable to the reader because they require a level of personal, physical involvement that is not possible in more traditional works of fiction. Tan (1994, p. 29), for example, claims that emotional states directed towards the fictional world (what he calls 'F-emotions') are best understood as *emotions of witnesses*, elicited through the observation of 'mere spectacle'.

Kreitman (2006) claims that despite having feelings for fictional characters, they are not the same as those for the non-fictional people we know, even though our emotional expression is in response to the authenticity of the fiction. They differ in terms of the type of emotion and/or its intensity because:

- we have only *selective* detail about the character (relevant to the narrative/ plot) – nothing mundane;
- there is nothing to do but observe the story as it unfolds (focused and passive engagement);
- our relationship to the characters is asymmetrical and unidirectional (we have feelings for them that are not reciprocated).

With VR interfacing, however, virtual interactions with characters are not only possible but are, indeed, an integral part of the fictional narrative and gameplay: one is being more than a mere witness to the unfolding drama.[3]

In 2005, Tavinor described how, as a character in the video game *Grand Theft Auto 3*, he was able to pay for the services of a prostitute whom he then went on to mug: something he admitted to later feeling *guilty* about. From personal experience, Tavinor came to realize that within the context of video game fiction it is possible 'to feel guilty or ashamed for *what one does in the fictional world*' (2005, pp. 24–25). Moreover, the interactive nature of these environments 'alters the character of our interest in them' (p. 25); and, it would seem, based on his confession (that of feeling guilty), the nature of our emotional involvement and investment. Games such as *The Sims* and *Fable II* allow players to create and engage with their own virtual family and therefore engage in fuller interactions, including the 'mundane'; and to experience (at least the impression of) reciprocal affection.

'BELIEVING IN' WHAT THE VIRTUAL REPRESENTS

If one compares the expression of fear demonstrated by a movie-goer like Charles with someone trying to evade the pursuit of a wild and ferocious beast, then one is immediately struck by the differences in their respective behaviours. (I am assuming that the person trying to evade capture is fleeing.) Importantly, 'fleeing' is not a result of fear; rather, it is a demonstrable component of it. Conversely, Charles's failure to flee is not evidence that he lacks genuine fear. Instead, because of the context in which it occurs, it is seen as *appropriately expressed*. Cultural norms and context therefore help the categorization process: we learn to recognize in others, and likewise adopt ourselves, those culturally and context-dependent coping strategies that constitute one component of our emotional state. Indeed, fictions are culturally accepted, even 'sanctioned' (Kreitman, 2006, p. 616), outlets for emotional expression (for Mar and Oatley, 2008, they even provide the means by which we can experience the world indirectly, thereby facilitating greater understanding and empathy towards those perceived to be different). However, unlike Charles, some people do leave the cinema. But even in such cases, to say that they leave *because* they are afraid is not to say that their leaving is a response to fear so much as it is their way of expressing it. Equally, when confronted by a deadly foe, some people freeze rather than flee (see also Suits, 2006). Either way, the emotion is genuine, even if in some cases the coping strategy is a little idiosyncratic.

The fact that Charles does not flee, then, can be explained with reference to context-dependent coping strategies, rather than by relegating his 'fear' to an incoherent or quasi-emotional state. Individual differences in how we express fear (or any emotional state) are an inevitable consequence of emotions as complex occurrences. So are the emotions typically expressed in each domain commensurate and therefore transferable?

In attempting to answer this question, consider the following study. Slater *et al.* (2006) partially replicated the infamous Milgram obedience study carried out in the 1960s (see Milgram, 1974), only this time using a virtual 'learner'. As with the original study, Slater *et al.*'s findings suggest that participants were typically stressed by the situation and even showed signs of caring for the well-being of the avatar. Slater *et al.* (2006, p. 5) therefore concluded that 'humans tend to respond realistically at subjective, physiological, and behavioural levels in interactions with virtual characters': this, despite the participants' 'cognitive certainty' that the virtual character – the 'learner' – was not real.

Despite being left in no doubt about the learner's virtual constitution, Slater *et al.* nevertheless recorded physiological changes in the participants' skin conductance levels (SCLs) and heart rate: measurements that corroborated participants' subjective awareness of certain physiological changes in themselves (based on a self-assessment questionnaire), such as starting to perspire or tremble. Moreover, anecdotal reports from Slater *et al.* suggest that participants behaved as if the learner were real: they obeyed the learner's request to speak louder, they showed frustration at incorrect responses and they experienced uncertainty about whether to continue when the learner objected; some even emphasized the correct response, presumably to aid the learner. Many participants also reported 'negative feelings'; and many said that they had considered stopping.[4] The negative feelings were elicited, we suggest, either directly through the image and sound of the learner's discomfort, or less directly by participants reflecting on the situation and asking themselves: What if this were real?[5]

In the original Milgram study (see Milgram, 1974), it is generally accepted that the participants believed that they had genuinely administered shocks to the learner. This is clearly not the case here. Yet, in terms of subjective, physiological and behavioural responses, there is strong evidence to suggest that the negative emotions experienced by participants in Slater *et al.*'s study are proportionate to those in Milgram's original study. The exact nature of the 'negative feeling' experienced by the participants is not made explicit in the report's findings, although the physiological responses are. It is our view that what the participants experienced was different at different times because the intentional object that their feelings (emotions) were directed towards was likewise different at different times. Initially, one could claim with some justification that negative feelings were elicited as a result of what was occurring to the virtual learner – participants were distressed by what they saw happening to the learner. At other times, when reflecting on the events (either during or afterwards), perhaps participants felt guilt or shame. Why? Because of what their actions *represented* or *symbolized*. Remember, for Kreitman (2006), our affect-laden responses are elicited by the authenticity of the characteristics of fiction. This includes, we suggest, the authenticity of the symbolism underscoring the action. Although one does not have to believe that the character is real, one nevertheless *believes in* the symbolic realism of the virtual encounter; in what it authentically represents.

The virtual learner's response is perceived to be authentic because of the realism captured within the virtual representation. It is this realism – this authenticity – that is being appraised and this which triggers the affect program response. The appraisal mechanism and affect program do not concern themselves with existential commitment. Consequently, the physiological response elicited by the VR interaction is generalizable to the non-virtual world – a fact corroborated by the findings of the virtual study. But the physiological response alone is not the whole emotion: even Walton (1978) agreed that Charles underwent genuine physiological changes when observing the on-screen slime. What made Walton conclude that the emotional state was merely quasi, then, was (a) Charles's lack of existential commitment and (b) his failure to exhibit what Walton deemed to be a more appropriate 'fear response' – fleeing the cinema, or some such thing.

We have already discussed why a lack of existential commitment is not sufficient to justify Walton's assertion that emotions elicited by fiction are quasi-states; and further argued that the behavioural 'response' should be understood not as a response to the emotion but as a manifestation of it. This manifestation *is* context dependent; and it is this context dependency that may prove a stumbling block for the view that disgust is an appropriate measure of moral wisdom in VEs. To understand why, consider further the behaviour of the participants in the Slater *et al.* study.

There is a degree of similarity between the behaviour of the participants in the original Milgram study and Slater *et al.*'s virtual study. In both cases, many of the participants carried on administering 'shocks' despite their heightened physiological arousal and negative emotional state. The fact that many participants in the virtual study kept reminding themselves that what they were doing was not real, attests to the authenticity and realism of the underlying symbolism involved. But, importantly, this fact – that they were reminded that it was not real – also contextualizes the study, and helps to explain why many continued when they had thought about stopping, and *in the knowledge that they could stop anytime they wanted to* (something that was less apparent in the original Milgram study). The majority carried on because it was not real, just as the majority of horror fans remain in their seats. But this fact does not undermine the genuineness of the emotional state; rather, it provides insight into how the complex occurrence that is an emotion is expressed.

Affect programs trigger physiological changes, but the appraisal that triggers this neural mechanism also engages coping strategies that are affected by context – another important component of the emotion. It is the extent to which this context modifies the coping strategy that will determine the degree of generalizability possible across domains. As a basic guide, but beyond the scope of this chapter to explore further (see Chapters 14 and 15 for discussion on moral management), the extent to which the participant *believes in* the symbolism captured by the virtual interaction should correlate with the generalizability of the virtual research findings.

In conclusion, if we allow that virtually elicited emotions are real emotions, as we have argued, then what it means to study 'virtually real emotions' is, importantly, to study *real* emotions virtually (that is, elicited from within a VE), as opposed to the study of virtually (as in, 'not quite', 'simulated' or 'quasi') emotional states. This has important implications, we contend, for the use of gamespace as an environment where, virtually, anything is permissible. To say that it is 'just a game' is not to downplay the genuineness of the emotional involvement or even investment a player may have within the gameplay, but it is to contextualize the emotion and concomitant behaviour, which then requires that we proceed cautiously when considering the transcendent quality of each to the offline world. The degree to which the individual believes in the authenticity of the representation and virtual interaction, and the potential consequences of this, is something we will discuss further in Part 3.

In the next chapter, we begin to consider why someone would want to engage in STAs. As a first step towards addressing this question, we discuss the topic of *play* and examine the idea that cyberspace is a virtual playground. As such, is engaging in STAs just a form of play?

7   On the nature of play

Cyberspace as a virtual playground

In order to discuss in more detail the potential psychological impact of engaging in or simply witnessing STAs, we need to consider further the nature of the space in which they occur. In this chapter we argue that many virtual spaces are playful spaces. Given this, we believe it instructive to introduce some general theories on the psychology of play, including factors that will assist us in determining whether play (including STAs) is likely to have a healthy or detrimental effect on the individual. In addition, we will consider those theorists who have applied theories of play to the Internet, and claimed that cyberspace constitutes, for many at least, a virtual playground. Then, as part of our discussion on the potential detrimental effects of play, we will briefly turn our attention to a relatively new phenomenon found on the Internet – *Chatroulette* (mentioned briefly in Chapter 2) – and consider the extent to which such a 'playful' space can be psychologically healthy.

INTRODUCING THE VIRTUAL PLAYGROUND

Rheingold (1993) was possibly the first to talk about the Internet as being a virtual playground: a space where cooperative play can take place. Danet *et al.* (1998) have also written about the playful qualities of computer-mediated communication (CMC). To quote from Danet *et al.* (1998, p. 41):

> Computer-mediated communication (CMC) is strikingly playful. Millions of people are playing with their computer keyboards in ways they probably never anticipated, even performing feats of virtuosity – with such humble materials as commas, colons, and backslashes. Not only hackers, computer 'addicts,' adolescents and children, but even ostensibly serious adults are learning to play in new ways.

Whitty and her colleague (see Whitty, 2003a; Whitty and Carr, 2003, 2005, 2006a) also argue that cyberspace is a playful and imaginative space. They state that although cyberspace is generally understood to be a space generated by software within a computer that produces a VR, one should nevertheless take the ontology of this space to lie somewhere between that occupied by '*real individuals*' and '*fantasy individuals'* (Whitty and Carr, 2006a). As was discussed in Chapter 2, through virtual immediacy, new bodies can be created almost instantaneously (or certainly with relative ease) in a space that has the *appearance* of an illusory world – a world separate from ordinary activities. Moreover, the contingencies of this space – for example, its rules and temporal qualities – may make it a safe space to experiment with constructions of self, as well as to experience the world in a unique way. Thus, virtual worlds have the potential to be spaces where individuals can experience any number of diverse and novel activities, ranging from acts of saintliness to acts of depravity. As noted earlier, one can fly, kill or even rape within these spaces; objects can take on different meanings and individuals can 'excogitate new identities' (Whitty, 2003a, p. 339). These spaces are not limited to visual spaces, however; rather, it has been argued that bulletin boards, chat rooms, MUDs and MOOs (MUDs, object oriented) should also be understood (potentially, at least) as virtual playgrounds. That said, what should also be apparent is that when we interact with others in cyberspace, we are not always engaging in play. Whitty and Carr (2006a) recognize that cyberspace is not a homogeneous space and not all online spaces are playful. Writing an email to a work colleague, for example, even an amusing one, is typically conceived of as far less playful than, say, engaging in cybersex in *Second Life*.

In this chapter we ask the question: If play is maintained in a space of its own and never intrudes on the rest of our lives, then should we be able to engage in any activity when we play? The theories we draw from in this chapter suggest that although play is not an ordinary activity, neither does it take place entirely in a vacuum. Virtual worlds, like other play spaces, are connected in some way to the real world. Individuals bring personal characteristics to the space as well as their personal history. Play, we believe, is connected to what is continuous or ordinary, and although virtual worlds may appear cut off from reality, like any other space, an individual (self or other) is affected by the activities that take place therein, even if that activity is playful in nature. Engaging in cybersex in virtual worlds, for example, might cause 'real' upset for one's 'real-life partner'. As a consequence, even if these encounters are understood to be play, might they still have a psychological effect on individuals? We note that there is a paucity of available research on how individuals are affected by their encounters with taboo activities within virtual worlds. Given this, we provide a few examples and draw from theories of play to speculate on how individuals *might* be affected.

CONCEPTUALIZING PLAY

Before considering the psychological effects that might result from 'playing' in virtual spaces, we need to understand what play is. This is not an easy task to undertake; especially given that there has been much disagreement on how to operationalize play (e.g. Caillois and Mehlman, 1968; Fink, 1968; Sutton-Smith, 2001). The cultural historian Huizinga, who is well known for his work on play, summarizes it in the following way:

[T]he formal characteristics of play we might call it a free activity standing quite consciously outside 'ordinary' life as being 'not serious', but at the same time absorbing the player intensely and utterly. It is an activity connected with no material interest, and no profit can be gained by it. It proceeds within its own proper boundaries of time and space according to fixed rules and in an orderly manner. It promotes the formation of social groupings which tend to surround themselves with secrecy and to stress their difference from the common world by disguise or other means.

(Huizinga, 1992 [1950], p. 13)

He further contends that play is universal, common to both animals and humans, and to be found in law, art, war, poetry, ritual and philosophy. In fact, Huizinga takes the universality of play one step further by claiming that it existed prior to human culture. In a potentially radical move, he argues that play and culture were once connected in an intimate way, such that 'culture arises in the form of play' (p. 46). To explain: for Huizinga, all forms of play are competitive and so present themselves as contests – from things as diverse as crossword puzzles and tennis games, to those that were played to the death (e.g. the Mayan precursor to what we today recognize as football). Out of these contests, social hierarchies evolved around which a given society would construct its values. As time passed, societies eventually changed and started to marginalize play.

Critics have argued against this view, however, stating that Huizinga's historical outline comes from an elitist perspective that focuses purely on the 'leisure class' (Henricks, 2006). Huizinga has also been criticized for focusing solely on the competitive aspect of play (Ehrmann, 1968). Caillois (1961) expanded Huizinga's definition to include four basic categories: competition, chance, simulation and vertigo. He also maintained that play could be controlled (*ludus*) or spontaneous (*paidia*). Ehrmann (1968), in turn, criticized this view, stating that Caillois was being too categorical in his conception of play, and that play does not fit neatly into these classifications. Despite disagreement on how to define play, Huizinga's successors have taken on board many of his viewpoints. These we will discuss in more detail now.

Many scholars agree, for example, that play is an activity separated from ordinary life. This is evident in the quotation by Huizinga (above), to which can be added: 'play is not "ordinary" or "real" life; rather, it is a stepping out of "real" life into a temporary sphere of activity with a disposition all of its own' (1992 [1950], p. 8). For Huizinga, to play is to commit oneself to an artificial, fictional version of the world (often thought of as engaging within a *magic circle*; see also Salen and Zimmerman, 2003). The psychotherapist Modell also understands play to be separate from ordinary life, which he believes takes place in a different space:

Playing takes place in a certain space and has certain limitations regarding the duration of time, as in games that are 'played out' within a certain limit of time. Yet playing may have its own quality of timelessness. Playing is also separated from ordinary life by the 'rules of the game': all play has its rules that pertain to the temporary world in which playing takes places. Rules are in effect a means of containing a space in which illusions can flourish.

(Modell, 1996 [1990], p. 27)

Ehrmann (1968), however, criticizes the view that play is in some way the antithesis of reality; adding that play is not a commentary on reality, nor is it a variation or reproduction of it. The point Erhmann makes is important to our own investigation: for if play is conducted purely in its own space, and the activities that occur therein are contingent on that space and therefore deemed to be *not real*, then one might wish to argue (or at least conjecture) that (a) the morality of the activity should be judged using a moral system born of that space and no other and (b) there can be no psychological impact from playing out these activities once the person returns to 'ordinary life'. Whilst we accept the first conclusion *with qualification* (to be outlined as the book progresses), the second is not a conclusion we wish to endorse.

Simmel (1950), we suggest, offers a more useful conceptualization of play. He too believes that play is an activity isolated from ordinary life, but this isolation needs qualifying. He recognizes that successful play is characterized by feelings of separation and distance. Playgrounds, for instance, are often physically marked off with clear boundaries. In fact, related to the notion of separation, Huizinga goes so far as to state that, even in early childhood, play surrounds itself with an air of secrecy. When one plays, it is made clear that others are not included. Some are in the know and others are not. This air of secrecy, Huizinga (1992 [1950], p. 12) contends, can enhance the experience: for 'inside the circle of the game the laws and customs of ordinary life no longer count. We are different and do different things'. Yet, for Simmel, too much separation can destroy play by its sheer irrelevance. Play, he insists, cannot take place in a vacuum; instead, there needs to be a connection between it and that which is continuous or ordinary. This connection has been emphasized by Whitty and her colleague (e.g. Whitty, 2003a; Whitty and Carr, 2003, 2005, 2006a) in their theorizing about the playful activities that take place in virtual worlds (see below).

In addition, Huizinga argues that another characteristic of play is that it is a voluntary activity. He believes that humans and animals choose to play because they enjoy it. Play is not imposed on individuals, Huizinga tell us, nor is it a moral duty; instead, it is an activity engaged in during one's 'free time'. However, although freely chosen, for Huizinga, play is an 'unproductive' activity; and given that play is outside the realms of reality, it is an 'activity connected with no material interest, and no profit can be gained by it' (1992 [1950], p. 13). Other scholars have also made this point (e.g. Callois, 1961; Marcuse, 2005 [1956]). Marcuse (2005 [1956], p. 195; emphasis in original) states that 'play is *unproductive* and *useless* because it cancels the repressive and exploitive traits of labor and leisure; it "just plays" with reality'. Not all scholars agree that play is unproductive, however. In particular, researchers of the Internet have argued that playing in cyberspace can in fact be *psychologically* productive (Whitty and Carr, 2006a) precisely because it is not disconnected completely from reality. (Again, this will be discussed in more detail below.)

Of all of the features of play noted above, Huizinga considers the most important to be its *spatio-temporal* separation from our everyday existence (Bateson, 1955, and Goffman, 1974, use the term 'frame' to capture this unique separation). For Huizinga (1992 [1950], p. 9), play is an activity; that is, 'distinct from "ordinary" life as to locality and duration . . . "played out" within certain limits of time and place'. Thus, when one enters into play, one adopts a new understanding of space and time. Indeed, as Whitty and Carr (2006a) point out, play (and children's play in particular) can begin at one moment and be concluded at another when it is deemed that play is 'over'. In the case of certain games, the rules may declare that play occurs within a specific time limit and within a specific space. Other games, in contrast, are simply 'played out' in time limits determined by how play takes its course. But even when play is 'taking its course', Huizinga (1992 [1950], p. 21) draws our attention to its labile nature, and reminds us that 'at any moment "ordinary life" may reassert its rights either by an impact from without, which interrupts the game, or by an offence against the rules, or else from within, by a collapse of the play spirit, a sobering, a disenchantment'.

To support this claim, Huizinga recounts a story that was told to him by a father about his four-year-old son. The father found his son 'sitting at the front of a row of chairs, playing "trains". As he hugged him, his son said: "Don't kiss the engine, Daddy, or the carriages won't think it's real" ' (ibid., p. 8). This story is indicative of a child at play; but at the same time reveals how fragile and ephemeral the quality of *illusion* in play is. Modell (1996 [1990], p. 27; emphasis in original) notes that 'the connection between playing and illusion has long been recognized and, as many have noted, is revealed by the etymology of the word *illusion*, which can be traced to *inlusio, illudere,* or *inludere,* which means literally in play'. In a more adult context, for some, the illusion of play may be broken by a sudden encounter with a taboo activity – when required to torture a game character for information, for example, or shoot hostages, or even rape another character (examples we shall return to in later chapters), all of which may be determined by, or at least permitted within, the rules of the gameplay.

Huizinga recognizes that successful play must have rules. Rules allow individuals to repeat the activity as well as to communicate with others in joint play (Henricks, 2006). In fact, Huizinga suggests that the play world collapses when rules are transgressed, leading to the end of a game. He states: 'the umpire's whistle breaks the spell and sets "real" life going again' (1992 [1950], p. 11). A 'spoil-sport' is therefore someone who breaks the rules or ignores them; and by doing so destroys play: for 'by withdrawing from the game he reveals the relativity and fragility of the play-world in which he had temporarily shut himself with others' (ibid.); and by doing so, this person 'robs play of its *illusion*' (ibid.; emphasis in original). Huizinga further believes that the spoil-sport breaks the 'magic world' and, as a consequence, needs to be ejected from the playground.

Simmel (1950) also discusses the limits of play. He points out that although play might seem like an escape from reality, players nevertheless impose limits on their endeavours (see also Calleja, 2010). People play on a team and that team might be represented in some way (e.g. shirt colour, type of race or guild in *World of Warcraft*, etc.). The rules also help elucidate social order; what, in Chapter 9, we refer to as *status functions*. They also assist in seeing objects in a new way (the 'opposition', for example, or legitimate 'targets'). In sport, this may lead to what Bredemeier and Shields (1986) call *bracketed morality*, meaning that although moral obligation within the field of play may deviate from certain everyday norms (one may legitimately try to intimidate or even physically hurt one's opponent, for example, as is the case in boxing or rugby), the 'bracketed' aspect within the term indicates that what may be legitimate in sport is still grounded on (or bracketed to) an awareness of everyday prohibited action. It is still frowned upon to cheat, for example, or to intentionally inflict *serious* injury on your opponent. In terms of STAs, this might consist in viewing those virtual characters who one is trying to kill as obstacles to be overcome rather than victims (see the discussion on moral management in Chapter 14).

In their work on play, Whitty and Carr (2006a) argue that rules are especially important to creating and maintaining the separation of play from ordinary life. They state that:

> Play depends upon rules and other factors related to space and time, but in so doing we can note than an interesting paradox arises. On the one hand, the fundamental essence of play is the freedom, the license to create and be set apart from ordinary life. Yet, on the other hand, for this to be accomplished, constraint is required in the form of rules and other factors related to space and time. Thus, in an interesting twist of logic, freedom is created only through constraint.
>
> (p. 58)

The rules of a game may be complex, of course, or few and far between; there may even be rules that permit much, if not all, of what is deemed taboo offline to occur within a given gamespace. Rules to this effect may be explicitly stated – you *can* kill opponents or rape or torture – or they may be made evident through what is allowable by the game mechanics. Confusion arises, however, when what is deemed permissible may be inferred from the fact that there is no explicit rule outlawing it (something that may be more applicable to multiplayer VEs – see Chapter 9). On such occasions, the claim that 'It's just a game' or 'I was only playing', with the corollary statement 'No harm done', may not satisfy all who occupy that space – namely the virtual community who have most likely interpreted any alleged ambiguity in the rules differently from the putative offender.

Related to this last point, the seriousness of play is also emphasized within Huizinga's writings. He argues that 'the contrast between play and seriousness proves to be neither conclusive nor fixed' (1992 [1950], p. 5). For Huizinga, although play may be a departure from ordinary life, this does not mean that it is necessarily preoccupied only with trivial matters. Instead, he believes that play could address both sublime and morally serious issues. In fact, drawing from object relations theory (see below for details), some theorists have argued that play *transcends* the serious and non-serious oppositional binary (Carr, 2001; Whitty and Carr, 2006a, 2006b). As claimed earlier, play can be *psychologically* productive; for there is a great deal that individuals can learn about themselves and society by engaging in play (Whitty, 2003a; Whitty and Carr, 2003, 2006a). In this respect, play is anything but trivial.

So far, we have considered factors that contribute to what makes play the thing that it is. Its degree of separation from ordinary life is a contested issue, as is its productivity and triviality. Play is certainly distinct from ordinary life, but this does not mean that it is unconnected to it, nor does it make it necessarily a trivial activity. However, the degree of connectivity to ordinary life, and the extent to which play is, for the player, a trivial matter are important contributory factors in determining the likely psychological benefit or harm rendered by play, particularly where STAs are concerned. In the next section, we move beyond contentions in the definition of play and look to theorists who have attempted to enunciate the psychology of play.

PSYCHOLOGY OF PLAY

Much that has been written on the psychology of play has focused on children. According to some theorists (e.g. Ellis and Scholtz, 1978; Piaget, 1951), children progress through a serious of complex social stages as they grow older, during which time they experience and understand play at different levels. A few psychologists have focused their attention on adult play, however (see Mos and Boodt, 1991; Schaefer; 1993; Winnicott, 1971a, 1971b [1951], 1971c, 1971d, 1971e [1968], 1971f [1967], 1971g). Schaefer (1993), for example, believes that play in therapy assists in reducing the need for defensiveness and thus allows the individual to explore new ways of feeling and behaving. Winnicott (1971a, 1971b [1951], 1971c, 1971d, 1971e [1968], 1971f [1967], 1971g) and Mos and Boodt (1991), for their part, argue that play is fundamental to the development of self in both children and adults.

In contrast to the majority of psychologists, philosophers and other social scientists have centred much of their theorizing about play on adults. Simmel (1950) believed that individuals enter the sphere of play with their own unique characteristics, curiosities, desires, anxieties, etc. However, and as a caveat, he claimed that play should not be understood as shaped solely by those individuals who engage in the activity, but in conjunction with the rules and the qualities of the objects within the sphere of play: for as Henricks (2006, p. 130) points out, 'players drive the interaction forward but they do not do this just as they please'.

Like theorists highlighted earlier, a psychodynamic view on play contends that play is all about illusion, and that this illusion can only be sustained provided that play is kept within a frame of its own – that is, a frame separate from ordinary life. In considering play in this way, psychodynamic theorists have argued that what happens in this transported world is very serious indeed. The idea that play fits into a dichotomous world or binary opposition of serious and non-serious activity is therefore firmly rejected: for it is not that play contrasts with what is serious but with what is real. Freud (1985 [1908], p. 132) makes this point strongly when he asserts:

> [E]very child at play . . . creates a world of his own . . . .. It would be wrong to think he does not take that world seriously; on the contrary, he takes his play very seriously and he expends large amounts of emotion on it. The opposite of play is not what is serious but what is real. In spite of all the emotion with which he cathects his world of play, the child distinguishes it quite well from reality; and he likes to link his imagined objects and situations to tangible and visible things of the real world. This linking is all that differentiates the child's 'play' from 'phantasying'.

The psychodynamic take on play is that it is a therapeutic activity. Play helps individuals deal with personal internal conflict and can be used as both a diagnostic screen and a cure. Winnicott is credited, by many, with making a very significant contribution to a psychodynamic understanding of play. His notions of *transitional objects* and *potential space* are particularly important in the context of understanding play. Winnicott (1971a), in keeping with Freud, argues that play transcends the serious and non-serious oppositional binary. He also views the play of infants as spontaneous and occurring in an environment of trust and the safety of parents, particularly the mother. Highly significant for Winnicott is what he takes to be the intermediate territory between an individual's inner and external worlds. He noticed, for example, how an infant would suck and hug a doll or blanket. He suggests that the doll or blanket does not represent a doll or blanket as such but, rather, is an *as-if* object. The infant makes use of the illusion that although this is not the breast, treating it as such will allow an appreciation of what is 'me' and what is 'not-me' (Winnicott, 1971d, p. 41; Winnicott, 1971g, p. 107). Although referred to as a transitional object, 'it is not the object which is transitional' (Winnicott, 1971b [1951], p. 14); rather, the object is the initial manifestation of a different positioning of the infant in the world. The doll or blanket thus connects to subjective experience whilst remaining in the objective world.

The *potential space* between subject and object is where, for the infant, play takes place. Germane to Winnicott's argument is that potential space is a safe space: a place where one can be spontaneous and experimentation can take place. He argues that in order for an individual to be able to play, there needs to be trust. The potential space is therefore an area of intermediate experiencing that lies between inner and outer worlds: 'between the subjective object and the object objectively perceived' (Winnicott, 1971f [1967], p. 100).

Importantly, according to Whitty and Carr (2006a), whilst the notions of transitional objects and potential space are raised within the context of infancy, Winnicott (1971b [1951]) insists that they are not simply confined to the experience of infants; rather, each is something that 'throughout life is retained in the intense experiencing that belongs to the arts and to religion and to imaginative living, and to creative scientific work' (p. 24). We come to rely on our own resources to experience culture and to expand our understanding of the world.

This, Whitty and Carr (2006a) argue, includes incorporating new technologies such as the Internet into our pool of resources; and, in doing so, further develops our capacity to generate potential space. As Winnicott (1971f [1967], p. 100; emphasis in original) notes: 'The place where cultural experience is located is in the *potential space* between the individual and the environment (originally the object). The same can be said of playing'. Moreover, and in a manner reminiscent of Huizinga, he adds: 'Cultural experience begins with creative living first mani-fested in play' (ibid.).

Winnicott therefore views play as *creative communication*, not occurring in the context of the subject alone but, rather, as inherently intersubjective. Play takes into account other subjectivities and the environment as it responds to the subject. Like others, Winnicott also views play as creating and sustaining illusion, which, as noted earlier, can be maintained if kept within a frame of its own – a frame that separates it from ordinary life. In short, for Winnicott, potential space is not pure fantasy, nor is it pure reality. However, '[i]n the absence of potential space, there is only fantasy; within potential space *imagination* can develop' (Ogden, 1985, p. 133; emphasis added).

CYBERSPACE AS A POTENTIAL SPACE

According to Winnicott, the 'good enough' mother starts off with an almost complete adaptation to her child's needs; however, with time, she gradually adapts less completely, allowing the infant to grow and deal with her failure. Winnicott believes that, given a 'good enough' environment (i.e. the provision of a safe space by the mother to allow the child's transition to become more autonomous), the interplay between the inner world and external reality promotes the develop-ment of self and facilitates growth. It is a space where we can develop, psycho-logically, to integrate love and hate and to create, destroy and recreate ourselves (see Winnicott, 1971d, p. 41). Without this 'good enough' environment, the child is likely to neglect ego needs and the 'true self' might not emerge.

Applying this to the Internet, Whitty (2003a, p. 349) has argued that virtual worlds can be productively understood as incorporating 'potential spaces' between 'real individuals' and 'fantasy individuals'; a space that is 'somewhere outside the individual but is still not the external world'. In being a potential space, virtual worlds would hold the possibility for psychological growth. Cyberspace thus provides individuals with not only the opportunity to be all that they might poten-tially be, but also, arguably, a safer space for this to *happen*. Moreover, there are more opportunities for an individual to be creative and experiment with identity, sexuality and love than offline, and with added immediacy. Whitty and Carr (2006a) illustrate their point by examining flirtation. They argue that although cyberflirting could undeniably be seen as a type of play (analogous to the married man or woman who flirts at a party in order to be reassured that they are still attractive, but with no intention of taking things further), cyberspace nevertheless creates more opportunities for the type of play described by Winnicott. This type of play requires that one sustain an illusion; and they propose that this is easier to maintain in an online environment than offline.

According to Whitty and Carr (2006a), the computer and the other computer periphery objects (e.g. avatars) are the transitional objects that allow individuals to position themselves in a given space and explore the 'me' and 'not-me', and the significance of these objects in context. They argue that the many playful spaces available in cyberspace provide individuals with a unique opportunity to explore and examine the self (the components of this self will be discussed further in Part 2). Virtual worlds, they believe, provide greater opportunity online for *fantasy*. In many online spaces, individuals can inhabit any body they desire, be it a youthful body, an attractive body or even the body of a member of the opposite sex. In addition, they can invent how their fantasy partner looks, feels, and even feels about them. Participants can *fantasize* that they are attracted to others, and in turn, others are attracted to them. Therefore, whilst clearly the body is not *physically* present during online interactions, *embodiment* of some kind still matters. In this 'potential space', participants are open to play with a variety of identities, including their embodied identity. The potential psychological impact of this on the individual will be examined further in Part 2.

Aitken and Herman (1997, p. 74) have suggested that Winnicott's framework 'allows the possibility of a flexible manipulation of meanings and relationships'. They argue that objects, cultural practices and self-images may become elements of this space. Moreover, they suggest that these elements can be altered 'as an individual adjusts and updates knowledge throughout a lifetime' (p. 74). In Winnicott's potential space, reality is plastic and meanings can be reconstituted; to the point where even society's rules can be reconfigured through play. Applying this to cyberspace, it could be argued that the potential space provides opportunities for individuals to play and experiment with traditional cultural meanings of self and gender, or even *moral* norms. Hamlen (2011) notes how adventure-based computer games afford and perhaps even encourage boys to try on new identities as they explore imaginary virtual worlds. Such games may even encourage them to make decisions that are appropriate within a given fantasy world (that make sense there, if nowhere else). In these spaces, one may develop a sense of what constitutes the social norm and, through the flexibility of the virtual, what does not. Online play can challenge stereotypical gender roles, for example, or in some spaces perhaps endorse or even exaggerate them! In other spaces, one may role-play the character of a healer or, alternatively, an assassin. The point being, through virtual immediacy in cyberspace, Winnicott's potential space seems to have *even more potential*. In other words, although it was possible before the Internet for an individual, through play, to try out different identities and even different activities – in order to discover (in the words of Winnicott) what is 'me' and what is 'not-me' – with the Internet, the scope for play, and subsequently for discovery, seems that much greater.

Others have made a similar assessment to Winnicott. Turkle (1995, p. 30), for example, suggests that 'the computer can be similarly experienced as an object on the border between self and not-self'; and that '[p]eople are able to see themselves in the computer. The machine can seem a second self' (p. 30). When viewed in this way, it makes sense that we should invest emotion towards such objects (e.g. the avatar I choose to represent *me* in these spaces). In line with the problems associated with the development of self online and identification with characters, Whitty and Carr (2006a) argue that we need to consider how we emotionally experience virtual worlds and how this experience transfers to other spaces. To aid our understanding, they draw on the writings of Bollas (1987, 1992) who, through an extension of Winnicott's work, argues that transitional objects, like all objects, leave a trace within us.

Some objects, Bollas argues, appear to have much more meaning for us than others, and seem to unlock unconscious thought processes and affective states. In a sense, these objects are 'transformational' and may act like 'psychic keys' (Carr, 2003; Whitty and Carr, 2003). By acting as psychic keys, the objects appear to enable past unconscious experiences to be released to inform present behaviour. Alternatively, playfully creating a new body for myself (for example) allows me to experience other ways of being. These, along with the ensuing behavioural change, might be incorporated into, and thereby contribute to, a new sense of self. This type of play has significant implications for therapeutic outcomes. Alternatively, individuals might see these experiences as separate from who they are when not in this space. Importantly, emerging evidence suggests that *some* individuals identify more with these avatars than others and, in doing so, invest more emotion towards them than others (see Caplan *et al.*, 2009; Liu and Peng, 2009). Moreover, some even end up investing more in these spaces and in these people (*qua* avatars) than they do people and interactions offline. As well as therapeutic benefits, then, the converse potential for psychopathology (or at least psychological harm) as a result of this form of identification cannot be discounted, and indeed is discussed in detail in Chapters 14 and 15.

Drawing from the work of Bollas, Whitty and Carr (2006a) argue that when an individual engages in a virtual space, psychologists ought to be concerned with what an individual brings to that space as well as what they take from it: for although what is being experienced is taking place in a space outside the realms of the ordinary world, these experiences leave a trace within the individual. This is particularly important to consider, we contend, when evaluating whether individuals should engage in STAs. It is also important to present this 'trace' within a more robust and articulated psychological framework. This will be our aim in Part 3. As a precursor to further discussion on this topic, however, we will apply what we have discussed so far to a relatively new phenomenon emerging on the Internet (mentioned briefly in Chapter 2): namely *Chatroulette*.

ENGAGING IN TABOO AND SYMBOLIC TABOO ACTIVITIES IN VIRTUAL WORLDS

There is a range of taboo activities one can engage in online, including activities that would be considered not only taboo offline but also quite possibly criminal. Take, for example, a fad that has emerged in the last two years, *Chatroulette*. In this space, strangers are randomly paired to engage in web-based conversations. They can opt to use voice, webcam and/or text. Strangers continue to chat until one decides to move on to the next stranger. Bilton (2010, p. 1), in *The New York Times*, describes his experience using the website:

> At one moment I was sitting in the living room with my wife, and on entering the site, we were siphoned into a dimly lit room with a man who told us he was in Russia. Moments later we were watching a woman dance half-naked in a kitchen in Turkey, and then we stared in shock at a gaggle of laughing college students in a dorm room somewhere. With each click of the mouse we were transported into a stranger's life — then whisked along to another jarring encounter.
>
> After five minutes, we disconnected and sat in silence, disturbed by the rawness of some of what we had seen . . . [Another time, we] clicked Next and there were three naked men in Amsterdam dancing to Rick Astley music . . . Then a man told us he was in jail . . . It's very strange, and not just because you are parachuting into someone else's life (and they yours), a kind of invited crasher. It is also the eerie thrill of true randomness — who, or what, will show up next?

Chatroulette is clearly a playful space, and satisfies the components of play detailed above. It is a space separate from ordinary life, played out within certain limits of time and place and is ephemeral. It certainly has an air of secrecy. Its gameplay allows individuals to engage in activities that would be deemed taboo and possibly criminal in other spaces (e.g. exposing yourself in front of strangers), and seems indicative of what Suler (2004) calls *toxic disinhibition*.[1] The question we pose, then, is: To what extent can individuals psychologically cope with this type of play? If one is able to completely dissociate from this space then one might argue that there is no harm done. However, we have argued in this chapter that it is very difficult to completely separate play from the ordinary world.

Individuals may find engaging in certain activities in this space a liberating experience – perhaps they do not strip down naked or dress up in fancy dress in other spaces and perhaps they are happy to contain this behaviour in this space. This might not be the self they aspire to be in other spaces. Individuals might feel freer to express this more creative, extroverted side of themselves, and decide that they wish, and are able, to transfer this newfound aspect of self to other spaces. Alternatively, participants, despite finding the experience enriching and fun, might nevertheless be content with that, and leave the space feeling exhilarated with no wish to pursue what they engaged in offline. However, there are potentially harmful effects. Experimenting with different presentations of myself might unexpectedly reveal to me that I am either an exhibitionist or a voyeur. This is problematic given that such behaviours are mostly not permitted in other spaces and are often deemed illegal. Another potentially negative effect might be that I unexpectedly experience shame and that this shame leaves an emotional trace. The act cannot be undone and so I am left to deal with this shame. Currently, there is no available research on the psychological impact of interacting in *Chatroulette* and so we can only speculate at this stage. However, we welcome further investigation.

In conclusion, like the alleged passive voyeur of Chapter 5, the air of randomness experienced by Bilton and his wife may mask a level of complicity that must inevitably accompany engagements in spaces such as *Chatroulette*. Certainly, the potential activities that could be witnessed and/or 'performed' and the complicity inherent even in the act of viewing, at present, constitute a legal and moral 'grey area'. But similar to the conclusion of Chapter 5, perhaps a way to avoid being tarnished with the tag of 'accomplice' is to restrict one's activities to engagements that have a purely virtual genesis.[2] As noted in Chapter 5, the most common example of this is the video game.

In the final two chapters in Part 1, we consider STAs within video games: first in the context of single-player games and then in relation to those that comprise multiplayer online communities. Our aim is to show that, within gamespace, the permissibility of STAs should be judged by a system of morality born of that space, concerning acts afforded by that space, and not by something imported from offline. In Chapters 8 and 9, we conclude our case against the relevance of offline moral systems to judgements about the permissibility of STAs. We also contend that as it is the player of these games who necessarily transcends spaces, rather than the game's content or online moral code, we must direct our focus towards an examination of the impact of STAs on the psychological well-being of the gamer – how he/she is able to manage and ultimately cope with online taboo violation (or not) – and the relevance of this to the question of STA permissibility, rather than whether STAs are right or wrong *per se*. The final two chapters of Part 1 prepare the groundwork for this argument, which is then developed throughout the remainder of the book.

8 Single-player games

What is and perhaps what should never be

In this chapter we present actual and hypothetical examples of STAs within single-player video games, and consider whether disgust in response to STAs is an appropriate measure of moral wisdom or whether it is in fact a further example of moral fallibility. In addition, we discuss reasons for and against the view that there are in fact some STAs that should not be permissible even within the realm of single-player gamespace, before moving on to argue that the permissibility of STA in gamespace should in fact be based on what we can cope with, psychologically, rather than the morality of the act itself.

'WHAT IS' IN THE WORLD OF SINGLE-PLAYER GAMES

The popularity of computer-mediated VR games has steadily increased over the years (Ryan *et al.*, 2006; Yee, 2006a, 2006b). This is perhaps testament to their growing affordability and technological sophistication; the latter evidenced by advances in the types of virtual interactions afforded within the gamespace. Computer-mediated single-player games (hereafter, single-player games) are packaged in many forms, and contain a diversity of plotlines, narratives and gameplays. Each constitutes an *interactive* virtual space; and whilst it is true that not all contain graphical representations of violence, a large proportion certainly do.

In numerous games it is commonplace to maim and kill, even murder (e.g. the *Left 4 Dead* series; or others such as *Kill Zone* and *Soldier of Fortune*), and in a growing number mutilate and even torture (e.g. *Reservoir Dogs*, *24*, *The Punisher* and arguably *Brink*, and *Red Faction*). It is even possible to target little girls for extermination (*BioShock*). For some games, such acts of violence are an integral part of the plotline and gameplay (e.g. *Manhunt 2*, *Postal 2*, *MadWorld*). There are even flash games available in which the sole purpose of the game is violence – specifically, torture (e.g. *Torture Game 2* and *Torture Time*). (The focus of this chapter, however, is on games with a wider, more commercially viable, audience.) In a few cases, it is even possible to witness the cannibalization of victims. The *Resident Evil* series, *Evil Dead* and *F.E.A.R.* (*First Encounter Assault Recon*) all feature cannibalism, although more in the form of a threat to the player than something they engage in themselves. However, in the withdrawn game *Thrill Kill*, it was possible to drink the blood of a victim one had just decapitated; and in *Rebel without a Pulse*, the player takes on the role of Stubbs the Zombie who engages in cannibalistic activities. In the latter example, the act of cannibalism seems much more central to the gameplay (recall, also, the example from Chapter 2: *Cannibal Warrior*). It is rarely the case, however, that characters engage in acts of rape or incest. Exceptions to this are *Phantasmagoria* where rape is possible and, from the 1980s, *Custer's Revenge*. In *The House of the Dead: Overkill*, incest is implied by an action, and in *No More Heroes* it is a feature of the game narrative but not interaction. Rape is, however, a key feature within *Battle Raper* (see also *Battle Raper 2*) in which defeated female opponents can be raped and sexually assaulted; and in *RapeLay* the entire gameplay centres on hunting down and raping/sexually assaulting a mother and her virgin daughters, although it is also possible to rape other women.

According to Jansz (2005 p. 224), the popularity of video games with increasingly violent and graphic gameplays is a strong indicator that 'gamers are not thwarted by the responsibility of committing violent acts in the virtual world of the game'. He goes on to suggest that the games' strong appeal must supersede any moral reservations on the part of the gamer. Even bullying has appeared as a central feature of one game (the somewhat controversial *Bully: Scholarship Edition*, available on Wii). To date, however, there are no single-player games that involve child sex, bestiality or necrophilia (although child sex and bestiality have featured in *Second Life* – see Chapter 9). Perhaps part of the reason for this can be put down to, amongst other things, the way different countries approach child protection issues and obscenity laws (see Chapter 4), and therefore the problems that would be encountered by online games violating certain countries' laws but not others.

PERHAPS WHAT SHOULD NEVER BE

In Chapter 4, it was noted how virtual child pornography is permitted in the US but not in the UK. For the sake of argument, then, let us say that in the US I am able to play a new computer game in which I adopt the role of a paedophile (McCormick, 2001, considers a similar example involving the holodeck of science fiction wherein one can engage in holo-paedophilia). As part of the gameplay, my character engages in a number of virtual acts of paedophilia. Would such (virtual) behaviour elicit in others moral repugnance? Should it? Should my virtual interactions (my STA) be seen as vile and deeply disgusting? As was noted in Chapter 5, no *real* child is harmed at any point in the game. Is this not therefore just another example of the sort of moral dumbfounding we encountered previously, where our sense of disgust overrides the right to allow individuals to do as they please so long as no one is hurt as a consequence?

For some, an obvious question might be: Why would anyone want to play such a game? (A question we will return to.) Perhaps such incredulity sits hand in hand with our disgust. As a first response, it could be said that the motivation for the act is independent of the act itself. Therefore, irrespective of motive, is engaging in gameplay involving virtual acts of paedophilia morally defensible? After all, as we saw in Chapter 7, play is not an activity restricted to childhood, and so it seems reasonable to ask why adults should not be allowed to play *any* character or game they desire; especially as play is arguably an illusion that sits within its own frame, separate from ordinary life, and as such can be said to represent a 'differentiated level of reality' (Modell, 1996 [1990], p. 25). Yet we also made the argument that the psychological impact of play does not necessarily remain separate from ordinary life; instead, what we experience and what we learn from playing in virtual playgrounds can transcend spaces.

Perhaps with this last point in mind, Brey (2003) argues that it is precisely because VR typically contains simulations or representations of physical and social reality that it warrants moral policing (see also Brey, 1999). As such, the manner in which characters or events within a game are represented, the behaviours they simulate and the interactions permitted them, should all come under moral scrutiny. A recent example of this scrutiny was the withdrawal of the Apple iPhone game, *Baby Shaker*, which occurred as a response to numerous protests from outraged parents' organizations (Arthur, 2009). The 'game' involved shaking a noisy baby in order to stop it crying: potentially shaking it until it dies, which is represented by Xs over the baby's eyes. Similarly, the planned video game *Six Days in Fallujah*, whose gameplay centred around one of the fiercest encounters of the 2004 Iraq war, was withdrawn before its release following angry protests in the UK and the US (the historical events depicted were held to have occurred too recently to be recreated in a game, and doing so was said to be in bad taste; *Sky News*, 2009). But from a moral perspective, should we distinguish between simulations already permitted within games and those not currently available or for the most part banned? In other words, if it is permissible to carry out STAs that involve killing, torture, mutilation and murder, then should it not be *equally permissible* to engage in acts of rape (including necrophilia), cannibalism, bestiality and child sex (including incest)? Equally, if it is not permissible to engage in STAs of this nature, then how can *any* legally (if not morally) prohibited action be permitted within gamespace? If one is of the view that paedophilia or rape is not an appropriate topic for a game (which is why the rape game *RapeLay* is banned in a number of countries), then surely the same must be said of killing, an event that is a regular feature of many gameplays, let alone torture and murder.

With this last point in mind, imagine a new game entitled *To the Victor the Spoils*. Within the gameplay, points are awarded for the rape and enslavement of captives, general pillage and the torture and brutalization of combatant and non-combatants alike. Alternatively, imagine playing *Long Pig*. Here, one is set the task of hunting down and cannibalizing one's victims, alive or dead. From what has been discussed so far, these hypothetical examples do not seem to be that far removed from what is already available. In which case, let us extend the fiction. Perhaps one might be tempted to engage in virtual animal sex in *Fun at the Zoo*, or virtual necrophilia in the hypothetical game *Cold Pleasures*. Such fictitious examples are not meant to be flippant; rather, we consider that they highlight the importance of the question: Should cyberspace, and specifically within this chapter, gamespace, be a taboo-free zone (at least with regard to established offline taboos)? If we can virtually murder, torture and mutilate in games, then why should we not also be permitted to virtually cannibalize or rape – be it adults, children or dead people? (For an insightful discussion on differences between virtual murder and virtual paedophilia, see Luck, 2009.)

THE PRINCIPLE OF SANCTIONED EQUIVALENCE

In judging what constitutes a suitable topic for gameplay, or at least in judging what is not totally inappropriate, one might be guided by the principle of *sanctioned equivalence* (Young and Whitty, 2011b). Killing, for example, can occur in legitimate or illegitimate ways. A sanctioned equivalent of killing is state-authorized execution, or the death of combatants during wartime. Torture has been justified in the past by legitimate authorities (Costanzo *et al.*, 2007; Soldz, 2008) and in some cases still is; or at least its legitimate use is debated – in the ticking bomb scenario, for example (Brecher, 2007; Opotow, 2007; see also Sample, 2008, for a detailed discussion on torture in video games). The unofficial 'Law of the Sea' maintains that cannibalism is acceptable, or is at least tolerated, when one's life depends on it and the victim is already dead, or was selected through the mutually agreed drawing of lots. (A similar scenario was famously debated by Fuller (1949) in his paper The case of the Speluncean Explorers.) In real life, passengers of Uruguayan Air Force Flight 571 (which crashed in the Andes Mountains on 13 October 1972) survived by resorting to cannibalism. All were Catholic and all received absolution from the Catholic Church. However, it is difficult to think of a sanctioned equivalent in the case of rape or necrophilia, or of cases in which one's life depended on an act of incest or bestiality. Of course, it might take little effort to conjure up a hypothetical scenario in which one's life did depend on such an act. However, the point we are making here relates to social norms, rather than one-off extreme and hypothetical examples. Sanctioned equivalence differentiates between equivalent outcomes that are either legitimate or illegitimate. All legitimate outcomes are judged to be essentially *instrumental* – a means to an end. On the other hand, actions that do not have sanctioned equivalence appear *pathological*, an end in themselves.

Gameplay killings are regularly enacted against a more traditional 'enemy' (e.g. *Call of Duty 4: Modern Warfare* or *Ghost Recon: Advanced Warfare 2*), against hordes of fictional evil mutants and against alien or demonic beings (e.g. the *Left 4 Dead* series, *Gears of War*, *Fallout 3*, the *Halo* trilogy and the *Resident Evil* series). In *World of Warcraft*, it is possible to cannibalize opponents, but this is carried out in order to re-energize one's life force. (We recognize that *World of Warcraft* is not a single-player game. However, it serves as a useful example of what might be permissible, in light of sanctioned equivalence, in single-player games.) Such actions fall within the remit of sanctioned equivalence, and therefore constitute an acceptable form of gameplay (Smith, 2006). Less clear is the justification for taking on the role of a contract killer (e.g. *Hitman*) or serial killer (*Postal 2, Manhunt 2*), irrespective of whether one's character is realistically depicted or presented in fantasy alien or demonic guise (e.g. *God of War*). As Cohen (2001, p. 251) notes, 'media studies of identification must account for the production of identification targets as well as the identification of audiences with them'.

What makes a serial killer a likely identification target within a game? For a possible explanation, we might consider society's apparent fascination with true crime, and the fact that there has long been a tradition in cinematic story-telling to provide fictional representations that mirror real-life events. On-screen serial killers can be found in all guises – Norman Bates in *Psycho*; Michael Myers in *Halloween*; and, more recently, John Doe in *Seven* or the Firefly family in *The Devil's Rejects*, to name but a few. Each provides us with a fictional representation of criminal behaviour that is only too real, even if it is sometimes exaggerated for effect. Even television drama seeks to satisfy this fascination, as is evident by the success of such series as *Prime Suspect or Messiah* in the UK. Games similarly reflect this interest, allowing the gameplayer not only to adopt the perspective of the killer, but also to explore (in a more *agentic* way) the sorts of actions characteristic of contract or serial killing. This richer, more 'in-depth' characterization is often contrasted with the somewhat cursory portrayal of the victim, which often leads to the depiction of the killer as *cool* and the victim as anonymous. Consider Jules and Vincent in *Pulp Fiction*, or Mickey and Mallory in *Natural Born Killers*. More recently, consider the characterization of the serial killer in the television drama *Dexter* – a serial killer who preys on other serial killers (a distorted form of sanctioned equivalence?). (According to *IGN.com*, plans are under way to produce a video game based on the character *Dexter*.) The victims in virtual gameplays appear to receive the same cursory treatment often evident in other works of fiction. We can even see this fascination directed towards the perpetrator of cannibalism. Has Hannibal Lecter in *Silence of the Lambs* provided us with our first cool, sophisticated cannibal? If so, then how far are we from Nero the necro, or Sylvester the molester?

According to Cohen (2001), with more traditional media, identification with a character is not so much about creating one's own identity as it is about internalizing the identity of the character portrayed through the media – making their point of view your point of view. In addition, Cohen (2001, p. 252) tells us:

> Identifying with extremely negative characters who are evil or very violent may evoke some understanding or even sympathy for them during reading or viewing but strongly identifying with such a character is likely to cause dissonance, guilt, or even fear.

In the case of traditional media, then, one may feel guilty about identifying with the negative character's evil intentions. With video games, however, the goal of the gamer may be simply to win the game. This may be the gamer's main or even sole focus. Thus, they may not be (as) aware of the virtual character's intention, or perceive it as merely incidental to winning the game, or progressing to the next level. We will have more to say on this in Chapters 14 and 15 when discussing player identification further, and the issue of moral management.

COMPARING OTHER MEDIA

As noted in Chapter 5, before the birth of computer-mediated gamespace, works of fiction occupied their own alternate virtual spaces. Even today, literary or cinematic fiction creates a space for the narrative to unfold. In these more traditional mediums, however, the narrative is the work of the author and/or director (depending on the medium); it is his/her story to tell, and in the telling of it, typically, the author/director invites you to bear witness to the unfolding drama – to the position he/she has adopted – and in doing so seeks to provoke a reaction (see Lack, 2008; Mey, 2007). The structure of the narrative, including the images presented, aims at communicating a message, and it is this message that more often than not you are asked to bear witness to and judge. As passive as one is when engaged with these more traditional fictions, in their more traditional virtual spaces, the 'work' is not vacuous. By inviting a response, the author/director is providing the opportunity for the audience to engage with the message. One may not agree with or even like the stance presented within the book or film, but *one expects there to be one* (Nussbaum, 1992). The 1999 film *Audition*, for example (directed by Takashi Miike), is reported to have prompted mass walkouts when premiered at the 2000 Rotterdam Film Festival owing to its extremely graphic and violent scenes (http://www.indiepixfilms.com/festival/75/2000). Other critics, however, have responded much more favourably to it (see Mitchell, 2001).

If a perspective is not perceived – that is, if the fiction appears to be vacuous – then typically it is judged (rightly or wrongly) to be bad fiction. Independent of any moral issues that may arise as a result of this vacuousness, the fiction is derided as a bad example of the art form – although we recognize that some may argue that in addition to the poor quality of the art form, the vacuous and/or gratuitous nature of the content may have moral implications. Just such a criticism was directed by Di Muzio (2006) towards *slasher* or *gorefest* films, specifically the original 1974 version of *The Texas Chainsaw Massacre*; however, it could just as easily be applied to later films such as *Friday the 13th* (1980), *Halloween* (1980) and *A Nightmare on Elm Street* (1984), or even more recently to what is sometimes referred to as *torture porn* (Edelstein, 2006) – in reference to films such as *Saw* (2004), *The Devil's Rejects* (2005), *Wolf Creek* (2005) and *Hostel* (2005). Di Muzio's objection to this type of graphic horror – which characteristically features prolonged terror, sadistic torture and human mutilation (Johnston, 1995) – is that it is immoral. However, these films are not immoral simply because they contain images of extreme violence, for as Di Muzio (2006, p. 280) notes:

> [O]ne would want to resist the thesis that it is wrong to read and enjoy Homer's *Iliad* because it contains violence, gore and death. Depictions of

violence do not *per se* belong in the category of the morally objectionable only because many instances of real violence do.

Instead, for Di Muzio, such films 'not only contain representations of violence and death, but are *devoted primarily or solely* to representing violence and death' (p. 281; emphasis in original). So much so, he continues, that a slasher film like *The Texas Chainsaw Massacre* 'makes the point of having no moral point' (p. 290).

What Di Muzio seems to be objecting to is that (in his view) slasher films (including torture porn – we do not believe that Di Muzio would object to its inclusion here) present violence and gore as an end in itself: as entertainment. They do not seem to provide (allow, perhaps) the opportunity for the viewer to reflect on the violence graphically represented on the screen, or certainly the depictions of violence do not appear to be instrumental to this reflective end.

Of course, one could challenge Di Muzio's interpretation of the role that violence plays within these films, or whether they are in fact, as he tells us, devoted primarily or solely to representing violence and death. This is the tack used by Kreider (2008), who argues that the depiction of violence is not typically an end in itself, and that often reasons for the violence are contained within the narrative, usually waiting to be uncovered as the story unfolds. Moreover, Kreider (2008, p. 153) argues that 'most people would agree that an artistic context does justify or at least mitigate some things that we would otherwise find objectionable'. A view shared by Poole (1982, p. 40) when stating that the depiction of 'morally and emotionally shocking situations might be tolerable if the author intended to create a work of art'. (Recall the discussion on obscenity in relation to art in Chapter 4.)

Essentially, what is captured within the exchange between Di Muzio and Kreider is the same issue of gratuity raised in relation to the alleged passive voyeur who viewed images of body horror on sites like *ogrish.com*. What is also evident from Kreider's comment on the importance of artistic licence, which contextualizes the depiction of, in this case, graphic violence, is that it is compatible with the argument presented above in which the artistic worth of the fiction is to be judged independently of the morality of what is represented; or at least any moral judgement should be informed by the intentions of the artist (be they director or author) to challenge the viewer to bear witness to what they are seeing (or reading). Thus, we are left to consider how the world the author/director invites us to enter is represented, and the manner of our invitation (Dillon, 1982). In short, good literature and art (including films) invite us to consider the point of view proffered by their creator, and will perhaps even challenge our own. They do this irrespective of whether we take up the challenge or succeed in being edified.

Within computer-mediated gamespace, the player is able not only to view fictional (*qua* virtual) characters engaged in virtual acts but also to interact with them, and within certain constraints develop his/her own narrative. But unlike more traditional works of fiction, there is no obligation to an *art form*. Virtual may be synonymous with fictional, but it is not synonymous with literary. There is no form to adhere to or even corrupt, or the form is so new that there is no established narrative template to be compared against. Having said that, the US publishers of the ultra-violent video game *Manhunt 2* (originally banned in the UK and Ireland) did describe it as a 'fine piece of art' (*BBC News*, 2007; see also Gee, 2006), so perhaps a normative structure is beginning to emerge, or there is an attempt to recognize gamespace as an emerging art form (see Woods, 2004, for a detailed discussion on whether video games could ever be a vehicle for critical creative expression and achieve the 'emotional depth' of other media, even when the subject matter is, for example, power, violence or death). Moreover, we note that the British Academy of Film and Television Arts (BAFTA) now has its own video game awards. Nevertheless, as things stand, when engaged in gamespace, one is not *required* to bear witness to the unfolding narrative, although we accept that it may be possible in some cases, or even be part of the gameplay, to do so (see Chapter 14).

SYMBOLIC TABOOS AS SOCIALLY SIGNIFICANT EXPRESSIONS

We will return to the topic of narrative below. In the meantime, irrespective of the presence (or lack thereof) of an invitation to bear witness to the unfolding 'drama', Powers (2003), like Brey, recognizes the symbolic significance of VR *representation*. Using the example of rape, he distinguishes between the physical act – of unwanted intercourse – and the sense of offence felt by the victim. Offline, unwanted intercourse is sufficient for a charge of rape, irrespective of any offence caused (a person may be unconscious, for example, or be of sufficiently low mental ability to be incapable of feeling offended). But in gamespace, Powers notes, the event seems to be subordinate to the offence taken. But who is being offended in single-player games? Where the 'violation' is directed by the gamer towards a virtual character controlled only by the computer software, any offence, it would seem, must be felt by the onlooker, perhaps in the abstract form of 'the moral majority' (recall the community standard measure of obscenity discussed in Chapter 4). An explanation of why the onlooker might be offended is offered by Powers (2003, p. 193): 'what a person intends to do and achieve by acting and uttering, is really part of the world . . . [and] is the subject matter for moral judgement, even when his or her agency is mediated by computers'.[1]

What the gamer is communicating, even through the virtual nature of their action, Powers (2003, p. 193) tells us, is 'socially significant expression': an expression that, in the absence of sanctioned equivalence or an invitation to bear witness, may be judged vacuous and therefore gratuitous by the onlooker. Similarly, Castronova *et al.* (2009, p. 686), on a related point, ask whether a virtual sword (for example) becomes 'invested with some kind of socially constructed realness as a result of playing a role in human communication and exchange'. Yet within the games presented here – actual or hypothetical – has it not to be recognized that what the gamer intends, and the social significance of their expression, is strictly context dependent – that is, restricted to the gamespace?

Contrast the games discussed so far with what are being referred to as 'serious games': games designed to act as a medium for a particular form of social change/

action, rehabilitation or learning (Peng *et al.*, 2010). In a study by Peng *et al.*, US participants were measured on their willingness to help the Darfurian people caught in the conflict in Dafur (Sudan) after interacting with a flash game entitled *Dafur is Dying*, compared to receiving text-based information on the real-life situation and the hardships faced by the refugees. Peng *et al.*'s findings led them to conclude that 'interactive digital games are more effective than noninteractive presentation modes at influencing people's empathic reactions to social issues' (2010, p. 735). The flash game used in Peng *et al.*'s study was designed to represent an actual conflict and people in genuine need of help. Here, it may well be stated with some justification that the content was designed to have socially significant expression. However, if the intention and its social significance are based on a contingency relation that is specific to the gamespace, then should not the moral system used to evaluate the gamer's engagements be born of the same space? One must therefore question whether the onlooker's sense of disgust and condemning moral attitude towards STAs is in fact appropriate. After all, adherence to the art form in traditional works of fiction, or even its deliberate corruption, occurs largely for the purpose of edification: that we may somehow 'grow' as individuals or a society as a result of contemplating the message (*qua* a challenge or an ideal) conveyed within the artistic expression. In the case of gamespace, however, as noted earlier, no adherence to an art form or motivation towards edification is required. As such, one might claim that judging a particular gameplay to be morally vacuous is wholly inappropriate, because its nature is such that it does not invite nor even require us to bear witness to its alleged socially significant expression from outside the gamespace.[2] What we are engaged with, here, is play, not art. Of course, we recognize that there are games that do provide the gamer with moral decisions to make, which then impact on the unfolding drama, including future options available to the game character (e.g. *Heavy Rain*). We will have more to say on the game as a moral object in Chapter 14. The point we are making here is twofold: (a) that the appropriateness of an action is context dependent (built on the contingencies of that space) and, related to this, (b) that a space may not seek to be burdened with the responsibility of socially significant expression, and doing so, especially in light of (a), is inappropriate.

In support of the importance of context, King *et al.* (2006) found that when an action was considered appropriate to the context, participants exhibited excitation in the same areas of the brain irrespective of whether their behaviour was aggressive or compassionate. In other words, irrespective of whether they acted aggressively towards one character (shooting a non-human assailant) or compassionately towards another (an injured human avatar), when this behaviour was considered to be appropriate to the situation (normative action), excitation of the ventromedial frontal cortex and amygdala occurred, compared to when participants were asked to engage in contextually inappropriate behaviour (healing the non-human assailant and shooting the injured man). It may be that in the case of King *et al.*'s study, both the normativity of the action (based on its context) and the social significance of its expression are compatible (to act compassionately towards injured humans and aggressively towards non-human assailants is also appropriate social expression). Nevertheless, they need not be; particularly if we adhere to the argument that the two spaces are independent – that is, the online space in which the interaction occurs is independent of the offline space from which one derives the supposed social significance of the expressed virtual interaction. An interesting empirical question is: Might the same areas of the brain signify 'appropriate' (normative) action in the context of a game in which one is meant to indiscriminately kill, torture or even rape? In this context, the appropriateness of the online interaction and the appropriateness of any alleged socially significant expression would seem to part company. Yet should we burden such games with the responsibility of monitoring what they express in terms of action and representation? Are we not unwittingly demanding from such games socially significant expression that is not there or that they do not seek to communicate? To reiterate, what is occurring in these spaces is essentially play and not art/literature.

Booth (1988) directs us to distinguish between two components of a fictional narrative: *nonce beliefs* and *fixed norms*. Nonce beliefs are those we are required to hold for the duration of the fiction; they may even stem from a willing suspension of disbelief. For example, I may be required to believe that in a galaxy far, far away, a rebel alliance is battling against the dark forces of the Empire. In addition to this, contained within the fiction are fixed norms – such as being honourable, treating people with respect, good triumphing over evil, etc. The fixed norms provide the backdrop against which we are to judge the exploits of the protagonist (and others); they provide the moral of the story, and are what we are expected to take away from the fiction. It may be here that the author attempts to provoke us, by subverting these norms and inviting us to bear witness to the consequences. In gamespace, like other fictions, the nonce beliefs can take many forms. But must the fixed norms transcend the gamespace as socially significant expression? Suppose there is no 'take home message' that we have argued is more a necessity (artefact perhaps) of traditional fictional spaces. Suppose the fixed norms are entirely context dependent, such that in *this* virtual space I can kill indiscriminately, torture or rape, or engage in virtual incest/paedophilia, cannibalism or necrophilia: because it is *just a game*. The fixed norms of this virtual space are incommensurate with other spaces – certainly with my offline world – because they are constituted out of a contingency relation that does not exist offline. As such, the fixed norms of this space have no bearing on my offline world.

TRANSCENDENT AUTHENTICITY

So why do games featuring STAs – actual or hypothetical – elicit a feeling of disgust from some onlookers? Recall from Chapter 6 how, according to Kreitman (2006, p. 614), emotional responses to fiction can only occur if a number of preconditions are in place: preconditions that enable the 'affect-laden, prereflective knowledge of the [individual] . . . to be brought into play', (a position compatible with Damasio's *somatic marker hypothesis* discussed in Chapter 3). Thus, although the characteristics and constructs applied to works of fiction are arranged in novel ways, they are nevertheless derived from, and are therefore compounds of, actual experience. Fictions, including those constructed within gamespaces, constitute an 'unreal entity with real characteristics' (p. 616). Real-world authenticity, then, transcends the space marked out by real and virtual worlds, and is measured by the number of attributes of a certain kind possessed by the virtual object.

For Kreitman, the emotional response elicited by the fictional object is triggered by the meaningfulness of the constituent properties. The properties we attribute to virtual objects and events are meaningful to us *because* they exist in our offline world. Moreover, because these virtual attributes are authentic – have *transcendent authenticity* (Young and Whitty, 2011a) – we have already acquired pre-reflective, affect-laden knowledge of them through our various encounters with objects and events with similar attributes offline (although often they are arranged in novel ways when encountered in gamespace). Kreitman's argument seems compatible with Knapp (2003) and Gert's (2005) view (from Chapter 3) that most objects and events that cause a sense of disgust in us do so because of social conditioning.

Through the authenticity of the constituent properties that make up the objects/ events in gamespace, we come to understand why some of the offline taboos violated within (actual or hypothetical) games might elicit disgust in onlookers who then adopt a condemning moral attitude. We understand the underlying process by which they may feel disgusted and subsequently offended, but the question we return to is: *Should* we be directed by such a response towards a condemning moral attitude? The authenticity of the component parts of the fiction is what we react to; it is this that transcends domains and is imported into the gamespace. But at the same time, no matter how authentically (and therefore successfully) the representation tries to capture the component features of the offline world, it does so from within an independent space that has its own unique contingencies, the most significant of which is the impossibility of harm befalling the object of these authentic constituent properties (the virtual victim), no matter how severe the moral violation directed towards them. Consequently, the problem of moral dumbfounding returns to challenge any normative stance we might wish to take here.

A QUESTION OF RATIONALITY, NOT MORALITY

Levy (2003) suggests a way to bypass such seeming moral irrelevance by arguing for judgements based on rationality rather than morality. He asks us to consider how we might 'think of the limits of human capabilities . . . [and] the boundaries beyond which we cannot go', and whether such boundaries are 'merely contingent restrictions which can and ought to be tested' (2003, p. 451). He then claims that our limits 'play an essential role in constituting our identities' (p. 452): for, 'in the absence of these limits, characteristic human activities lose their point' (p. 453). He further instructs us that some of these limits are born of our mortality; others, our physicality; and others still our culture; and that, together, they capture the boundaries of our *humanity*. Using the example of bestiality, Levy argues that such an act is identity-threatening in so far as the more someone engages in it, the more difficult it will be for them 'to retain a grip on [their] identity as a full member of our community, and we will find it harder to admit [them] to full membership' (p. 454).

Acts of bestiality or necrophilia, or rape, torture and mutilation, or incest and paedophilia, may be difficult to condemn morally, at least with any justification, if one restricts such acts to gamespaces in which they are performed on computer-generated objects only (see Luck, 2009). Most people's revulsion at such acts, even when carried out exclusively in virtual space, is vulnerable to a charge of moral dumbfounding, based as it is on social conditioning that is itself the product of particular offline contingencies (such as the *somatic marker hypothesis*). But perhaps there is room for the claim that what such action amounts to is an erosion of our humanity (a similar concern was voiced in relation to obscenity – that it led to depravity). Toronto (2009, p. 119) similarly considers whether interfacing with virtual worlds 'has the potential to change what it means to be human'.[3] Perhaps these acts are as Levy describes them – identity-threatening – even when performed solely in virtual space against virtual objects: for carrying out actions of this kind involves a deterioration of our identity as human beings, at least in the space in which they occur, and at least in relation to our contingent identity as it has evolved offline. The focus of the judgement, then, is not on what our actions are doing to others, but what they are doing to us (a point we shall return to). Clearly, there *can be* a moral dimension imposed on these events (irrespective of whether there should be), but Levy's point is that there need not be for them still to be deemed impermissible. A claim to inappropriateness does not have to be couched in morality, he tells us; rather, it can be rationally based. Why would we want to engage in activities that erode our identity as human beings?

Importantly, Levy does accept that a one-off act of bestiality (for example) is not identity-threatening (or perhaps is negligibly so); rather, it is prolonged activity of this kind that is threatening. It might be argued, then, that if occasional, relatively brief excursions into a gamespace that enables virtual acts of bestiality (etc.) to be performed are not identity-threatening, then they should be permissible. Or even if one's identity (one's humanity) is threatened *within this space* – say, as a result of more prolonged interaction of the kind described above – so what? Even if the arbiter of permissibility is transferred from the domain of morality to rationality, who is to say that gamespace should not be used for acts of alleged irrationality? After all, Levy (2003, p. 454) does acknowledge that 'the limits which define our humanity . . . are, by nature, contingent and shifting. To redraw the map of our limits . . . is to set for ourselves new boundaries within which human life takes on a new shape'. Moreover, in the potential space of play is there not room for the irrational?

A QUESTION OF PSYCHOLOGY NOT MORALITY

Perhaps one possible reshaping of our identity is one in which we have the freedom of space to engage in playful acts of irrationality. Consequently, perhaps permissibility should be guided neither by abstract notions of morality nor by rationality, but by the *psychological impact* that such altered contingencies have on the individual. In a gamespace involving sudden changes in contingency relations, acts that, according to Levy, erode our identity as human beings are possible (irrespective of whether they should be permissible). An important empirical question, then, is: How might engaging in this type of identity-threatening, taboo-violating behaviour, impact on the psychology of the individual? If psychological changes do occur, might they be damaging or liberating? Perhaps the switch between online and offline contingencies is psychologically problematic as individuals seek parity in their identity across domains. Our identity as human beings has been shaped by our contingent moral history; how might a sustained history of engagement in a taboo-free zone, or in a zone with markedly different moral contingencies, alter this 'characteristic' human identity? If such a change were to occur, would it necessarily initiate a change in our offline humanity as we seek parity of identity across spaces, or would we develop multiple identities across domains?

From a moral perspective, we can ask: Should we engage in all possible activities available to us in gamespace? Perhaps, from the perspective of the context dependency of the actions available, it is difficult to adopt moral values that transcend *all* of these spaces. Perhaps, then, rather than it being a moral issue, it is a psychological one. As such, and to reiterate a point raised in Chapter 4, it is not so much whether we should engage in all possible actions that is the issue, but whether, psychologically, we can. Might it be, in fact, that unrestrained engagement is psychologically damaging? Of course, violating taboos in certain types of gameplay might be psychologically beneficial, as indeed might some types of cyber 'spaces' for the expression of taboo subjects. Ogunyemi (2008), for example, writes about the use of cyberspace as a place where African women from the Sudan can talk about their rape experiences, a subject traditionally considered taboo.

Indeed, in the context of gamespace, Ryan *et al.* (2006, p. 348) have this to say: 'Whatever the concerns of critics, players themselves find games gratifying and pleasurable'. In addition, they consider that 'as emerging games are increasingly providing deeper and more long-lasting experiences for players, their potential for psychological impact is increasing proportionately' (ibid.).

MOTIVATION FOR SYMBOLIC TABOOS

In Chapter 3, we speculated over whether an offline system of morality would be ineffective as a means of judging behaviour within cyberspace because of the potential for varied contingencies within its different spaces, and the difficulty of utilizing moral values that are applicable across all possible contingencies. This view seems to be shared by McCormick (2001), at least in so far as he considers traditional utilitarian and Kantian approaches to morality ineffective because they focus on the act itself rather than the person carrying out the act (for a continuation of McCormick's discussion, see Coeckelbergh, 2007; Waddington, 2007; Wonderly, 2008). Within the gamespace, the act is (clearly) a virtual act, which is why no harm befalls the object of the action (the victim). As such, there is no negative utility (utilitarian approach) or failure to do one's duty (Kantian approach). Yet as McCormick (2001, pp. 284–285) points out when discussing a hypothetical example of virtual paedophilia:

> What strikes us about the example is that there seems to be something wrong with the activity without regard to what might happen outside the [virtual realm] at some other time. And there is something wrong with the act solely with respect to the person who commits it.

To return to an earlier question: Why would a player want to engage in virtual paedophilia, bestiality or necrophilia? *Possibly*, one might view it within a game-play as a means to an end: a task that has to be completed in order to move on to the next task/level, and nothing more; and certainly not something that one lingers over. Luck (2009) discusses an example in which the goal of the game is to steal the Crown Jewels from the Tower of London. One way of achieving this goal is to sleep with the Beefeater's 15-year-old daughter. But even this may not be considered sufficient justification. After all, it seems legitimate to ask: How is such an action integrated into the gameplay, particularly in light of the principle of sanctioned equivalence discussed earlier? Even more troubling, then, what if the act is an end in itself, as seems to be the case with the rape simulation game *RapeLay*? What if the goal of the game is solely to engage in the sorts of STAs mentioned above? Earlier, we introduced Levy's (2003) claim that such acts are identity-threatening. McCormick argues something similar, only in relation to virtue theory, claiming that simulated taboo violation erodes one's virtue. The virtue that McCormick is referring to is derived from Aristotle's *eudaimonia* (a kind of flourishing or well-being achieved through the application of reason). Within the gamespace, the object of one's intention may be virtual (the victim), as is the tool with which one executes the action (one's avatar/first-person shooter), but the subject of the intention (oneself) is not. The psychological composition of the gamer transcends the space, irrespective of the self they may wish to present within that particular space (special-forces operative, serial killer, rapist, paedo-phile). McCormick's argument is that engaging even in simulated taboo violations is corrosive, presumably because such actions *represent* vice rather than virtue; and one's intention, even if it is only to *simulate vice*, is damaging to one's well-being (eudaimonia). (Again, this can be linked to earlier concerns raised in relation to obscenity.)

McCormick's endorsement of virtue theory, like Levy's argument that it is irra-tional to engage in something that is identity-threatening, is normative. Each author instructs us on how we should conduct ourselves – either in a way that is not identity-threatening or in a way that does not erode our virtue. Yet such normative positions are vulnerable to the charge that they are simply trying to import into virtual space an ideal or socially accepted state of affairs that is contingent on our non-virtual world. Why should I not engage in irrational behaviour or vice in a space in which it is safe to do so? What is being suggested by these authors is that it is *not* safe to do so. Not because others are harmed – although this may be an additional consequence regarding persons offline (see Chapter 13) – but, primarily, because one harms oneself.

Interestingly, a similar argument is made by Di Muzio (2006) who we discussed earlier in relation to graphic horror films. Di Muzio asks us how we would react if someone felt entertained by watching a film depicting graphic child torture, or even if the viewer were sufficiently detached from what was being depicted to be able to pass comment on the technical prowess of the film maker in recreating such a scene. For Di Muzio (2006, p. 285), being entertained by such fiction, or even detached from it, only succeeds in 'working to cut the nerve of [our] humanity'. Such self-harm, he instructs us, acts against our own moral development, preventing us from tending to it (again, this echoes those concerns raised over the alleged depraved causal consequences of obscene material). Of course, the film maker and/or the editor must, presumably, have engaged with these scenes with a fair degree of technical detachment when editing the film, as would a student of film making be required to do when studying it. Does this make them morally corrupt? We seem to be returning to the issue of bearing witness to the scene – what is the take-home message the director is trying to convey, or what else is being learned from this fiction? But even if someone is purely entertained by the scenes just described, does that make *the scene itself* morally wrong? Perhaps the person, in being entertained, has missed the point of the scene – the director's take-home message. Being entertained by the scene does not make the scene itself morally wrong, we contend: for suppose the individual is also entertained by the violence depicted in the *Iliad*, or the beach scene in *Saving Private Ryan*. Might our intuitive concern for the individual entertained by a fictional scene of child torture be over the psychological state of this individual? If so, then the issue is not the fictional act itself but how we are coping with what we bear witness to, or interact with in the case of STAs within gameplays. As suggested earlier, the question becomes not what we ought to do in these spaces, but what we are capable of dealing with: the measure of which is our ability to maintain psychological well-being across spaces. However, the well-being we are seeking here is less exacting than that demanded by Aristotle's eudaimonia.

Playing VR games, even violent ones, holds a certain allure for an increasing number of people (they are gratifying and pleasurable). Within their 'private laboratories' (Jansz, 2005, p. 231), gamers can engage with different emotions and identities in relative safety – relative to the offline world, that is – and invest in their own form of psychological exploration. When one bloodies and brutalizes a stranger to the point of death with a kitchen utensil, as it is possible to do in *Manhunt 2*, or when one sexually assaults a defeated female opponent (watching her cry and hearing her anguish) in *Battle Raper*, one is enabled through the game to become what Jansz (2005) calls the architect of one's own disgust. Now, if we dismiss disgust's role (at least within gamespace) as a measure of moral wisdom, we can see, perhaps, how being able to experience disgust in the absence of moral condemnation might have a certain appeal, at least for some. Therefore, it is not our position to morally condemn gamers who engage in STAs (even of the sort not yet available commercially); rather, we seek to explore what gamers are able to deal with psychologically. We say 'explore', because, to date, there is little empirical evidence to inform our discussion either way.

Despite the paucity of research, it is nevertheless our contention that STAs are not *in and of themselves* psychologically unhealthy (a defence of this claim will be provided in the chapters to come). That is not to say that STAs will not have a psychological impact on the gamer. Exploring emotions and identities, exploring taboo and disgust, will each in its own way affect our psychological make-up, just as any form of engagement does, however negligible. The issue, then, is not whether, or to what extent, we are psychologically affected in one space compared to another, but how we are able to manage this impact across the different spaces we interact in. Because of this, when assessing the appropriateness of gameplays within single-player video games, it has been our aim throughout this chapter to show that questions dealing with what is or is not moral are the wrong sorts of questions to be asking. Instead, a more informative strategy for judging permissibility is to focus on what gamers are able to deal with psychologically.

Traditionally, research has tended to look for relationships between violent media (more recently, video games) and aggressive thoughts, feelings and behaviour (see Chapter 13). While useful, this is only one aspect of the potential psychological impact gamespaces may have on the player. Underlying any changes in the gamer's thoughts, feelings and behaviour, we contend, is the need to seek psychological parity across domains. This principle applies to any two spaces in which there is a (large) disparity between personas presented therein. The parity issue is, of course, just as important to the gamer who only plays the role of superhero (for example); however, the focus of this book is on those spaces in which one is able to violate offline taboos. In the absence of research findings on the impact of STAs on the gamer's need to maintain psychological parity or, indeed, in the absence of research looking at who is more susceptible to the effects of potential disparities across spaces, we are required to build a picture based on what we do know. In gaining insight into the question of how we cope, psychologically, with the freedoms available within certain virtual spaces, especially when we have to return to the relative constraint of the offline world, and particularly when these virtual freedoms are becoming more realistically represented and more readily accessible, we need to examine further the nature of the self that frequents these virtual spaces. This we do in Part 2. In the meantime, and in concluding Part 1, we consider online multiplayer gamespace, and ask: What, if any, additional issues exist regarding psychological parity and the enactment of STAs within massively multiplayer online role-playing games (MMORPGs)?

9 Multiplayer games

Are we all agreed?

In the previous chapter we concerned ourselves with the manner in which characters or events within single-player gamespace are represented, the behaviours simulated and the interactions permitted. We considered whether, from a moral perspective, we should distinguish between those acts already permitted within single-player games and others – actual or hypothetical – not currently permitted or available. We concluded that there are no sustainable moral arguments for distinguishing between such acts; arguing, instead, that questions of morality are the wrong sorts of questions to ask, at least with regard to the act itself. Rather, we should concern ourselves with the psychological impact that any potential freedom from moral prohibition might have on the gamer. The question therefore becomes not so much whether, morally, we should engage in all possible actions, but whether, psychologically, we can.

In this chapter we switch our attention from single- to multiplayer gamespace (see also Young and Whitty, 2010a). Massively multiplayer online role-playing games (MMORPGs) allow players to create and develop their own unique avatars. (We will use the term MMORPGs for convenience and to be consistent, rather than interchanging it with MMOGs or MMOs, which may be used by other authors we refer to.) Gamers choose from among a range of features to help define the identity and attitudes of their character, including occupation, gender, race (or even species), sexual orientation and religious/spiritual allegiance (the last of these acting as a broad measure of morality). According to Smyth (2007, p. 718), the added multiplayer dimension has changed the nature of the game from 'a solitary or small group activity into a large, thriving social network'. Does the fact that opponents are real people *offline* (not players generated by the game's software) make a difference to (a) what should be permissible within the virtual gamespace in terms of both representation and interaction and (b) the psychological impact of STAs? In addition, how might changing the contingency relation to a virtual interactive space that is not typically regarded as a gamespace (namely *Second Life*) alter the response to (a) and (b)? (For discussion on a forerunner to *Second Life* – namely, *The Palace* – see Suler, 1996.)

INTRODUCING MULTIPLAYER GAMES

In MMORPGs, players take on the role of a fictional character, typically (but not exclusively) in a fantasy world, and have agency over many of their character's actions. The worlds created in these games continue to evolve even when the player is absent from the game – examples include *EverQuest*, *World of Warcraft*, *Final Fantasy XI* and, more recently, *Warhammer*. Like single-player games, the popularity of these games continues to grow.

More recently, the nature of the interactions afforded within these multiplayer spaces has become more 'adult' based; and whilst violence within MMORPG gameplays is not at the level of some single-player games (e.g. *Manhunt 2*), it does seem to be catching up and indeed sought (if the number of subscribers is anything to go by). *Age of Conan*, *Warhammer* and *Requiem: Bloodymare* (for example) provide increased opportunities for extreme violence and more graphic depictions of violent outcomes; and, according to some (see Stefanescu, 2006), *2 Moons* offers perhaps more blood and gore than ever before – the game's slogan being 'No mercy for the weak, no pity for the dying, no tears for the slain'.

Continuing the adult theme, *Sociolotron* promotes itself as a world with different values and rules in which you are allowed to explore your 'darker side' (*Sociolotron 2* was still under construction at time of writing). Virtual sex, both consensual and non-consensual, is permitted and graphically represented, as is politically incorrect behaviour, including blasphemy and all forms of discrimination. The general philosophy of the game seems to be that if you are given the freedom to express yourself within this space then you should allow others to do the same (if you want to 'dish it out' then you should be able to take it, we are told). Exempt from this freedom, however, is any form of simulated paedophilia. It is explicitly stated on the game's homepage that this is unacceptable (a point we shall return to). Similarly, in *Pangaea*, a game originating in Korea, sex is either a main feature of the gameplay, or appears indirectly in gambling and fantasy battle options – female warriors lose their clothes when hurt or wounded, for example, becoming fully naked when killed. Continuing the cybersex theme is *3 Feel* – launched as the first English adult MMORPG. Here, the main purpose of the game is to engage in sexual behaviour.[1]

Like single-player games, MMORPGs contain *simulations* or *representations* of many aspects of offline physical and social reality, even when set in futuristic and/or fantasy/alien worlds; and as we noted in Chapter 8, according to Brey (1999, 2003), even mere simulations warrant moral policing, especially when they are simulations of prohibited offline behaviour. Killing is a common occurrence in many of the gameplays mentioned, with murder and the brutalization of one's victims not only permissible but, in some (many?) cases, an enticement to play. Moreover, we have seen how rape features within *Sociolotron*. In addition, *World of Warcraft* permits the cannibalization of one's victims as a means of restoring health; and in *The Art of Persuasion* (again, from *World of Warcraft*), the use of torture is possible, even required.

SOCIALLY SIGNIFICANT EXPRESSION REVISITED

What these examples illustrate is that, like single-player games, MMORPG game-plays regularly involve the enactment of prohibited offline behaviours, often in enhanced or exaggerated ways. Powers (2003) recognizes this when examining what he claims is the symbolic significance of VR representation. Recall from the last chapter how, using the example of rape, he distinguishes between the physical act – of unwanted intercourse – and the sense of offence felt by the victim. However, in that chapter we questioned the appropriateness of this idea of offence, arguing that within single-player games – even those allowing torture and mutilation, or rape, murder and cannibalism – the 'social significance' of the representation and therefore of the potentially (or allegedly) offensive expression is strictly context dependent, based as it is on a contingency relation that is specific to that game-space. By importing a given society's moral values and subsequent sense of offence into the gamespace, including our socially conditioned sense of disgust in the face of taboo violations, we are vulnerable to a charge of moral dumbfounding.

To illustrate, suppose instead of playing a computer chess game using virtual representations of the traditional chess pieces, the board contains virtual persons, animals and objects (bishops, castles, knights on horses, etc.). Suppose further that when 'taking' an opponent's piece, each figure is rendered ineffective in a violent and gory spectacle.[2] A knight taking a pawn (or footsoldier), for example, might be represented by the latter being hacked to death. Alternatively, a knight could be burned alive at the stake when taken by a bishop. The queen could be beheaded or raped to death, etc.

For some, this new version of chess may cause unease, even a strong sense of revulsion. Perhaps onlookers would be repulsed by its more literal take on the game. But whether engaged with a more traditional chess set or our hypothetical version, the actions and *what* they represent – namely eliminating the opposition – are game specific; they differ only with regard to *how* they are represented within the gameplay (either by having pieces 'toppled' and removed, or in the more graphic way described above). However, and importantly, altering how the actions are represented does not mean that those playing the hypothetical game are suddenly engaged in socially significant expression, any more than their more traditional counterpart is. Each is just playing chess. There is no society outside of the gamespace that either player is trying to appeal to. One must therefore question whether any moral condemnation directed towards the use of the newer chess set is in fact appropriate.

Irrespective of which set is used, the rules and objectives of chess remain the same. All that has changed is how one wishes to represent the pieces within the game and the act of having a piece 'taken'. In fact, it could be argued that what is being proposed here is merely an extension of chess sets already available offline that use more intricately carved mediaeval or fantasy characters. Graphically representing the act of 'taking' an opponent's piece changes nothing within the rules and strategies of the game; in the same way that using more intricately carved pieces changes nothing. After all, chess can still be played even with the most rudimentary objects representing each piece. Therefore, both the addition of more intricate pieces and the new graphic proposed here are gratuitous to the *literal* playing of the game. However, an objection to the use of more intricate chess pieces because they are gratuitous might be considered rather weak and, in the end, a matter of taste. Could the same not be said of any objection to the hypothetical chess set – that it is likewise just a matter of taste, rather than morality?

Unlike the example of computer chess described above, and in fact unlike all other single-player computer games, the multiplayer element of MMORPGs means that the gamespace contains its own *actual* social structure. In other words, this independent virtual space – this temporary world of play – has its own socially mediated rules, which help define the gamespace in which the illusion (implicit to play) is generated, and the extent to which it can flourish. This includes the social significance of what is expressed within that space, and the extent to which it is context specific. For unlike single-player games, MMORPGs attract the attention of not only the onlooker ('society') but, by definition, the community of players who share and thereby make up a particular domain.

COMMUNALLY AGREED STATUS FUNCTIONS

As we saw in Chapter 7, the fundamental essence of play is the freedom and licence to be creative, and to be set apart from ordinary life. Yet we saw how play also depends on rules and other factors contingently related to a given space and time. Consequently, an interesting paradox arises in which freedom within play is created only through constraint. As an example of such constraint, virtual objects/ events are assigned a mutually accepted *status function* – this is used to establish coherent play within a cohesive gaming community – formally presented by Brey (2003, p. 278) as 'X counts as Y (in context C)'. Thus, in keeping with our last example, two chess players may agree that when playing with *this* chess set (context C), which has a missing king, a wine cork (X) counts as the king (Y). More generally, and more relevant to MMORPGs, it might be established that within the context of a given gamespace (context C), action X (or actions X_1 and X_2, etc.) counts as Y (something it is permissible to do). However, if the status function of an object/event is not clearly indicated to the satisfaction of all parties (does X_3 also count as Y in this context?), then a conflict born of ambiguity often ensues and the game risks losing it coherence, and the community its cohesion. The potential for status function ambiguity is nowhere more apparent than in the types of social interactions possible in MMORPGs. Owing to the game-like quality of the events played out in these environments, an element of make-believe inevitably accompanies player interactions. However, recognizing when these social encounters involve simulation compliant with status function and when they involve interactions that have an ontological status that transcends the virtual is not always easy, and, indeed, may not always be something that some players want to make clear (Turkle, 1995). As Brey (2003, p. 281) notes:

Interestingly, users of virtual environments sometimes appear as if they want to keep the dividing line between reality and role-playing fuzzy, so as to have the benefits of real-life social interactions while always having the fall-back option of claiming that it is all make-believe.

The status function will likely be linked to taboos, even offline taboos that have been imported into the gamespace. As such, gamers might be expected to react with a sense of disgust towards those who have violated certain prohibited behaviours – raping the avatar of a fellow gamer, for example. The community-agreed status function constrains the freedom inherent within the virtual space. Those who fail to abide by this constraint may be regarded as virtual pariahs, to be ejected from the community whose status function they have flouted.

As noted earlier, unlike single-player games, MMORPGs may fall under the scrutiny of two independent social audiences, constitutive of two independent social spaces – those that make up the community within the game and those that represent 'society' looking on. Reference to these two communities is implicit within an objection raised by Richard Bartle (on his blog in 2008) to the act of torture carried out within *World of Warcraft: The Art of Persuasion*. Bartle is initially concerned by the lack of alternatives available to the player: that a non-torture option is not made available for those who might morally object, even as their character, to the torture. However, Bartle goes on to claim that the socially significant expression (to utilize Powers', 2003, phrase) evident here is that the only consequence of torture is positive, because within the game it is the only means of progression. Bartle's objection can be seen to draw implicitly on the concerns of these two separate social groups – gamer and society. The gamer might be concerned by the lack of choice; society by what the player might 'learn' about the usefulness of torture within a given society, something which they may transfer from the virtual to non-virtual domains (that torture is beneficial/has positive outcomes, and is therefore acceptable).[3] Those gamers who reject Bartle's objection, respond by claiming (correctly) that the torture is virtual, and so should be judged within the context of the game only – what one might call the 'what's the big deal' response. Within this objection, one can see the *context relatedness* of their argument: that the action is contingently related to the gamespace. As no one is actually tortured, attempts to impose moral prohibition could be viewed as evidence of moral dumbfounding. This same response can be directed towards those who object to violence within single-player games. Of more legitimate concern to the gaming community, however, is Bartle's initial objection that the game does not provide alternatives for the player. In other words, the moral choice within the game is unnecessarily and, in fact, inappropriately restrictive. The concern, therefore, is not that torture is wrong but, rather, that a lack of choice is unacceptable to the gameplay. In short, a critical position might be: let me torture because I choose to do so, not because I have no alternative.

Using this example, in context C (*World of Warcraft* 'torture scenario'), X (enforced act of torture) counts as Y (only means of progression) within the gameplay. However, if the status function of the torture scenario (that it *should* count as the only means of progression) is not accepted by all within the gaming community – because it is preferred that alternative means of progression should be made available, even if they are not taken up by all – then conflict (*qua* dissatisfaction) *relative to that space* is likely to ensue. Importantly, then, if alternatives are permitted, such that torture is not the only option, then gamers who accept the new status function of the scenario must also accept that torture is a *possibility* within the gameplay – it is, after all, one of the options. In the absence of removing torture as an option altogether, this means that within the community of gameplayers, there is the possibility (likelihood) that some will torture and some will not. Now, whether one opts to torture or not, the important point is this: all gamers who enter this particular space acknowledge not only the possibility of torture being used but also consent to its *permissibility* within the gameplay. The social expression within this community, then, is that torture is allowed, even if not indulged in by all.

Recall how, in *Sociolotron*, a permitted feature of the gameplay is sexual assault and rape. Here, the avatars of offline players may engage in acts of simulated non-consensual sex, either as victims or as perpetrators. For the social group looking on ('society'), such actions may provoke moral outrage, even deep disgust; but, as already noted, such a position is vulnerable to a charge of moral dumbfounding – at least based on the fact that, within the *virtual space*, no one is physically harmed (we will consider the *psychological* impact in Chapters 14 and 15). However, and importantly, for the community of gamers who frequent this space, the contingency relation is such that, even if not indulged in, it is accepted that it is permissible to rape – much as it is accepted that smoking tobacco or drinking alcohol is permissible (although not mandatory) for people of a certain age in England. But recall, also, that it is expressly forbidden within *Sociolotron* to engage in simulated acts of paedophilia. Why is this? One likely reason is the differing restriction on virtual child abuse and pornography, as noted earlier, which would make the global availability of this game with such permissible interactions problematic (however, see Chapter 15 for an 'insider view' on STAs based on interview data from players of *World of Warcraft* and *Sociolotron*).

If, within a community of gamers who occupy a particular gamespace, it is permissible to violate any number of offline prohibitions (STAs) – such as direct extreme racist and sexist comments to other members of the community – and indulge in any number of simulated illegal and morally proscriptive behaviours, then why not, *in principle*, permit virtual paedophilia? If, as an offline adult, one can enter a virtual space occupied by other offline adults – let us call it the kingdom of *Actus Reus* (meaning wrongful or guilty act) – and virtually maim, torture, rape, murder and mutilate, even cannibalize, then why can one not also within this space, and exclusively within this space, engage in acts of paedophilia, necrophilia or bestiality? Let us say, for the sake of argument, that it is agreed among those who frequent this space that when one's avatar dies, which could occur because it is a space fraught with danger, one's virtual cadaver can be used for sex, food or both – by either one's friends or foes – or that, when alive, one can engage in sex in animal or hybrid animal–human form, or even take on the form of a child. *If* one is in a virtual space (context C) in which *X* (paedophilia) counts as *Y* (a permissible activity to simulate), then is it not the case that any outside abhorrence to this communally accepted status function, as with our earlier example of hypothetical chess, is really just a question of taste rather than morality?

TABOOS AND IDENTITY

The contingent relation between the behaviour and the space in which it occurs makes the imposition of moral values imported from a space outside of the game difficult to defend, unless they violate the basis for a communally agreed status function. What this means is that, morally, it is difficult to challenge the permissibility of an otherwise prohibited activity that is (a) restricted to the space in which it occurs and (b) accepted as permissible, even if not exhaustively indulged in, by the community who occupy that space. However, this is not to say that we should not be concerned by some of these activities, or hold that they are risk-free behaviours.

Recall from the previous chapter how Levy (2003) argues that violating taboos is potentially *identity-threatening*. Levy's argument for the inappropriateness of an action is not couched in morality; rather, it is based on the need to maintain some semblance of rationality: for, according to Levy, rationality constraints 'play an essential role in constituting our identities' (p. 452) and, in their absence, 'characteristic human activities lose their point' (p. 453). But recall, also, how in Chapter 8 we argued against rationality as a normative constraint within virtual space, noting that perhaps one possible reshaping of our identity is one in which we have the freedom of space to engage in (playful) acts of irrationality. In addition, unlike single-player gamespace, within a multiplayer environment, indulging in *permitted* acts of virtual bestiality (for example), or whatever STA is preferred, means that the community occupying the particular environment is endorsing the status function of the otherwise prohibited action. Within this social space, offline prohibited action – be it in the form of murder, torture or rape, or even bestiality, necrophilia, cannibalism and paedophilia (including incest) – is not identity-threatening but identity-*enhancing*, perhaps even identity-*defining*. If nothing else, it forms the basis for the individual's admittance into that particular community, not their rejection.

Of course, in games such as *World of Warcraft* it should be made clear that not all who play the game wish to engage in activities such as torture, or define themselves by it, or even describe themselves (their character) as a torturer. Recall that an objection to the torture scenario in *The Art of Persuasion* was partly based on the lack of options available for progression for those who did not wish to carry out the task. So even in games in which it is permissible to engage in certain activities, not all gamers may choose to do so; or may object if an option for not doing so is unavailable. Here, even if engaged with, the action (torture) seems to be instrumental; and, to reiterate, objections may focus on the lack of alternative means to the same end, rather than any particular one that *is* available and therefore deemed permissible within the gamespace.

But what if the goal of the game is solely to engage in the sorts of STAs that feature in *Sociolotron* (which seem to be an end in themselves)? It seems difficult to understand how such actions would not become a defining feature of one's (character's) identity *within the gamespace*; something Levy thought would be detrimental to identity. We discussed (in Chapter 8) how McCormick (2001) argued something similar, only in relation to virtue theory, claiming that simulated taboo violation erodes one's virtue. Within the multiplayer gamespace, the *object* of one's intention is virtual (the other player's avatar, say), as is the instrument with which one executes the action (one's avatar); but, importantly, the *subject* of the intention (oneself) is not virtual, nor is the other gamer – the person 'behind' the object of one's intention (the other avatar). The psychological composition of each gamer transcends the space in which their virtual actions are carried out, irrespective of the self they may wish to present within that particular space (e.g. special-forces operative, dragon-slayer, serial killer, rapist, paedophile). For the sake of brevity, however, we are interested here only in the gamer who is the agent of the action, not the recipient.

Can the gamer separate out – compartmentalize even (Suler, 2004) – those identities that are shaped by the altered contingencies of virtual and non-virtual space, and the communities that occupy these spaces? Or must it be that in constructing our identity we seek parity of self across domains, such that our identity necessarily transcends spaces? We noted in Chapter 2 that different selves can be presented whenever we interact within a different environment, regardless of the influence of virtual technology, and accept from Chapter 8 that different selves can be presented even in single-player games. However, what we are claiming in this chapter is that the potential for disparity between environments is so much greater and so much more immediate within multiplayer gamespace compared to variations in offline social environments, or even within single-player games. As such, does this potentially large and immediately accessible disparity mean that psychological parity is difficult to achieve or maintain, especially after prolonged bouts of social engagement within MMORPGs?

Similar questions occupied the thoughts of Turkle in the 1990s, with regard to similar spaces known as MUDs and MOOs:

> In virtual reality, we self-fashion and self-create. What kind of personae do we make? What relation do these have to what we have traditionally thought of as the whole person? Are they experienced as an expanded self or as separate from the self? Do our real-life selves learn lessons from our virtual personae? Are these virtual personae fragments of a coherent real-life personality?
>
> (Turkle, 1995, p. 180)

A response to these sorts of questions will be considered in much more detail in Chapters 14 and 15. In the meantime, we will prepare the ground briefly for the discussion to come.

Yee (2006b) reports that everyday, millions of individuals interact with each other in MMORPGs, and that these individuals are on average 27-years-old and typically spend around 22 hours per week in these virtual spaces. Research into MMORPGs has focused mostly on social elements (e.g. Griffiths *et al.*, 2003; Lo, 2008; Yee, 2006c), online identities (e.g. Blinka, 2008; Smahel *et al.*, 2008), the addictive nature of this space (e.g. Charlton and Danforth, 2007; Grusser *et al.*, 2007) and the relationship between gaming and aggressive behaviour (e.g. Grusser *et al.*, 2007; Kim *et al.*, 2008). Of significance, then, is the available psychological literature suggesting that some individuals identify, at least in part, with their online characters, be it in role-playing games such as *World of Warcraft* or less game-based environments such as *Second Life*. In a survey that included 532 players, Blinka (2008) found that over 20 per cent of adolescents and young adults believed that they possessed the same skills and abilities as their character. More-over, he found that over 35 per cent of adolescents and young adults would prefer to be like their character. Such results suggest that some individuals place signifi-cant emotional investment in their avatar and the social communities they belong to (Whang and Chang, 2004).

This being the case, we need to consider seriously whether all activities carried out within these communities are psychologically healthy; not because some of the attitudes and actions expressed within them are morally proscribed in other spaces, but because they are likely to be congruent with an identity that is psycho-logically disparate to that typically exhibited offline (although this need not be the case or need not be problematic, as will be discussed in Chapters 11 and 12). In addition, because of the nature of multiplayer environments – which, compared to single-player games, involve a form of *actual* social engagement – there is more opportunity for one's online identity to develop, and in more complex and socially integrated ways than some players might be comfortable with offline (Cole and Griffiths, 2007). This development is likely to involve a degree of experimenta-tion: perhaps more explicitly in relation to one's avatar, but with the suggestion that this involves some expression of one's identity (again, see Chapters 11 and 12 for discussion on the positive and negative ramifications of this).

Explicit or even implicit experimentation is thus a feature of multiplayer game-space; but in this domain, must there be the same acquiescence to authenticity as found in other spaces (e.g. dating sites)? After all, it is just a game: a potential space of play. As already noted, MMORPGs are games that enable, and often require, complex social interaction and cooperation as part of the gameplay. Being a dragonslayer, for example, may not be an authentic element of who I consider myself to be; but perhaps some of the characteristics the dragonslayer is imbued with are – strength, courage, honour, etc. It is these characteristics that not only enable me to slay virtual dragons, but also provide me with the confidence to engage in the kinds of social interaction that I would be less willing, even unable, to enter into offline. For some players, then, the gameplay's intrinsic appeal, *as a game*, is in fact incidental to its perceived instrumental value – as a means of realizing one's 'ideal' characteristics. As Bessière *et al.* (2007, p. 534) note when discussing *World of Warcraft*: 'its anonymity and fantasy frees players from the yoke of their real-life history and social situation, allowing them to be more like the person they wish they were'.

MANAGING IDENTITIES ACROSS SPACES

To become more like the person I wish to be is to move closer, psychologically, to my *ideal self*, which, if *authentic*, should promote psychological well-being. (We will discuss these terms in more detail in Part 2 and, for now, accept that they are in need of further clarification.) However, the realization of one's ideal self *within gamespace* is context specific and perhaps even context *dependent*, and so it is the transcendent quality of this newly realized (ideal) self that must be considered (see Chapters 11 and 12). MMORPGs such as *World of Warcraft* are, of course, explicitly game based: for although players have a certain freedom to develop their character and pursue certain activities, they are nevertheless restricted by the game mechanics – that is, 'quests' devised by the game's manufacturer. *Second Life*, in contrast, has no such gaming agenda and, indeed, for many of its users is not perceived as a game at all. When given the freedom to create one's own avatar, and a wealth of spaces in which to integrate one's new self, it is reasonable to conjecture that the tendency for identification with one's virtual character will be that much stronger. As such, the *potential* for psychological discrepancy (if one imbues one's character with one's ideals) is likely to be that much greater if one is unable to transfer this newly realized ideal self to the offline realm.

Now, it may be that certain experiences available in *Second Life* cannot transcend domains: offline, one cannot experience flying unaided, for example, or travel instantaneously to a distant virtual land. However, certain activities may be more amenable to such transcendence; and here we find a potential for concern (or *more* concern – we accept that all forms of discrepancy have at least the potential to raise concern). In those virtual spaces where STAs are actually or hypothetically permissible – where they constitute part of an agreed status function – the issue of psychological parity becomes an even more pronounced issue.

Rape, as we have discussed, is permissible within certain gamespaces (e.g. *Sociolotron*), and is not a totally unheard of practice within other MMORPGs, including *Second Life* (McCabe, 2007). In fact, in 2006 it was reported that add-on software (*Rapeplay* 1–4) could be purchased, which enabled one avatar to rape another in *Second Life* (Mohney, 2006). Discussion on the rights and wrongs of virtual rape has tended to focus on whether permission has been obtained from the player about to be raped (Laurenson, 2005) and the psychological impact on the 'victim' if permission was not.[4] What is required is both players' acceptance of the status function of rape within the gameplay. Controversy is courted whenever the status function is ambiguous or disregarded (as in the infamous LambdaMOO case reported by Dibbel, 1993 – see Chapter 2). More recently, a different STA has become (relatively) popular within *Second Life* – namely bestiality (Tan, 2007), including a fad involving sex or possible rape and impregnation by a unicorn (Zjawinski, 2007). Such activity has led Linden Lab (the creators of *Second Life*) to initiate a tougher 'crack-down' on 'broadly offensive' behaviour (Tan, 2007), which has seen the removal of the virtual ageplay space, *Wonderland*, because of alleged paedophilic activity (Russell, 2008; *Sky News*, 2007). ('Ageplay' is the adopting of a virtual child persona by adults.)

Owing to the lack of adequate policing of the *Wonderland* space, of immediate concern was the possibility of offline minors being asked to engage in simulated behaviour that is prohibited offline, or the danger of contact with minors occurring offline as a result of encounters in the virtual space. However, whilst accepting that these are important issues, they do not concern us here. Instead, we return to the question posed earlier concerning paedophilia. In a space frequented by *adults only*, is there a moral case to answer regarding virtual child sex? Is not any abhorrence to this based on a disgust response and negative moral attitude that is contingent on a different space – namely our offline world – in which minors are minors, and not adults presenting as virtual minors?

Part of the problem with trying to import moral values from our offline world into the virtual spaces available to MMORPG users is that they tend to focus on the action itself (e.g. utilitarian and Kantian approaches). What we have argued, here, is that in those spaces in which offline taboo violation is an agreed part of the status function within that space, no moral code is broken. To be clear, we are not arguing for the total absence of moral values/taboos within virtual space; rather, it is our contention that what morals and taboos there are should be born of the same contingency relation as the space itself, not imported from some other space. In MMORPGs, the psychological and social trappings of the individual gamers are, to varying degrees, imported into the virtual space (see discussion in Chapter 14 on the gamer-subject): norms of eye contact, spatial orientation and gender-related interpersonal distances are unconsciously adhered to (Yee *et al.*, 2007; see also Yee *et al.*, 2009, for discussion on the height and attractiveness of avatars and their impact on gaming performance).

A critical aspect of engaging in STAs, then (or in fact of any prolonged engagement within a virtual world in which one's persona is somehow altered – likely enhanced), is not whether they violate one's offline moral values, but whether they impact negatively on one's need to maintain psychological parity (which could be facilitated by having the same moral values across spaces, of course). There is a likely risk that some users will seek parity across domains and, importantly, between what are incommensurable psychological identities (serial killer–university lecturer, for example). Ultimately, this may lead the gamer to favour and even fixate on their virtual persona, resulting in the psychological dominance of the virtual over the non-virtual – a persona that, if constructed around violence and STAs, is certainly incommensurate with our offline world. If the non-virtual identity transfers across domains into a world where taboo violation is morally and perhaps legally proscribed, then this has potential dire consequences for the individual. Alternatively, and in its own way unfortunate, if the allure is away from the offline world towards the virtual world of gamespace, then the motivation will be to spend more and more time in that space – where one's identity and what one is permitted to do are congruent. For when gamespace 'becomes a seductive alternative that breaks with ongoing experience' (Toronto, 2009, p. 121), video game addiction (Bryant and Davies, 2006; Gentile and Anderson, 2003; Wood, 2008) is a possible (likely?) outcome of any attempt to redress psychological parity in favour of one's virtual persona, as are other forms of what is sometimes collectively called *problematic Internet use* (see Chapter 14). Psychologically, the 'gamer' who adopts their online persona may dwell (and socialize) much more in the virtual space of their choice but, physically, remain anchored to this world: a world where, according to Smyth (2007), they may suffer from poorer physical health than non-gamers, or gamers from other (single-player) groups.

To date, there is limited research that specifically targets the issue of psychological parity (although recent research is discussed in Chapter 15). However, according to newspaper reports, the psychological effects of the disparity between virtual and non-virtual space are beginning to emerge. The 'allure of the virtual' and the psychological impact this can have on the individual was allegedly felt shortly after the release of James Cameron's *Avatar* (Piazza, 2010; Sandler, 2010). Apparently, movie-goers began experiencing depression and suicidal thoughts after disengaging with the film's immersive environment. To be emotionally moved by fiction, of course, is nothing new (as discussed in Chapter 6), although to feel (allegedly) depressed and suicidal may seem like an extreme reaction. Even more extreme is a rare condition discussed by Ballon and Leszcz (2007, p. 211) that has some relevance here: *cinematic neurosis*, which amounts to 'the development of anxiety, somatic responses, dissociation, and even psychotic symptoms after watching a film'. Ballon and Leszcz note how persons vulnerable to the condition 'include those who have issues with their identity' (p. 212), which can be influenced by the symbolic, often horror-based, nature of the film narrative. Perhaps, cinematic neurosis is an extreme clinical manifestation of the much more ubiquitous issue of divergent spaces and psychological parity alluded to above. By 'ubiquitous issue' we mean simply that the need for parity is not elicited solely by horror symbolism or taboo violation, but also by any space in which the discrepancy between the possibilities for action within that space and the space one typically occupies are more extreme. The degree of immersion that is becoming possible with advances in virtual technology is also of concern: for if such effects as those described above (with the *Avatar* example) are being felt by someone in the relatively passive position of 'movie-goer', then how much more might they be felt when one is actively engaged as a character in virtual space? How much greater would the psychological effects of *Avatar* be if one could be a character immersed in the filmspace and so interact with others in that space and develop the narrative?

In conclusion, like single-player games, research looking at the effects of MMORPGs on players' thoughts, feelings and behaviours has tended to focus on their potential harm, or has offered caveats to that effect. It is our contention, however, even if only speculatively so at this stage, that underlying any changes to the MMOPRG player (and the single-player gamer) is the need to seek psychological parity across domains. Those players who do not identify in any strong or longlasting way with their avatar, or who perceive it to be imbued with the same/ similar traits as themselves, are unlikely to seek psychological parity – there is no need. However, for those who do identify with their avatar, *and* judge their avatar to possess traits valued by themselves *and* perceive that the only means of realizing this ideal self is through their avatar, the need to seek parity will be strong, we contend. This will occur by either transcending domains, such that the qualities of the avatar are transferred to the gamer offline, or by the gamer seeking to spend more time in the space in which their ideal self can be realized.

The need to maintain psychological parity is particularly acute, we suggest, in MMORPGs because of the social element integral to these gameplays. Here, one has a greater opportunity to 'develop' one's sense of self along ideal lines while engaging in actual (even if virtually based) social interactions. The loss of such a self when one re-enters what may be for some a socially impoverished offline world is therefore all the more salient, and the motivation to return to the virtual world, and for longer, even greater.

In the next part of this book, we begin to make the case for the importance of psychology rather than morality to gauging STA permissibility. As a first step to this end, we discuss in more detail the issue of identity within virtual spaces, including what is involved in presenting and experiencing one's ideal self, and the potential for the development and 'progression' of this self – *qua* embodied identity – in authentic and inauthentic ways, and how one might manage the transition of one's self across potentially disparate spaces. Before then, however, let us consider what some have held to be a more radical alteration of self within cyberspace – namely, disembodiment.

Part 2

The nature and authenticity of selves within cyberspace

10 Disembodiment

A meeting of minds

In Part 1, we presented cyberspace as a place of altered contingencies; a place where the possibility for representation and interaction is virtual and, in many cases, immediate. The discussion that followed was, in part, a response to the general question: If the way we represent ourselves and interact with others is contingent on a particular space, then what possibilities present themselves in these different spaces and how should we police them? In Part 1, we explored this question with an emphasis on the *act* of taboo violation and presented a case supporting the claim made in Chapter 2: that, ultimately, questions about the morality of virtual acts are the wrongs sorts of questions to ask, at least when trying to determine what should be permissible within a given virtual space.

As a continuation of our defence of this claim, in Part 2, we shift focus away from issues relating directly to the morality of virtual representation and interaction in favour of an examination of the psychological impact of STAs on the individual who transcends the offline world. Part 2 therefore entails an examination of psychological issues relating to the *self* in cyberspace, which we embark on in order to defend the argument that the permissibility of STAs should be informed by psychology, rather than by a system of morality imported from our offline world. Our reasoning for such a move is as follows: If the altered contingencies characteristic of a given virtual space have a direct bearing on the way we choose to represent ourselves within that space, and the way we represent ourselves contributes to the likelihood (or not) of engaging in activities that would be considered taboo offline, then the extent to which we can alter ourselves in these spaces needs to be explored further in order for a greater understanding of the connection between space, representation and action to be achieved. A psychological study of the self in relation to these other factors should not be viewed in isolation from its moral implications, however. Instead, it should be seen as the *basis* for decisions regarding the permissibility of virtual representations and interactions. To flout such psychologically driven prohibitions might be to the detriment of those deemed more susceptible to the potential impact of STAs and other moral freedoms on their sense of self and, in particular, on what we will later refer to as *psychological parity*. This, in turn, may have moral ramifications offline. What this detrimental effect might be and who is more or less susceptible to it will be considered further in Part 3.

In the meantime, let us begin our examination of the self by considering what is perhaps its most rudimentary – some might even say fundamental – form: the *disembodied* (Cartesian) mind. The legacy of Descartes (the eponymous author of Cartesian dualism) is still felt today in much of our everyday thinking about the self; consider, for example, the implicit dualism evident in the difference between the expression 'I hate my body' and 'I hate myself'. Because of the influence of Descartes on Western thinking, it is necessary to take a brief philosophical excursion through aspects of his work; not only because he provides a springboard for later discussion on embodiment (see Chapters 11 and 12) but also, more immediately, because his thinking about the self has already been applied, albeit in a diluted form, to cyberspace. In this chapter, then, we consider whether cyberspace is in fact a suitable place for a meeting of minds. Our conclusions will help inform discussion in the chapters to follow.

IN PURSUIT OF THE CARTESIAN SELF

In the early days of the Internet, much was written on the role of text-based *computer-mediated communication* (CMC) as a medium for disembodiment. Early researchers claimed that being disembodied presented individuals with certain advantages; some even arguing that the Internet was able to provide users with the space to free themselves from the sorts of bodily constraint endemic within offline interactions, allowing, instead, disembodied engagement characteristic of a utopian ideal. Moreover, according to Ajana (2005), cyberspace was hailed by some as the perfect environment for the realization of *Cartesian dualism*; with advances in digital technology concomitant with hyperbolic claims about the untapped potential of cyber-reality, the allure of existential freedom and the removal of bodily constraint (Dery, 1994). The words of 'Anthem', a well-cited MCI commercial, echo this sentiment: 'There is no race. There is no gender. . . . There are no infirmities. There are only minds' (MCI, 1997; cited in Boler, 2007, p. 145). Similarly, Kupfer (2007, p. 44) reports the experience of a cyber enthusiast: 'What I loved about the internet was . . . the feeling of being without a body, of . . . a mind touching other minds'.

The early scholars who argued that individuals can be disembodied online endorsed a view of virtual interaction much as the cyber enthusiast described above: as minds touching minds. Levine (2000) even claims that people can connect romantically online via the same 'meeting of minds'. She writes that 'the beauty of the virtual medium is that flirting is based on words, charm, and seduction, not physical attraction and cues' (p. 565). Rollman *et al.* (2000, p. 161) add that 'by eliminating time, distance, and body, the architects of the Internet have created an unhindered medium that connects the mind and spirit'. In each of these examples, the importance of the body is downplayed.

Not all early scholars agreed with this view, however. Whitty (2003a, p. 344) expresses her opposition thus: '[T]he view of cyberspace as . . . a place where there is no body is a very narrow construction of how we should conceive of this space and the activity that occurs within it'. Whitty believes that rather than cyberspace being a place for a pure meeting of minds, the body still matters. As such, she suggests that researchers ought to be interested in the reconstruction of bodies online and how these online activities transfer to one's offline sense of identity (a point we consider below and develop in Chapters 11 and 12).

Moreover, despite the fervent endorsement of disembodiment by a number of early theorists, few of them make anything more than a cursory reference to Cartesian dualism (a noticeable exception is Ajana, 2005; see also Young and Whitty, 2010b, for further discussion). Therefore, in this chapter, we consider the possibility for disembodiment within cyberspace in more detail and, specifically, go in search of the Cartesian self. This does not mean that we are hoping to find an immaterial essence of being, 'floating' around in virtual space. Instead, our search will take the form of a considered evaluation of the extent to which CMC provides the opportunity for users to *experience* disembodiment compatible with Descartes' conceptualization of the mind as disembodied, but, importantly, without the problematic ontological baggage that accompanies strict Cartesian dualism. Of course, we recognize that an assortment of activities can occur within cyberspace, and that the physical body is quite obviously represented in photographs, cartoons, pictures, videos and so forth; nevertheless, our focus in this chapter will be exclusively on CMC, in the form of online textual exchanges, which are accompanied at least superficially by an absence of the body. The disembodiment *we* speak of, then, is not characterized by any form of ontological division; it simply refers to a particular experiential state, the nature of which will become apparent as we progress.

A rejection of Descartes' ontological claim is certainly a major departure from authentic Cartesian dualism. So what value is there in pursuing this line of inquiry? Our motivation is twofold. First, according to Descartes, the mind and body are contingently related. Therefore, while each of us happens to be related to one particular body like no other (which we call 'mine'),[1] this unique relation is merely contingent. Likewise, we each typically (but not always, as we shall see) *experience* our mind and body as intimately connected. Presumably, this fact is also contingent. An interesting and important question, then, is whether the virtual immediacy constitutive of cyberspace (as discussed in Chapter 2) provides the means to alter this contingency. Might it be that in cyberspace the subject has the opportunity to experience themselves as disembodied? If so, then would this self not be Cartesian in spirit (no pun intended)? In other words, if the contingency relation were different, owing to the virtual nature of the environment, might this environment lend itself to experiences of disembodiment?

In addition, we also intend to engage in a more thorough examination of Descartes' position. However, the aim of this chapter is not to endorse Descartes' ontological distinction, neither is it our intention to revisit the many arguments advanced against it. Rather, we wish to address the more contemporary issue of whether evidence documenting the manner in which people engage in putatively disembodied communication within cyberspace is consistent with Cartesian dualism, at least at the experiential level. If so, then perhaps we can salvage the

Cartesian self (*qua* experiential self within cyberspace), and support an experience of disembodiment *based on a contingency relation unknown to Descartes in his day*; if not, then perhaps any notion of cyberspace as a medium for disembodiment should be recognized as hyperbolic and finally laid to rest.

UNDERSTANDING CARTESIAN DISEMBODIMENT

When Descartes announced to the world *cogito, ergo sum*[2] (I think, therefore I am), in that instant his essential being was transformed, reduced even, to a disembodied mind.[3] Critics, however, were quick to challenge the credibility of his ontological claim: not only in terms of the manner in which he arrived at his conclusion, but also with regard to the fundamental division this produced between immaterial mind and material body, and the problematic nature of their interaction. Thus, through the *cogito*, Descartes equated his own existence with the act of thinking; an act that carried with it a certain credibility: for there is no thought which negates the power to think, and therefore no thought which negates the act of one's own existence.[4] In his search for certainty, Descartes reasoned that the most fundamental epistemic truth, on which his philosophy could be founded, was synonymous with the self-evident nature of his own existence. This reasoned self – this self that is able to withstand the most stringent sceptical inquiry – was given its own ontological status, to the extent that the 'I' of the cogito was stripped of any and all corporeal trappings.[5] In short, for Descartes, thought was the product of a disembodied mind whose existence was independent of the world (Haugeland, 1995).

Importantly, however, this picture of independence – of ontologically distinct minds and bodies – does not stem from Descartes' own day-to-day experience; rather, it stems from his recourse to reason. Having said that, Descartes recognized the dissimilarity between the more intimate manner in which the mind and body appear in everyday experience and the dualism articulated throughout his Meditations. The concession he makes to experience is to admit that he (as his mind) is most highly bound to his body and not, therefore, present merely as a pilot is present in a ship.[6] Importantly, then, Descartes acknowledges that bodily sensations constitute something that one is not aware of simply at an intellectual level (a point we shall return to). On the contrary, he accepts that one *feels*, for example, the searing pain of a blade, or the dull ache of a blow to the torso.[7] Moreover, Descartes acknowledges that the intimacy shared by the mind and body is not something that one can deduce through reason alone: it does not represent an *a priori* truth. As he admits in the sixth meditation, the fact that I am aware of the sensations of my body and not of another's, or the fact that the feeling of hunger causes the desire to eat, are facts the truth of which I cannot attain other than to admit that 'nature taught me so'[8] – that is, to concede an *a posteriori* connection.

In addition, a simple act of reaching is typically experienced *non-spectatorially*; it does not involve an experience of oneself causing the action (the bodily movement) to occur. As Gardner (1994, p. 41) explains:

Willing one's body to move is not like finding that pulling a lever just happens to cause a door to open. The fact that it is no surprise to find one's body attuned to one's will implies some sort of accompanying awareness of the relation of will to body, without which physical agency would be experienced as marginal and oneself as intervening in the world in the manner of God performing a miracle.

Yet despite this concession to experience, there still exists within Descartes' philosophy an insurmountable divide between experience and reason, to the extent that the intimate relationship that the subject has with his body is ultimately mediated: it still occurs through the act of cognition, and therefore requires a form of interaction with the body that is never satisfactorily explained. In the end, despite the incongruent nature of his experience with his thesis, for Descartes, reason prevails: the outcome of which is a conception of mind and body as co-extensive, intimately entwined but fundamentally distinct.

TOWARDS AN EXPERIENTIAL BODY

To avoid committing the same intellectual fallacy, opponents of Cartesian dualism argue that it is important to incorporate within one's understanding of self, the very bodily dimension of experience that Descartes holds apart. Ilyenkov (1977 [1974]), for example, argues that we do not acquaint ourselves with two Cartesian halves – thought in the absence of body and body in the absence of thought; each is an equally fallacious abstraction.[9] Consequently, a depiction of self as captured through one's experience necessitates not only the rejection of the privileged Cartesian mind but also, importantly, the lesser and somewhat caricatured Cartesian body. For although it is no longer posited as the mechanistic housing for the Cartesian mind, the body nevertheless remains (erroneously, we suggest) the silent partner in many scientific accounts of consciousness. With *growing* confidence the scientist declares that the body has been conquered, and its workings catalogued and explained. Thus, with true reductionist fervour, the body is passed over as *nothing but* a mass of blood, flesh and bone that is synonymous with the cadaver on the anatomist's slab, bereft of that extra and still illusive ingredient we call consciousness.[10] The body that the anatomist's examinations have revealed to us, however, is not the body that is experienced from first to last.[11] The cadaver is far removed from the experience we have of our body as it encounters the world on a daily basis. We do not know the body in experience as it is depicted in the medical journals – for this constitutes an alien description that lacks the first-person quality we are used to. Instead, we know ourselves as we experience ourselves, as embodied agents engaged with the world.[12]

> As far as the body is concerned, even the body of another, we must learn to distinguish it from the objective body as set forth in works on physiology. This is not the body that is capable of being inhabited by a consciousness.
>
> (Merleau-Ponty, 1962 [1945], p. 351)

For Merleau-Ponty (1962 [1945]), the body is not the passive host of an imma-terial mind but, rather, an experiential body that engages with the world.[13] This body, unlike the hollow flesh posited by Descartes, constitutes the locus of human existence, and as such is the *sine qua non* of experiential content. Radley (1998) likewise argues that embodiment, and not merely the body, is the locus of one's psychological life. Gallagher (2005b) (following Metzinger, 2004) refers to this as *Leib*, to be contrasted with *Körper* (objective body). Merleau-Ponty therefore rejects the disembodied nature of cognition and claims, instead, that the basis for thought is in fact the accumulated performances of this experiential body (or *Leib*) expressed in relation to its environment. It is not, then, by virtue of the occupying Cartesian consciousness that the world is known. Instead, it is the embodied subject who, in being cut from the same fabric as the world, encounters it inten-tionally (Merleau-Ponty, 1962 [1945]).

In short, Descartes set himself the seemingly impossible task of joining together an immaterial mind with a material body, which resulted in the untenable position we call Cartesian dualism. Merleau-Ponty, in contrast, recognized the significance of the inherent intentionality within the body's orientation towards its environment. Descartes, for his part, failed to recognize that the body we typically experience is in fact the fundamental means by which we shape and are shaped by our world. In short, he failed to identify embodiment as the existential condition that necessitates the possibility of self, culture and, for Descartes, that most misconceived form – reflective (Cartesian) consciousness.

PATHOLOGY AND DISEMBODIMENT

Despite the undoubted appeal of embodiment (*qua Leib*), and its resonance with our everyday experiential state of being, there are nevertheless times when our experience of ourselves as embodied is lost, or certainly falls short of the intimacy espoused by Merleau-Ponty: occasions, then, when our experience *is* more like that of a pilot in a ship. Perhaps these states of experiential dissociation are indicative of different sorts of contingency relations, the peculiarity of which produces in us a sense of disembodiment that satisfies the experiential require-ments of a Cartesian self. By way of illustration, atypical, and often quite severe, examples (although no less pertinent for that) can be found from within the annals of psychiatry. Namir (2006, p. 218), for example, describes a patient who self-harms:

> Alienated from her abused body, she experienced her body only when cutting it. Feeling it cut off from her affective and sensual aliveness, cutting her skin gave her both. Reclaiming her body from its deadness threatened to kill her.

Similarly, Sims (1995, p. 153) documents the experiences of a patient suffering from delusions of alien control:

When I reach my hand for the comb it is my hand and arm which move, and my fingers pick up the pen, but I don't control them . . . I am just a puppet who is manipulated by cosmic strings. When the strings are pulled my body moves and I can't prevent it.

And again in the case of depersonalization disorder:

I feel as though I'm not alive, as though my body is an empty, lifeless shell. I seem to be standing apart from the rest of the world, as though I am not really here . . . I seem to be walking in a world I recognise but don't feel.

(Phillips and Sierra, 2003, p. 157)

In these example, the subject appears to be a spectator, although not, we would say, a disinterested one (the significance of this last remark will become apparent as we progress). In contrast, a more typical example of an altered contingency relation between experience and physical system is sickness: something that, according to Brody (1987, p. 27), likewise produces a 'spectatorial' experience of disembodiment:

[I]f sickness leads us to see our bodies as being something foreign, thwarting our will by their intransigence and unmanageability, then sickness has fundamentally altered our experience of self and has introduced a sense of split and disruption where formerly unity reigned.

In the face of such experiential evidence, Burwood (2008, p. 264) concedes that it may seem to me (as the subject of the experience) that 'my body is a material reality in its own right, with an identity separate to and external to mine, and with its own agenda, which may frustrate me in the pursuit of my goals'. Moreover, such examples demonstrate that embodied experience, 'far from being unfavourable to dualism, may actually promote its central thesis that we are not, in some important sense, our bodies' (ibid.). Burwood goes on to discuss the inherent ambiguity in such experiences of dissociation, which he claims are well captured by the word *Unheimliche* (which translated means 'unhomely' or 'uncanny').[14] However, he resists the claim that an 'uncanny' experience is one of total bodily separation. To claim that I am not my body is perhaps to claim that I am not *fully* my body (this ambiguity is not lost on Burwood). The sense in which I experience *having* a body remains in need of further qualification, then, but does not, Burwood maintains, result in a loss of a sense of 'my-ness', or indeed for this to be replaced by a radical sense of 'otherness'.

Despite the seeming support for a form of experiential dualism brought about by cases of dissociation, and regardless of how debilitated my body appears to me, I am nevertheless 'drawn to recognize all this in the context of the inescapability of my particular embodiment' (p. 275). In other words, the negation of intimacy between mind and body, experienced in cases of dissociation, is made salient precisely because it occurs against a backdrop of normative embodied existence.

I do not experience a *lack* of intimacy; rather, what is made salient (to me) is its sudden *loss*. The salience of this loss is a measure of the discrepancy between how it is that I now experience myself and how I should experience myself. For the comparison to be meaningful – that is, salient as loss – the underlying sense of ownership ('my-ness') within the experience must remain. As such, the subject of the dissociation is not altogether disinterested (to return to the point introduced earlier): for it is argued that the body is not just any other body; rather, it is my body that, despite its debilitation, is still mine.

To borrow the terminology of Gallagher (2005b), to experience the uncanny body is not to experience a *Cartesian Körper* – an animate, objective, but ultimately autonomous, body. Neither is it to experience a *Cotardian Körper*,[15] bereft of animation. The uncanny body, we suggest, is more in keeping with an experience of Merleau-Ponty's 'lived body' or Gallagher's '*Leib*' that has simply gone awry. To reiterate: This feeling of going awry, for it to be made salient, must occur against a backdrop of normative embodiment. There remains a degree of connectedness that transcends any physical change or feeling of oddness; of things being different. For there to be an experience of difference, there must be, at the same time, recognition that it is the *same thing* that has changed.

Let us now turn our attention to the question of cyberspace and whether it, unlike the examples of altered contingency presented above, is conducive to the realization of the Cartesian self.

ALTERED CONTINGENCIES AND THE EXCOGITATED SELF

The constraint my embodiment places on my experience, Descartes would argue (we contend), is a contingent fact, even in cases of pathological dissociation. Typically, I experience myself as intimately related to my body like no other. This experiential closeness is a product of one particular contingency relation, whereas the experience of dissociation is simply another (or so we have argued). Yet, in cases of pathological dissociation, the 'uncanny' feeling experienced by the subject is not sufficient to produce a complete sense of disembodiment. If we are to salvage the Cartesian self, perhaps we need to alter the contingency relation further. Perhaps the experience of disembodiment indicative of the Cartesian self is dependent on a certain sort of contingency relation, until recently unavailable. Perhaps it is dependent on cyberspace.

Could it be, then, that cyberspace provides the means to make the realization of the Cartesian self attainable? Is it truly indicative of the contingency relation we have been pursuing? Not according to Ajana (2005, p. 4), who considers 'the possibility of a neo-Cartesian split through cyberspace [to be nothing but] a naïve delusion', which produces, at best, 'pseudo-disembodiment'.[16] So which is it to be? Is cyberspace the medium through which abstracted, disembodied cognition holds sway over corporeality,[17] or is it merely an environment of pseudo-disembodiment, as Ajana suggests, in which one experiences a different sort of uncanny self? Let us consider the evidence further.

Early theorists, especially more radical feminists, believed that people could be disembodied (e.g. Haraway, 1991; Plant, 1992; Stone, 1992, 1996). However, these theorists did not argue that bodies were not present online, but rather that one could escape one's own physical body and completely re-invent new bodies and identities; that the Internet provided real opportunities to create postmodern selves (we will have more to say on this in the next chapter). They believed that all physical aspects of identity could be abandoned and new identities could be excogitated. Feminist theorists were especially hopeful that individuals could escape the sorts of gendered expectations placed on them on an everyday level. As Klein (1999, p. 202) writes:

> [I]n postmodern and cyberthinking, the categories of 'women' and 'men' (or young and old or white and black) have lost any meaning . . . it is up to the individual to be whatever s/he desires – including donning the body/ies s/he wishes to appear in, at a given time – some sort of an eternal fancy dress ball, one might think.

The Internet has therefore been seen by feminists as a way to overcome patriarchy. Van Loon (2008, p. 98) describes cyberfeminism as:

> A take on power that does not resort to 'a slave morality'. Cyberfeminism does not base its critique on the nature of women as being victims. The process of 'becoming other' is more complicit, it cuts across the divides that create gender, race, humans versus animals, humans versus machines, and is therefore never clear cut. The other must, therefore, not be idolized or fixed; the other does not hold a moral superiority.

Discussion on the *cyborg body* reached its peak in the 1990s; nevertheless, more recent research has found some support for the earlier theorists' claims. Hugh-Jones *et al.* (2005), for example, identified a narrative of personal development with women who exhibited their bodies online. Escaping one's physical body could, however, have potential benefits for both men and women. The Internet may offer, for instance, a way for men to experience more freedom from traditional pressures and to claim ('feminized') identities that ordinarily would be considered taboo. In addition, it has been noted that many men prefer to consult online rather than face-to-face health services, suggesting that male vulnerability is something that can be more safely expressed in virtual rather than actual spaces (see Gough, 2006).[18]

For such theorists, cyberspace is perhaps a bastion for the disenfranchised self in need of emancipation from the constraints of the corporeal. Here, cyberspace is understood to be a place of embodied (rather than disembodied) experience, where the real or imagined constraints of the old body are removed, to be replaced by a sense of *self renewed*. What we are presented with is a description of a self that transcends the physical body, but not *embodiment*. One's experience of embodiment, it would seem, is no longer dependent on the old, contingent relation with the corporeal. To reiterate, new identities are excogitated.

This utopian ideal brought about much hope for scholars and Internet users alike. However, leaving one's identity completely offline was a challenge in the early days of the Internet, and remains even more so now that individuals increasingly enjoy using pictures and video (both synchronous and asynchronous). Our trade-mark flesh, it appears, permeates even into cyberspace. Thus, evidence does not seem to support the utopian ideal. Instead, research on how individuals flirt, engage in online sexual activities and develop and maintain online relationships demonstrates the importance of the body.[19] This might involve the accurate representation of 'real' physical bodies, but can equally take the form of reconstructed bodies. As noted in Chapter 7 when discussing play, 'although we do not have physical, tangible bodies in cyberspace, we do nevertheless have bodies' (Whitty, 2003a, p. 344). Importantly, then, transcending the physical does not 'eradicate body-based systems of differentiation and domination' (Balsamo, 1993, p. 129).

RECONSTRUCTED BODIES

If one were to peruse the textual exchanges on bulletin boards, discussion boards or chat rooms, one would find ample evidence of constructed bodies. Whitty (2003a) argues that even when the body is not present online, people still describe what their bodies look like and feel like; therefore, the body (embodiment) still matters. More specifically, what matters is how individuals elect to reconstruct theirs and other people's bodies. The significance of the body is illustrated in Hardey's (2002) example of an online dater who routinely delays describing his offline physical disability. Despite this delay, he nonetheless talks about the need to reveal his 'actual' body prior to meeting face to face:

> Once I put that in my general description [being in a wheelchair following a motorbike accident] but I found I got 'sympathy' mail. In my experience women find it difficult to get beyond the chair if they don't know you and you just meet casually in a pub or whatever. Now I hold off a little before I explain about the accident and that I'm in a wheelchair. The advantage of the system is that it allows me to decide when to reveal this aspect of my life which I don't want potential girlfriends to see as the thing that defines me. So I've got to know a girl and to some extent come to trust that once she knows about the chair we can get that over with and decide whether to keep in touch or move on.
>
> (2002, p. 577)

Online dating sites continue to increase in popularity. As they become more sophisticated, individuals are opting to display more photographs and videos (not always their true depictions; see Whitty, 2008a, for a more detailed discussion). But even when these sites were more text based than pictorial, researchers found that the body was not altogether obliterated (Hardey, 2002). Scharlott and Christ (1995), for example, carried out a study on a text-based online dating site. On this site, users were required to select an option indicating how attractive they were; most would also write a *physical* description. Interestingly, Scharlott and Christ reported that no one rated their looks as below average. They also noted that the way women described their physical appearance affected the likelihood that men would contact them. Of the women who rated their appearance above average or very good, 57 per cent of them received messages from more than 50 men.

When relating online, especially with regard to developing romantic relationships, evidence indicates not only that descriptions of the body are important, but also that talk about *how* bodies meet in virtual space is of equal importance. This is illustrated in the following extract from an email sent to an online lover:

> Very quietly, because the night is so very quiet a hundred miles from all other humans, of the lake. We lean up against each other for warmth, I have my arm around you to hold you close. The sense of waiting becomes almost intolerable. . . . We reach out to touch the reflections and our hands meet in the sparkling water. Breathless from the transformation of night to day, I turn to you and our lips meet.
>
> (Gwinnell, 1998, p. 59)

Such evidence, Whitty and Carr (2006a) argue, refutes Levine's (2000) claim (noted earlier) that romantic connections amount to a meeting of minds. But what of those individuals who are more concerned with how the other thinks than with their physical appearance? Is the *intention* to be disembodied sufficient to produce the Cartesian self?

CAN WE BECOME DISEMBODIED?

Boler (2007, p. 154) describes the putative disembodied communication within cyberspace as 'digital Cartesianism with a twist': the 'twist' being her way of articulating the subject's ultimate deference to the body as a way of establishing meaningful communication. Around this time, subjects typically enquired about age, sex and location ('asl'); each of these 'markers' standing in defiance of the disembodiment promised. It seems that, in cyberspace, the physical body and its social meaning has not been transcended, or 'technologically neutralized' (Balsamo, 1993, p. 128). On the contrary, evidence appears to support the view expressed by O'Brien (1999, p. 85) (and endorsed by Boler in her paper) that 'reference to the body as connected to self will still be evoked as the basis of meaningful communication'.

This seems to be borne out by the evidence presented so far; but we are also interested in whether CMC and the 'overly cognitive nature of electronically produced experience' (Kupfer, 2007, p. 44) provides the *opportunity* for the Cartesian self to emerge. *If* such a self were to emerge then might it be linked to the intention (on the part of the subject) to become disembodied: an intention that is absent from the pathology case studies we looked at earlier? With this in mind, consider the following extract taken from a bulletin board.[20] Here, users discuss the appropriateness of requesting information about age/sex/location (asl).

> *soby18* Wots with everyone's first question always asking about asl . . . I just want to have a chat with someone . . ..
> *nanasangel* it burns me up when the first question is always asl? what ever happen to hello? . . .
> *winterborn_44* I feel like every body i don't want a date i just want a chat.
> *Foxxie73* Hey, I understand where you are coming from, but also try and look at it this way . . . When you are chatting with someone wouldn't you want to kinda know what age group there in so then you have some idea of what to talk about?

Within this brief discussion there seems to be a desire on the part of *some* of the users to disregard the trappings of embodiment. The practice of requesting 'asl' is seen almost as an affront to the realization of the disembodied ideal – a meeting of minds. What is apparent from the comments by *Foxxie73*, however, is that there is an equal need, by some, to embody their fellow users in order to communicate in a meaningful way. (Other users endorse this 'convention', as can be seen in Boler's (2007) original transcript, not presented here.) In keeping with the focus of this chapter, then, let us consider the evidence available for when individuals interact exclusively via online text. Are such individuals able to engage *intentionally* as Cartesian selves?

Even when individuals attempt to disguise their offline identities and sex, evidence indicates that these are often revealed through their writing style. Researchers have found that complex gender information can be transmitted via text, with certain linguistic cues distinguishing men's conversations from women's (Lea and Spears, 1995). Thomson and Murachver (2001) found that women are more likely to make references to emotional and personal information online. Moreover, these researchers found that participants in their experimental study were able to identify the gender of the person they were communicating with online. Witmer and Katzman (1997) found that women used '*graphic accents*' (which are essentially what most people refer to as emoticons) in their online conversations more than men. It has also been found that men's and women's messages are treated differently online. Herring (1993), for example, found that men were more likely to participate in discussion boards, and that their messages, for the most part, were much longer than women's.

Escaping from one's offline identity, it would seem, even for those with a desire to do so, is a challenge not yet met. Markers reveal the nature of our offline embodiment even when engaged in textual CMC. Moreover, evidence supports the view that when engaged in textual CMC, subjects typically seek to anchor their exchanges in some form of bodily architecture. This allows each communicating subject to present a certain self-*as-object*, towards which dialogue is fashioned. But even when the intention is to be disembodied, our *meaningful* discourse betrays our 'real', embodied identities.

In conclusion, for those within cyberspace whose goal it is to engage in a meeting of minds, the content of their correspondence has been shown to lack the purity of Descartes' *res cogitans* (thinking thing). The content of their putative disembodied dialogue is 'contaminated' by embodied categorizations. An empirical question has been answered – namely: Do people retain a level of embodied communication within cyberspace, even when their intention is to be disembodied? The answer, it seems, is yes.

What we have considered throughout this chapter is whether CMC is able to provide a context for the realization of the Cartesian self – that is, whether one might experience oneself as a disembodied mind whilst engaged in CMC. Evidence indicates that, at present, this is an unrealized dream. Moreover, much contemporary work within the field of embodiment suggests that, even in principle, one's experience of self will always be to some degree embodied. In short, CMC, as currently engineered, is not a bastion for the Cartesian self, and evidence based on the inclinations of cyber enthusiasts suggests that Cartesian dualism is not an experiential reality.

In his Meditations, Descartes struggled with the disparity between his reason and his experience. As already mentioned, he recognized that bodily sensations do not present themselves to the mind as pure intellect; rather, they are experienced in all their visceral salience. Descartes ultimately failed to reconcile this experiential union with his philosophy. In presenting different contingency relations, some involving dissociations, but mostly centred on the pursuit of disembodiment within cyberspace, we have likewise failed to find the Cartesian self. Thus, Cartesian dualism, *qua* experiential separation, cannot be salvaged by altering the contingency relation – at least not in terms of any alterations explored here. In fact, we would go so far as to say that the evidence and argument presented in this chapter further endorse what many already suspected (knew!) pre-cyberspace – that Cartesian dualism is an untenable philosophical position and experientially absent. It would seem, then, that this is still the case, even in the era of cyberspace: for in pursuing Descartes' abstracted mind into the virtual realm, we have learned not only that the intimate relation between mind and body is maintained and not transcended, but, moreover, that it is fundamental to meaningful communication, even in a world where embodiment appears, on the surface at least, to be less apparent. The more we try to disengage with the body, the more its importance is revealed to us.

In the next chapter, we consider the self as an embodied self, and explore what selves are possible in the spaces of altered contingency evident within cyberspace.

11 Embodiment

Cyber-relations and possible selves

In Chapter 10 we discussed how, in the 1990s, cyberspace was hailed by some as an arena for the realization of the disembodied mind and, the computer interface, the place where 'the spirit migrates from the body' (Heim, 1993, p. 101). The aim of these early Internet theorists seems to have been to champion 'disembodied technocracy' (Gunkel, 1998, p. 119) in an attempt to fulfil some form of Cartesian ideal: 'to live "purely" in the realm of the mind freed from [one's] corporeity' (Switzer, 1997, pp. 511–512). Towards the end of the last chapter, however, and following those who over the last 20 years have opposed this view, we argued that claims about cyberspace – that it represents a bastion for the Cartesian self, where personal identity could be experienced independent of bodily attributes, not fixed or limited by physical characteristics (Slater, 1998) – were in fact mistaken. Consequently, we rejected such 'incorporeal exaltation' (Gunkel, 1998, p. 118), judging it to be hyperbole and, instead, embraced a less accommodating view of disembodiment.

In this chapter we start from the premise that cyberspace is not a suitable environment in which to find Gilbert Ryle's *Ghost in the Machine* (that is, a Cartesian mind or 'ghost' interfacing with the 'machine' of cyber-technology). In fact, we attest that claims to the contrary (as presented in Chapter 10) amount to 'the worst kind of Cartesian thinking' (Gurak, 1997, p. 2). Instead, we endorse Balsamo's (1993) metaphor: that the virtual worlds of cyberspace provide a fresh arena for the staging of the *body*, on which new dramas are to be enacted. The self as *embodied* therefore becomes the focus of this chapter. Here, we examine different components of embodied identity within cyberspace, particularly with regard to cyber-relating and online dating. We also consider whether cyberspace is a suitable environment in which to cultivate possible selves.

WAYS OF CONCEPTUALIZING THE BODY

It is our view that virtual embodiment incorporates a number of key conceptualizations of the body. Therefore, when discussing embodiment within both immersive and non-immersive VEs, we wish to distinguish between different types of body. Perhaps the most straightforward is the objective body, which refers to one's physical form. Next is the virtual body, which amounts to a virtual representation of one's self in physical form – the avatar – that may or may not correspond closely to one's objective body. Finally, and allied more closely (but not exclusively) with immersive environments, is the body one experiences: more commonly referred to as one's experience of embodiment. Here, the user experiences having a particular (virtual) body of a certain size, shape and agentic status – that is, as being the cause of interactions within the VE. This sense of embodiment often includes the experience of being somewhere other than the location of one's objective body, a phenomenon commonly referred to as *presence* (Minsky, 1980). Lenggenhager *et al.* (2007), for example, manipulated the user's visual somatosensory input within an immersive VE, in order to demonstrate how the experience of one's embodied self can be 'dissociated from one's physical body' (p. 1098) and, instead, appears to be 'localized at an extracorporeal position' (p. 1097). In short, the experience of presence indicates that one's sense of being somewhere as an embodied agent need not correspond to one's physical location.

Following Gallagher's (2005a) lead, we also find it useful to discuss embodiment with reference to a person's *body-image*. Put simply, body-image is 'a system of perceptions, attitudes, and beliefs pertaining to one's own body' (Gallagher, 2005a, p. 24). Part of my body-image therefore stems from the fact that my consciousness has object-directedness, and the object that it is directed towards in this case is my body.[1] As such, I possess an image of myself as I would any other object. The product of this *reflective* act of awareness – of being aware of myself as an object – is known as the *self-as-object* (James, 1981 [1890]). In addition, my self is not *just* an object that I reflect on; it also constitutes part of my embodied experience (see Legrand, 2007). My body-image therefore forms part of my pre-reflective awareness of myself as an embodied agent. This pre-reflective sense of self, we refer to as the *phenomenal self.*

In what is to follow, the self-as-object refers exclusively to the intentional object of a reflective act of consciousness. In cyberspace, this equates to one's reflective awareness/conception of the virtual body in immersive environments, or simply the 2- or 3-D image and/or description one presents of oneself in non-immersive environments. In contrast, the phenomenal self refers to the subject's pre-reflective experience of embodiment, in or out of the VE. Importantly, then, it is our view that the self-as-object and the phenomenal self constitute different components of what Gallagher (2005a) refers to as the body-image.

The body-image should not be confused with the self-concept, however, which, although incorporating the self-as-object, also includes a number of other features, including attitudes towards self and others, hopes, fears, aspirations, even social-identity, status and esteem. To illustrate this difference, let us say that in a particular space I present myself as a healer because I have a desire to help people. My self-as-object therefore takes on the guise of a 'healer' avatar and conforms to how a healer would appear in this space, and is recognized as such by others. This 'healer' (*qua* self-as-object) forms part of my body-image as discussed, but is also a component of my self-concept (perhaps in the form of 'In this space I take on the

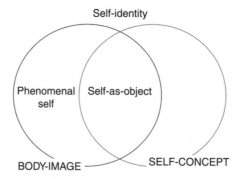

Figure 11.1 Schematic illustrating the components of one's self-identity.

guise of a healer'). In addition, my self-concept includes my pro-attitude towards healing and my desire to pursue this vocation, etc. (see discussion on possible selves, below). Finally, the terms 'self' and 'identity' (taken together or apart) are used synonymously with 'embodied self', and should therefore be understood to include the body-image and self-concept (see Figure 11.1).

ONLINE RELATING

For many, the Internet is perhaps the most common medium in which to engage with the virtual world. As a medium for communication, it provides the user with an ideal opportunity to present an alternative self-as-object, or perhaps even a plethora of alternative selves, to the one typically presented in face-to-face communication (e.g. Bargh, *et al.*, 2002; McKenna *et al.*, 2002; Turkle, 1995). As Slater (1998, p. 92) notes, 'we would expect the construction of new kinds of bodies, identities and connections between them, a liberation, an experimentalism or at least a diminished conventionality'.

These different presentations of the self-as-object have been examined in detail, especially in relation to the development of online relationships. Bargh *et al.* (2002) and McKenna *et al.* (2002), for example, examined the types of selves that individuals are more likely to present in newsgroups. McKenna *et al.* (2002, p. 12) reasoned that individuals who feel lonely or socially anxious when engaged in traditional, face-to-face interactions are more likely to feel better able 'to develop close and meaningful relationships' within this virtual space. McKenna *et al.* were also interested in whether these same individuals were then able to continue their relationships offline, and the extent to which their initial Internet communication better enabled them to make this transition into the offline world. They found that those who conveyed what they (McKenna *et al.*) referred to as their *Real Me* online – that is, who manifested traits or characteristics that they genuinely possessed but were otherwise unable to express offline – were able to develop strong Internet relationships and bring these relationships into their offline lives.

Two years after their initial study, 354 of the 568 participants were emailed a follow-up survey (also published in McKenna *et al.*, 2002). In line with the researchers' prediction, these relationships remained relatively stable and durable over the intervening period. (As an aside, in Chapter 12, we discuss McKenna *et al.*'s study in relation to what we call the *supermorphic persona*. The terms 'Real Me' and 'supermorphic persona' are not meant to be equivalent, although we accept that some overlap exists between them – to be clarified later.)

Pre-dating McKenna *et al.*'s work, in the 1990s, Turkle claimed that multi-user domain (MUD) players often constructed new selves through their online interactions (Turkle, 1995). Cyberspace was thus perceived by Turkle as a place where one could discover a deeper truth about oneself. She illustrated this with an example of a young man, Gordon, who did not 'fit in' at school: an example even more pertinent today, we would argue, following the transition from predominately text-based to more visually accompanied interactions. When discussing Gordon, Turkle (1995, p. 190) noted how 'MUDs allowed him to create a new character at any time [and, because of this,] he could always begin with a clean slate. When he changed his character he felt born again'.

It is important to understand, however, that although Turkle argued that people can 'experiment' by presenting different selves online, often these same individuals maintain a connection with both their online and offline identities (see discussion on psychological parity in Chapter 14). Again, in relation to Gordon, Turkle had this to say: 'On MUDs, [he . . .] experimented with many characters, but they all [had] something in common. Each [had] qualities that Gordon [was] trying to develop in himself' (p. 190).

POSSIBLE SELVES

According to Markus and Nurius (1986), possible selves are significant, personalized, yet ultimately social representations of ourselves that we either aspire to be like or fear becoming. They are intimately connected to our *now* selves (our current self-concept), and represent our 'hopes, fears and fantasies' (p. 954), derived from what we know of ourselves and the society in which we live. Possible selves are also understood to regulate – *qua* motivate or deter – future behaviour and constitute a means of evaluating and interpreting the status of our now selves. Markus and Nurius refer to these selves as the 'expected self', the 'hoped-for self' and the 'feared self'. The *expected self* is the person one believes one can realistically become and is said to act as the focal point for one's energies in striving for the future. The *hoped-for self*, in contrast, is further away from the present self and may or may not be realistic. Finally, the *feared self* is a possible self that one does not desire to become; it serves as a motivator, so that the individual takes action to *avoid* becoming that possible self. In short, possible selves may represent the desired continuation of the now self, or be a reaction to it; either way, they amount to what vanDellen and Hoyle (2008, p. 302) refer to as 'reference values against which the current self is compared'.

Importantly, however, for Markus and Nurius (1986, p. 955), apprehending possible selves, unlike race, gender or other habits, attributes or preferences, constitutes self-knowledge or 'views of the self that often have not been verified or confirmed by social experience'. They are ways in which we *conceive* of possible future selves – what Markus and Ruvolo (1989, p. 211) metaphorically described as 'a bridge of self-representations' between what we are now and what we might become – for better or for worse.

A similar position has been taken by Higgins and his colleagues (Alexander and Higgins, 1993; Higgins, 1987; Strauman and Higgins, 1987), although they apply the terms 'actual self', 'ideal self' and 'ought-to-self'. The *actual self* includes the traits or characteristics that an individual possesses and expresses to others in social settings; *the ideal self* includes representations of how someone would like to see their self, including hopes, wishes and aspirations; whereas the *ought-to self* represents the attributes that an individual believes they should possess. In his 'self-discrepancy theory', Higgins (1987) argues that too much discrepancy between the actual self and the ideal self is associated with dejection-related emotions – that is, feeling disappointed and dissatisfied with one's life because one's hopes, wishes and aspirations were unachievable. In contrast, a large discrepancy between the actual self and the ought-to self is associated with agitation-related emotions – namely feelings of fear, threat and restlessness because significant others believe that the person is behaving differently from the way they typically behave in most social settings. Higgins' approach to possible selves thus posits that it is not psychologically healthy to experience too much discrepancy between these different selves.

Given the greater opportunities available for experimentation with presentations of self within cyberspace, it is little wonder that researchers have been interested in which aspects of possible selves individuals are more likely to present in online spaces as well as the consequences for these decisions. Bargh *et al.* (2002), for example, found in their experimental study (focusing on newsgroups) that the actual self was more accessible in memory during face-to-face interactions with a new acquaintance compared with Internet interactions. More recently, Manago *et al.* (2008) found that users of *MySpace* tended to present idealized selves on their webpages. However, when studying a sample of *Facebook* users, Back *et al.* (2009, p. 373) found the opposite, concluding that 'there was no evidence of self-idealization'; rather, profiles matched closely individuals' actual personality profiles. Weisbuch *et al.* (2009) found a similar consistency across spaces in *Facebook* users, based on independent observers' first-impression ratings of participants' webpage profiles and corresponding face-to-face encounters.

It may be that users of *Facebook* typically transcend online and offline spaces on a regular basis (in as much as they communicate with the same people online as well as offline), an occurrence that helps regulate the consistency between the presentation of selves across these spaces, creating what Ducheneaut (2010) refers to as a fairly stable, 'synthetic' identity (see Chapter 14). In contrast, on online dating sites, researchers found that some online daters created profiles that reflected their ideal selves-as-objects (Ellison *et al.*, 2006; Whitty, 2007, 2008b;

Whitty and Carr, 2006a). An individual might describe themselves as a surfer, for example, even though they do not regularly surf, as this is ideally how they would like to see themselves. Researchers have also found that individuals are likely to describe an identity that they do not currently possess but hope to in the future (e.g. Whitty, 2008b; Yurchisin *et al.*, 2005). This is illustrated in an extract from a telephone interview conducted with a male online dater called Ben:

> I was a bit fed up with no return so I just made up something that I'm very wealthy, I'm some entrepreneur and used my friend's Porsche and pictures and stuff like that. I'm standing next to a Porsche 911 turbo and made it sound really exciting . . . I basically wrote down the profile of me of what I'd like to be in 10 years because I was getting no return, I was being very sincere with a lot of people so I put that profile in and guess what? I get returns, absolutely everywhere. I'm telling you it is coming like, I don't even have to approach people. People just come and I renamed myself as entrepreneur 23.
>
> (Whitty, 2008b, p. 246)

The above example illustrates not only an ideal self-as-object (albeit a very unrealistic one), but also, *because* it is so very unrealistic, a blatant misrepresentation. In Chapter 12 we discuss this example again in relation to what we refer to as an ideal*ized* (in contrast to 'ideal') self (see also Young and Whitty, 2011a). Applying Higgins' (1987) self-discrepancy theory, we would predict that *entrepreneur 23* might not cope too well, psychologically, if he continues to maintain an 'ideal self' that can never be actualised offline. Whitty (2007) therefore suggests that online daters should ensure that they represent their actual selves (*qua* self-as-object, in this case) in their online dating profiles, especially given that the first date is more of a screening process: for when there is a large discrepancy between the profile and the person they meet face to face, individuals are most likely to reject their dates immediately after their first 'meet'. It may be, then, that the online dater cannot afford such liberties as to present an 'ideal' self-as-object (again, we return to this point in relation to idealized selves in Chapter 12), but what of other online spaces?

The identities that individuals create for their characters within MMORPGs have also been studied and the theory of possible selves applied. Bessière *et al.* (2007) suggest that MMORPGs are ideal environments for individuals to create characters that imbue their ideal selves. These theorists stress that it is the anonymity in this space that facilitates these presentations of self (although we would like to suggest, instead, that it may well be the playful nature of the space that affords such a presentation, given that individuals are often known to their gaming friends). Bessière *et al.* found that individuals who score lower on measures of psychological well-being are more likely to create characters who are closer to their ideal self and less like their actual self compared with those who score high on measures of psychological well-being. The further consequences for psychological well-being that such a discrepancy causes – in line with Higgins' self-discrepancy theory – are discussed in Chapter 12, along with the question of whether there are or should be limits to how much one experiments with aspects of the self.

As the work of Higgins reveals, a discrepancy between ways of conceiving of the self can impact on our affective states. Our understanding of selfhood or identity, as we saw in Figure 11.1, involves more than the self-concept. In the sections below, we wish to state the case for the cultivation of possible selves within VEs, where, through virtual immediacy and altered contingencies, a whole host of potential future selves may be virtually realized. Importantly, however, these virtual realizations are not just conceptual, they will also have an experiential and therefore affective impact on us.

VIRTUAL POSSIBLE SELVES

Nearly a century before Markus and Nurius, William James alluded to the existence of possible selves when stating that 'men distinguish between the immediate and actual, and the remote and potential' (James, 1981 [1890], p. 300). James also recognized that some of these remote and potential selves may be mutually excluded from each other or from what is immediate and actual (one's now self), and so remain unfulfilled or have to be relinquished (see Comello, 2009, for a detailed discussion). As James (1981 [1890], p. 295) admits:

> [I]f I could, [I would] be both handsome and fat and well dressed, and a great athlete, and make a million a year, and be a wit, a *bon-vivant*, and a lady-killer, as well as a philosopher; a philanthropist, statesman, warrior, and African explorer, as well as a 'tone-poet' and saint. But the thing is simply impossible. The millionaire's work would run counter to the saint's; the *bon-vivant* and the philanthropist would trip each other up; the philosopher and the lady-killer could not well keep house in the same tenement of clay.

Having said this, Comello (2009) notes that James did consider the pursuit of certain (possible) selves to be context dependent. Similarly, McAdams (1985) talks of the self, structured within different narratives, in terms of a series of contrasting *imagoes*: sets of often dialectical opposite characteristics that help delineate the relationship that an individual has with others as well as him/herself. Perhaps, then, in contexts or narratives that are far enough removed from each other, one could *be* what are in effect mutually exclusive possible selves. Such contexts are, we contend, the potentially divergent (perhaps even incongruent) spaces of cyberspace. What it means to be a possible self *within* these spaces, as well as what it means to have this self transcend spaces and ingratiate itself within one's (amended) self-concept, are interesting questions, as is how one might cope with this change – questions we will pursue throughout the remainder of this book (particularly Chapters 12, 14 and 15). What we do know at present, however, is that entertaining a given possible self is likely to impact on one's current thinking about oneself and any ensuing behaviour or even long-term goals (Wurf and

Markus, 1991). Likewise, Markus and Nurius (1986) claim that *how* we interpret and evaluate now selves in relation to possible selves not only depends on the 'surrounding context of possibility' (p. 955) but will 'be particularly sensitive to those situations that communicate new or inconsistent information about the self' (p. 956). Any change in context will therefore impact on our evaluation of the possibility of possible selves and on their relation – positive or negative – to our self as a whole. Again, this is something we consider extremely pertinent to VEs, particularly those that afford the pursuit of STAs.

In addition, Mantovani (1995) regards possible selves as essentially private because people tend to react only to those aspects of our identity that are publicly accessible. Our thoughts about possible future selves, whether feared or hoped for, are aspects of our self-concept that others tend to be unaware of. As he further states (1995, p. 679):

> This means that possible selves, although forming our repertoire of identity alternatives, are poorly controlled by the social context surrounding us in everyday life. It is left to the individual alone to know and decide about her/ his possible selves, in relative secrecy and isolation from others, although always under the influence of the mass media conveying the normative social system in which s/he participates.

Thus, Mantovani holds that possible selves are private in the sense that they are our unrealized conceptions of possible future selves, which, as was noted above, tend to lack social validation. With the advent of VR technology, however, it is our contention that possible selves may become realizable and therefore more salient within environments previously unavailable to the individual. Such VEs, and the altered contingencies that characterize them, not only afford a person the opportunity to try out their possible selves and thereby obtain a degree of social and hence public validation (or not, as the case may be) but, equally, offer increased or otherwise unlikely (hitherto unavailable) opportunities for the expression of further possible selves. The individual may only become aware of these selves through access to this environment (see Chapter 15 for an example of this). In other words, the VE may afford a kind of virtual realization of possible selves that emerge from the much more immediate change in context. For Vignoles *et al.* (2008, p. 1195), however, irrespective of context, 'a desirable possible self is one that promises feelings of self-esteem, efficacy, meaning, and continuity'. For some individuals, these attributes may only be realized and/or socially validated in an environment with the kinds of altered contingencies available virtually.

Compatible with this idea is Erikson's (2007) view that a possible self should be more than an abstract belief held by the individual that a given state of being – a future self – is preferred or feared (etc.). In addition, he argues, a definition of possible selves should include reference to 'an experience of what it would be like to be in this state' (p. 349), which includes 'having at least some degree of agency in a future situation' (p. 352). This is also compatible with alterations or at least reference to one's phenomenal self. The intersubjectivity of possible selves is also emphasized – namely the importance of future selves interacting with others within a context of mutual understanding. As Erikson (pp. 354–355) states:

> Without our assumptions about intersubjectivity, phenomena such as role expectations, anticipated shame, or anticipated rewards would be meaning-less because they are based on the assumption that we can understand each other and that others relate to what we do or do not do.

Intersubjectivity and agency are, of course, integral to multiplayer virtual spaces, and mutual understanding can be achieved (potentially) through the estab-lishment of status functions (as discussed in Chapter 9). In addition, perhaps the what-it-is-likeness of the experience of a possible self is something that can be more easily realized within a VE: for might VEs provide a form of virtual social validation, thereby increasing or at least altering the impoverished nature of the self-knowledge (regarding possible selves) that Markus and Nurius referred to? To reiterate – *qua* one's phenomenal self – one is able to experience the virtual what-it-is-likeness of this possible self. Virtual immediacy and the altered contin-gencies of cyberspaces provide a much more extensive 'surrounding context of possibility' that possible selves are said to be a measure of. Of course, ultimately, the context of possibility we are interested in is that space which affords the possible self the moral freedom to engage in STAs. Before discussing this, however, and how one might cope with such freedom (see Chapters 14 and 15), further exposition is required.

Earlier, we briefly noted how possible selves motivate behaviour by guiding the subject towards certain goals or away from others. More specifically, this involves a process of self-regulation that vanDellen and Hoyle (2008) refer to as 'discrep-ancy reduction' or 'discrepancy enhancement'. Related to this, and when in the pursuit of possible selves, Granberg (2006, p. 122) states:

> When outcomes match social feedback, the match validates the possible self and verifies the new identity, facilitating its integration within the self-concept. When outcomes do not match social feedback, an 'identity interrup-tion' is created; this must be resolved before the new identity can integrated fully with the rest of the self-concept.

Pertinent to the issue of VEs, and particularly engagement in STAs, is a scenario in which social feedback (validation) is received in one space (a given VE) by the community who occupy that space, but not offline. If the virtual realization of a possible self receives social validation in the space in which it is realized, but not in any other (including, importantly, the offline space), then how does this discrep-ancy across spaces impact on one's self-concept?

Of interest, then, is the manner in which cyberspace may affect how one enter-tains such possibilities, in terms of both possible selves and the role cyberspace plays in shaping the context of possibilities. In other words, might the use of VEs transform possible selves from things we entertain, as Markus and Nurius conceived of them, to embodied representations of ourselves that are enacted virtually? If possible selves are provided with a certain virtual constitution within VEs, then this alters not only the type of self-knowledge we have of them but also the extent to which they can be socially validated (particularly if the VE is a multi-player space). In addition, it is worth considering how virtually realized, perhaps even socially validated, possible selves that engage in STAs might impact on one's identity as a moral or virtuous person (for example), particularly when such actions, if they were to be replicated offline, would be proscribed. Therefore, although not discussed in the context of VEs and STAs, the following questions raised by Erikson (2007, p. 353) are particularly apt:

> My view of myself today is enormously influenced by my belief of what will happen to me in the future. Am I changing or stable? Am I changing in a positive or negative direction, or is it negative or positive features that are stable? These are crucial questions when it comes to defining my present self-concept, and we answer these questions according to what possible selves we see as likely or unlikely in the relevant domains . . ..

In addition to Erikson's questions, we may consider the extent to which the possible selves realized within cyberspace are authentic expressions of one's self and, importantly, whether being authentic or not in these spaces is psychologically important (recall the discussion on play in Chapter 7, for example). To illustrate, when explaining their notion of possible selves, Markus and Nurius (1986, p. 954) use an example of someone wishing to lose 20 pounds in weight. Such a self, they declare, is not a vague or abstract possibility but is, instead, something much more vivid: a self that is 'thinner, more attractive, with an altogether more pleasant life'. If, through the process of virtual immediacy, one can (virtually, at least) realize this possible self and, in the process, receive some form of social validation, even if context specific, then to what extent is this possible self – *qua*, for example, one's virtual self-as-object – authentic? Equally, how might one experience oneself, based on the way others react to this self-as-object – that is, what effect will this have on one's phenomenal self? In short, what are the psychological ramifications of such authenticity or inauthenticity for the individual, and how might this further or more seriously impact on possible selves and their relation to the now self if one switches from talking about a change in weight (for example) to engaging in STAs?

In the next chapter we consider the realization of possible selves within the context of virtual immediacy, authenticity and *progressive embodiment*.

12 Progressive embodiment
The supermorphic persona

In this chapter we continue to explore the notion of embodiment within the context of Balsamo's (1993) metaphor: that the virtual worlds of cyberspace provide a fresh arena for the staging of the body. In Chapter 11, we discussed how virtual worlds can present, for the embodied subject, an opportunity for physical transcendence: a means by which the subject can transcend the limits of the physical body but not, importantly, the necessities of embodiment and, in doing so, virtually realize possible selves. Almost as a corollary, then, is the further belief that cyberspace provides the potential for *somatic flexibility* (Bateson, 1972). As Coyne (1994, p. 65) notes:

> Virtual reality is celebrated as a highly significant challenge to . . . the way we view our bodies and ourselves. According to some, we will find that with [virtual reality] it is possible to change from one body to another according to what the situation demands . . ..

The freedom Coyne describes is compatible with a further freedom permitted within cyberspace – to engage in *progressive embodiment* (Biocca, 1997). By 'progressive embodiment' we mean to extend the ideas discussed in Chapter 11 relating to possible selves by focusing on the enhancement of one's embodied *cyber*-self (mainly *qua* self-as-object and phenomenal self, but not excluding the self-concept) in a manner that corresponds to the potential afforded within a given space, which may include possible selves hitherto unavailable. In addition, relevant to the notion of progressive embodiment is the issue of authenticity briefly mentioned towards the end of Chapter 11.

An authentic presentation of a 'progressively embodied self' is that which one has the potential to realize given the 'right' environmental conditions, and therefore the 'right' contingency relations. This we refer to as an *ideal* realization of embodiment. Importantly, this is not to be confused with an ideal*ized* realization, which we equate with inauthentic embodiment: an example of which might be to present oneself in a manner congruent with culturally held ideals of beauty and desirability, irrespective of one's potential to realistically meet these ideals. As Vignoles *et al.* (2008, p. 1168) note: 'People imagine what is possible for themselves by comparing with significant others and by internalizing stereotypes and norms relating to important social identities'. Imagining such a possibility, only for the sake of being congruent with such stereotypes, norms and important social identities is to manifest a self that is idealized.

We wish to explore, within the framework of progressive embodiment, the extent to which the somatic flexibility said to be on offer as a result of a coupling between oneself and various forms of interface technology elicits either authentic or inauthentic presentations of embodiment. To do this, we need to consider whether the means by which we come to conceive of and experience ourselves as embodied offline are available to us within virtual space. In other words, to what extent do the *components* of our embodiment (particularly the self-as-object and phenomenal self) find equivalent expression online? If these components are realized within virtual space, then to what extent is this realization authentic or inauthentic? Second, we are interested in the psychological ramifications of authenticity. How might the freedom afforded by cyberspace for somatic flexibility impact on the identity of an individual – that is, their body-image and self-concept? Will individuals seek parity within themselves across domains, or will they be content simply to compartmentalize each identity (Suler, 2004), restricting it to the confines and context-specificity of each on- or offline world? If the former, then how might someone cope with this constraint – cope, that is, with the fact that one's identities are such that they cannot transcend domains? (Recall James' (1981 [1890]) mutually exclusive selves from Chapter 11.) Alternatively, if parity is sought, then what tensions will this create within an individual who seeks to express an identity that is authentic only in some spaces (contextually authentic) and inauthentic in all the rest (lacks transcendent authenticity – see below)? (Recall Higgins' (1987) self-discrepancy theory.) Will this lead to a dissatisfaction of self within other spaces? In short, will the individual experience a loss of prowess because their ideal*ized* self can only be realized within cyberspace, or some particular space therein? Or might the need to maintain parity of self across domains ultimately force individuals to express their *authentic* self across all spaces, on- and offline? If the latter, then the freedom that cyberspace affords for the discovery and development of a persona congruent with one's ideal self should be viewed in a positive light (but only *if* the persona is authentic). By developing one's ideal rather than ideal*ized* self, the authenticity constitutive of this identity is, we suggest, able to transcend domains, meaning that an individual is not restricted by where they can express it. The transcendent quality of authenticity is such that, rather than cyberspace constraining someone to certain context-specific spaces, it extends the repertoire of environmental and social encounters in which one's authentic self is *expressible*.

THE SUPERMORPHIC PERSONA

The issue of authenticity is raised by Slater (1998) when considering whether an identity built on the absence of *physical* bodily features could ever be falsifiable, and therefore could ever be inauthentic. Rather, who we are, he conjectures, would seem to 'turn on [our] resourcefulness in using tools of representation' (p. 91). This point is well taken and will be returned to throughout this chapter, particularly in relation to context authenticity. However, it is fair to say, even at this early stage, that we would be reluctant to deny the relevance of authenticity altogether. Alternatively, and as we have noted on occasion throughout this book, it could be argued that different selves are presented whenever we engage with a different social crowd, regardless of the influence of virtual technology. We are willing to concede this point. To reiterate, our interest in cyberspace stems from the relative ease with which one can enter the virtual community and construct a virtual self, and the potential scope within this environment for authentic or inauthentic embodiment, which stretches far beyond anything typically available in the offline world.

Supermorphia is a word we have created to capture the state of this progressive embodiment. It must be stressed, however, that supermorphia (or the supermorphic persona) is agnostic when it comes to the issue of authenticity. Instead, it merely indicates an attempt on the part of the individual to enhance their embodiment beyond that typically achieved or sought in the non-virtual domain. Supermorphia, then, is the realization of somatic flexibility, and the direct expression of the potential for progressive embodiment afforded by a given interface (or, rather, the space it creates), irrespective of the authenticity of this expression. The question of authenticity should therefore be considered independently from the tendency, as we see it (although not inevitability), for individuals within cyberspace to manifest supermorphic personas in one form or another. In addition, we are interested in the extent to which the realization of the potential for progressive embodiment – one's supermorphic persona – alters the individual's experience and understanding of embodiment across domains. Is the experience beneficial (psychologically healthy) or is the potential for progressive embodiment and the flexibility this is couched in likely to have a detrimental effect on the individual's non-virtual sense of embodied identity and psychological parity?

THE PROGRESSIVE SELF-AS-OBJECT

The body-image, *qua* self-as-object, is expressed within cyberspace as a kind of 'electronic persona' (Fisher, 1991, p. 109) through which users present various approximations of their physical form and underlying personality traits. The presentation of this form of body-image, as we have already encountered, can occur in chat rooms or on discussion boards, or even graphically as an avatar engaged in real-time activities within a three-dimensional community (e.g. *World of Warcraft* and *Second Life*). The fact that the virtual self-as-object is an intentional *representation* of some reflective, object-like conceptualization of the user's own embodiment raises an interesting empirical question – namely: To what extent is the virtual self-as-object congruent with the user's offline self-as-object? And related to this (and Higgins' (1987) self-discrepancy theory): What are the consequences of this high- or low-level congruence, both in terms of authenticity and psychologically?

Such questions are important because interactions within VEs are, according to Ford (2001, p. 662), 'real interactions that can affect the ways in which persons view themselves, their world, and others'. Balsamo (1993), however, offers a caveat pertinent to this issue: Within cyberspace, freedom from the physical body does not necessitate that people will exercise this freedom to be any other kind of body than the one they already enjoy. Whilst accepting this point, and by means of a continuation of the discussion started in Chapter 11, we nevertheless contend that cyberspace provides, for many, a medium for the realization of an alternative, predominantly supermorphic self-as-object. This may benefit the individual but, equally, could have a detrimental effect depending on whether the supermorphic persona constitutes an ideal/authentic or idealized/inauthentic expression of the self-as-object. Any beneficial or detrimental effect may also depend on the *experience* the individual has whilst exploring different alternative selves. I might, for example, whilst at play, decide to 'try out' an idealized/inauthentic self, and through my experience of this learn about ways to behave and attitudes to possess that will ultimately contribute to an authentic presentation of my self-as-object, derived from my newly amended self-concept. Such a view can be seen as a development of more general ideas about fiction expressed by Mar and Oatley (2008) in which we can learn about others different to ourselves by engaging with various literary narratives. In the case of the VEs discussed here, however, rather than being passively presented to the viewer (as with more traditional fiction), the narrative tends to be constructed through interactive engagements – to reiterate Ford's (2001) comment (above) – and so provides an opportunity for the user to learn more about *themselves* as well as others.

To illustrate, recall from Chapter 11 how, owing to the lack of traditional cues online, it was argued that, as a medium for communication, the Internet provides the user with an opportunity to present an alternative self-as-object to the one typically presented in face-to-face communication (Bargh *et al.*, 2002; McKenna *et al.*, 2002). Recall also how Bargh *et al.* and McKenna *et al.* examined the types of selves that individuals are more likely to present in newsgroups. These researchers argued that those able to present their 'Real Me' online were better able to sustain relationships and transfer them offline. Using these same study findings, it is *our* view that those individuals who felt lonely or socially anxious when engaged in traditional face-to-face interactions were more likely to express their supermorphic persona across the Internet compared to more traditional social environments and, as a consequence, were more likely to feel better able to develop closer and more meaningful relationships because of this within that space. Importantly, however, it is not necessarily the case that the 'Real Me' and the supermorphic persona are equivalent. The Real Me has intrinsic authenticity, whereas the supermorphic persona is neutral on the issue of authenticity.

It is therefore our contention that, in the McKenna *et al.* study, the authenticity of certain individuals' initial Internet communication better enabled them to make the transition into an offline relationship. Here, the supermorphic persona is compatible with McKenna *et al.*'s 'Real Me', but need not be. Those who did not present their 'Real Me' in the McKenna *et al.* study presumably were unable to sustain the relationships offline. What we are arguing, then, is that these individual still presented *a* supermorphic persona. However, owing to the inauthenticity of the self-as-object (in this case), there was no successful transference of the relationship to the offline realm. In short, McKenna *et al.*'s study found that those who conveyed their 'Real Me' – what we are calling an *authentic*, as opposed to inauthentic, supermorphic persona online – were better able to develop strong Internet relationships and bring these relationships into their offline lives.

In McKenna *et al.*'s study, it would seem that the somatic flexibility available through online communication afforded individuals the opportunity to present and ultimately embrace their authentic supermorphic self-as-object (that which they had the potential to bring forth given the right environmental cues). Supermorphia in this context should be hailed as a positive form of progressive embodiment whose authenticity is evidenced by the ease with which the ideal self-as-object was transferred across domains. In addition, recall from Chapter 11 how theorists prior to McKenna (and colleagues) argued that there are psychological gains to be made from experimenting with different forms of identity in online environments. Recall how Turkle (1995) conceived of cyberspace (*qua* MUDs) to be a space where people can 'experiment' by presenting different selves online and, as a consequence, discover a deeper truth about themselves. She illustrated this point with the example of Gordon, who did not 'fit in' at school. Despite the diversity of experimentation, Turkle believed that often these same individuals maintain a connection with both their online and offline identities. The deeper truth that Turkle advocated is compatible with the supermorphic persona as it equates to the realization of an ideal and therefore authentic self-as-object. Moreover, the need to maintain a connection between one's supermorphic presentation and one's non-virtual self-as-object, is testament to the more fundamental need to retain authenticity across domains (a point we shall return to).

ISSUES OF AUTHENTICITY WITH THE SELF-AS-OBJECT

Using a somewhat different approach, Ford (2001) evaluated the impact of VEs on those with various forms of paralysis. Like McKenna *et al.* and Turkle, he too (initially at least) identified a number of positives when presenting an alternative self-as-object within cyberspace (in the form of a 3-D avatar). As he notes: 'Through the careful selection of a virtual representation, a person with paralysis can mask her abnormal shape, lack of movement, and decreased stature' (Ford, 2001, p. 663). How this is construed as a positive is illustrated using an example of a wheelchair user: 'Unless I choose a particularly short graphical representation for myself, there is no such thing as being "two feet below" conversations in these new arenas of socializing' (ibid.).

Such an alternative (possible) self would be unlikely offline, but the possibility of this alternative self is made available through the use of VR technology. The masking of the person's offline self-as-object, and therefore those aspects of the embodied subject that are represented by it, enables certain differences between oneself and others to be redressed. However, and somewhat paradoxically, the same act of masking also *reveals* the discrepancy that exists between the user's supermorphic persona and offline self-as-object. This discrepancy is problematic for Ford, who argues that it amounts to an 'idealized' representation of embodiment, which serves to reinforce negative stereotypes held of disabled bodies, and that the preference for and value placed on the idealized representation is ultimately to the detriment of the disabled individual who will become more marginalized, more absent.[1]

It would seem that when evaluating the positive or negative contribution of progressive embodiment within cyberspace, specifically in relation to the body-image *qua* self-as-object, much depends on whether the supermorphic persona is a digital representation of one's ideal self, and therefore on how well versions of this new persona can be adapted offline (as Turkle's example of Gordon demonstrates), or whether one's supermorphia merely constitutes the manifestation of an idealized version of this component of the body-image. If cyberspace is utilized as a means of realizing one's potential to be authentic – in a manner one finds difficult to do in non-virtual social engagements – then in the context of relationships at least, if this supermorphic persona can be taken offline, evidence suggests that it can have a longlasting positive effect (as evidenced by McKenna *et al.*'s research). However, if the virtual self-as-object is merely a digital representation of one's own understanding of certain idealized standards of attractiveness and desirability within a given community, then there is a danger that this will lead to the pursuit of inauthentic expression, and ultimately to the marginalization of one's offline body-image. Perhaps it will even act as a stumbling block to any future realization of one's *authentic* supermorphic persona through the medium of cyber-technology.

As a way of illustrating some of these potentially negative consequences, we return to the topic of online dating discussed in Chapter 11. Whitty (2008a) found that the presentation of an 'idealized' self on online dating sites is not a sage strategy, noting that although a clichéd self appears on the surface at least to constitute the sort of self that would make an ideal[2] romantic partner, many online daters nevertheless felt that these individuals were simply not being 'real'. The online daters interviewed talked about looking for 'genuine' and honest people rather than some sort of clichéd individual, or what we would refer to as 'inauthentic supermorphia'.

Whitty also noted how some online daters admitted to presenting their self-as-object in more idealized terms – sometimes by exaggerating what they looked like or even telling outright lies. Deceptions often centred on aspects of their physical appearance, such as weight/size, age and height, or involved describing themselves as better looking than they actually were; some used out-dated photographs or even a photograph of a different person. These deceptions should not be trivialized, however: for Whitty (2008b) found that, in the main, exaggerations or lies about one's appearance (however slight) meant that participants were unable to move beyond their first face-to-face meeting.

The motivations for presenting oneself as an idealized and consequently inauthentic self-as-object may be diverse. The virtual worlds of cyberspace enable one to transcend the physical and explore various forms of embodiment and, for some, this may be motivation enough. However, some of the participants interviewed by Whitty (2008b) were more forthcoming about their motives. They made it clear that lying about their appearance and status helped enhance their self-esteem because of the increased attention they received, even if they never met others offline. However, if one's aim is to transfer the relationship offline, then evidence suggests that the larger the discrepancy between one's supermorphic persona and offline self-as-object, the harder will be the transference from one world to another (see Whitty, 2007). This was well illustrated in Chapter 11 by the example of a male online dater, Ben (a.k.a. *entrepreneur 23*). Recall how he made up a profile in which he was very wealthy, and entrepreneurial, with a Porsche (he used a photograph of his friend's car). As a consequence, he received considerably more 'returns' than previously.

In Ben's case, we suggest that his choice of inauthentic persona, in the super-morphic guise of *entrepreneur 23*, is condemning him to remain trapped within a virtual world of his own making. But what if we were to permit *entrepreneur 23* a degree of context authenticity, in so far as it is accepted that *within cyberspace* Ben is *entrepreneur 23*? What would such a concession achieve? Certainly it would not make the transition from cyberspace to offline world any easier, we contend. The absolute context dependency of this type of authenticity would be revealed as soon as Ben (as *entrepreneur 23*) attempted to present his supermorphic persona to the offline world and failed: something that we have already noted is less likely to occur when the supermorphia constitutes the realization of an ideal and therefore authentic self-as-object. Irrespective, then, of what level of context authenticity is bestowed on *entrepreneur 23*, Ben's virtual self-as-object would lack *transcendent authenticity* because even if permitted the stature of 'authentic self in situ', it is ultimately an idealized representation.

Whilst individuals who interact within online communities do not always seek face-to-face communication with cyberfriends, in the main, online daters prefer to meet the 'real person' behind the profile soon after connecting online (Whitty and Carr, 2006a). This is partly motivated by the need to avoid wasting time developing a relationship with someone who turns out to be deceptive; but what about cases where virtual interactions are not motivated by the desire to transcend domains? Does context authenticity find legitimacy in the self-contained and much more clearly demarcated world of *Second Life*, for example? Certainly the potential for the realization of an idealized self-as-object remains, as is briefly illustrated by Meadows (2008, p. 57):

> In 'reality' it was 8 a.m., and I was sitting in a small apartment above a canal in Holland. Outside the snow was gently falling on some ducks, which were huddled together from the cold. All I had in the fridge were a few pieces of waxy herring and some orange juice that had gone acidic days ago. And I was starting to shiver. Meanwhile, in *Second Life*, the party was winding down a bit. Korya and four others were still joking and dancing. It was 2 a.m. in Second Life . . . Eventually, I logged out and after warming myself in the shower I went to sleep as the sun headed for early afternoon.

The contrast between worlds is stark, as is the implied discrepancy between selves-as-object residing in each. Despite the contrast, however, perhaps what we are discussing here is nothing more than a pseudo-problem, and in fact there is no issue of authenticity to resolve. As things stand, there are simply two discrete worlds with two distinct selves-as-object, each with its own incommensurable authenticity, and with no desire for transcendence. If such a strict demarcation of selves were possible, then perhaps context authenticity would be sustainable as a legitimate measure of one's supermorphic persona. However, the ability of some users to keep these putatively discrete worlds and selves-as-object apart will be challenged in Part 3. As will become apparent, there is evidence to suggest that at the psychological level there is a need to transcend worlds and seek parity and unity between what we are presently contemplating as different context authenticities. Meanwhile, in the next section, transcendent and context authenticity will continue to be explored, this time in relation to that other aspect of the body-image, the phenomenal self; and with it one's *experience* of embodiment.

THE PROGRESSIVE PHENOMENAL SELF

The extent to which interactions are experienced as being 'in' the VE is often regarded as a measure of *presence*. What is of interest to us, here, is the form this presence takes within a framework of progressive embodiment. Specifically, we wish to address three questions:

- Does progressive embodiment equate to an *experience* of embodiment that is enhanced, perhaps in terms of interactive prowess and/or vividness – a super-morphic presence?
- If so, what impact will this have on the authentic nature of the experience?
- What impact will the authenticity issue have on the individual's need to maintain parity across domains?

The phenomenal self equates to one's experience of embodiment. Presence within a VE is inversely related to the phenomenal self's sense of proximity to the location of the objective body. The more immersed within the VE one feels, the more removed one is, experientially, from the objective body. The stronger the illusion of 'being there', the greater the sense of presence. What is interesting about the phenomenal self is that, even within a computer-mediated environment, it is experientially genuine. By this, we mean that *where* one experiences oneself may be illusory – one may not literally be exploring the inside of various body parts, for example as is the purpose of the VR game *Interskin* (Jones, 2000) – but the *experience* of being embodied at this virtual location is no less genuine, no less real. As an aside: because we are claiming that the experience is genuine/real, it is important to distinguish between VR experience and, say, hallucination. VR experiences are stimulated by external triggers – the virtual interface – whereas hallucinations are triggered by internal events. Despite this difference, each experience is no less genuine as an experience, but only the former is an experience that stems from an external reality – that is, a real physical source independent of the experiencing subject.[3] However, even if we were to accept that one's sense of presence – of being located within a virtual arena, interacting with other virtual bodies and/or inanimate objects – amounts to a genuine experience, and that one's phenomenal self is likewise experientially genuine, it is the issue of authenticity that concerns us here. (Some may wish to question the difference between a genuine and an authentic experience. The use of these two terms is merely to distinguish between the experience, itself, and what the experience is an experience of, as will become apparent as we progress.) Therefore, as was done with the self-as-object, we must distinguish between the ideal and the idealized, this time in relation to the phenomenal self.

ISSUES OF AUTHENTICITY WITH THE PHENOMENAL SELF

Relevant to this distinction is Ford's (2001, p. 678) talk of the modification – or 'smoothing out' – of a user's idiosyncratic postures and gestures through the process of computer-mediation filtering, which produces 'uniformity and generality in virtual postures' and 'styles of social interactions' that are contrived in comparison to non-virtual individual expression. To illustrate, consider Mooradian's (2006) example of virtual karate and how, *in principle*, through the use of a full-immersion body-suit, the user could physically orient towards, strike and block (etc.) a virtual opponent. Not only could these movements 'be gauged and reproduced to simulate a real fight in physical space' (p. 680), but when one physically throws a punch, for example, the motion could be matched to the closest stored strike and 'executed perfectly and with tremendous simulated force' (p. 681). Similarly, Mueller *et al.* (2007) describe a virtual game, *Breakout for Two*, in which a ball strikes blocks in a wall with the aim of dislodging them. The ball's impact intensity is mapped onto a three-point scale: the harder the ball is hit, the higher the intensity is registered on the scale and the more the block 'cracks'. However, what this means is that the *actual* intensity of the strike is 'filtered' down to one of only three possible levels of virtual strike.

As invigorating as the virtual karate experience may be, Mooradian tells us, it would nevertheless be lacking owing to its mere approximation to actual karate, an art form characterized by the precision with which each move is executed. (We can see the *emergence* of Mooradian's example at a commercial level in Wii games such as *Punch Out, Fight Night* and *The Circle*.) Mooradian's point is essentially that although the experience of virtual fighting is a genuine *experience*, it is not an *authentic* experience *of martial art combat*. Progressive embodiment could therefore be interpreted as leading to an experience of enhanced fighting prowess but not an experience of authentic fighting prowess. The measure of authenticity seems to be based on the level of discrepancy between what is occurring experientially and what is occurring objectively, at least in terms of the movement of one's objective body. But could it not be argued that just as the experience is a genuine VR experience (in this case, of oneself with enhanced fighting qualities), so it is also an authentic experience of martial art combat *within the context of the virtual arena*. Perhaps it is analogous to the way that someone lifting a heavy object using a pulley system is demonstrating authentic lifting prowess in that context. This is certainly a possibility if the virtual karate interface is simply a tool for the enhancement of an embodied experience, just as a pulley system is a tool for the enhancement of one's lifting capabilities.

Depending, then, on the purpose of the VR simulation, it may be that the virtual interface allows a degree of accessibility to a 'sport' that might otherwise be denied certain individuals. If the goal of the virtual activity is to provide the novice with an experience of enhanced fighting prowess marketed as, say, martial art combat, then perhaps a degree of approximation and, ultimately, enhancement is inevitable; and whilst the inauthentic nature of this experience in comparison to genuine martial art combat should not be overlooked, perhaps it is beside the point. Perhaps virtual karate is contextually authentic. Whilst willing to consider this point, it nevertheless seems reasonable to explore further the extent to which such virtual experience, as genuine as it may be as an experience, could ever acquire transcendent authenticity and, in doing so, match the authentic experience of a non-virtual sporting event. As Fairweather (2002, p. 241) points out, 'absolutely safe virtual sports would lose some of their point'. More specifically, it seems reasonable to question whether one's phenomenal self within cyberspace could ever transcend the virtual realm and sustain a level of authenticity across domains, or whether each phenomenal self is in fact context dependent and therefore incommensurable. This might have serious repercussions if, for example, the goal of the simulation is to train athletes to adopt authentic sporting posture and engage in authentic sporting action geared towards a successful outcome in the offline world: for under such circumstances, presumably the simulation would be made more controllable and therefore safer. As Fairweather (2002, p. 241) again notes, 'training in such a safe environment may induce competitors to transfer lessons "learnt" to the non-virtual practice of sport, and thus to take excessive risks when they are without the "safety net" of the simulator'.

The authenticity issue is not, however, whether one is prone to take excessive risks when the skills one experiences possessing in the relative safety of cyberspace are transferred across domains (although this may be a notable consequence – see, for example, Arnold and Farrell's, 2002, discussion on virtual training for surgeons); rather, it is about the extent to which the movement of one's objective body and one's VR experience of embodiment are isomorphic (in the same way as authenticity was a measure of the extent to which one's supermorphic persona and one's offline self were isomorphic when discussing the self-as-object earlier). Consequently, if, with the aid of virtual karate technology, one has the potential to become a Grand Master,[4] then one's phenomenal self should correspond experientially to the level of precision exhibited by one's objective body at any given stage in one's progression towards the realization of this ideal (this is assuming that the virtual technology can accurately map one's 'moves' onto the virtual stage).[5] The authenticity of one's phenomenal self, in this case, should transcend context (again, just as online daters were more likely to transcend context when their virtual self was authentic). But if one's self-as-object is idealized, and one's supermorphia inauthentic (one is not a Grand Master but presents oneself as such in terms of the avatar's persona), then the corresponding experience of *enhanced* fighting prowess, required for persona and experience to be congruent, would likewise be inauthentic in comparison to the actual capabilities of one's objective body and the actual experience of embodiment that is one's offline phenomenal self.

To illustrate this point, imagine fighting a virtual version of a real-life opponent. In the virtual arena, one experiences enhanced fighting prowess – a certain kind of phenomenal self. If this combat is then transferred to the offline world, where one engages the real-life version of one's virtual opponent, in the absence of technological enhancement one's embodied experience would be different, even though one's objective bodily movements are equivalent to those adopted during the virtual combat. But as noted earlier, if this occurred, or if one's sole aim was to *pretend* to be a karate fighter, even at the level of Grand Master, or to adopt enhanced fighting prowess solely within the virtual arena, then would it not be the case that one's supermorphia in terms of both self-as-object and phenomenal self was nevertheless contextually authentic? After all, one would be experiencing the embodied prowess of a *virtual* Grand Master in the context of cyber-enhancement. Moreover, within this context, would it not in fact be contextually *inauthentic* to present oneself as anything other than a Grand Master?

What these hypothetical scenarios highlight is that the issue of experiential authenticity, and with it the transcendent authenticity of different phenomenal selves experienced within different domains, is somewhat ambiguous. The potential for (or even likelihood of) discrepancy between these separate, context-dependent phenomenal selves brings its own 'psychological' risks. The experience of enhanced embodied prowess is only experienced as 'enhanced' in comparison to something else – something less. Therefore, when returning to one's original embodied state, one does not experience simply a lack of prowess but rather its loss. Recall Ford's caution when discussing the self-as-object: There is a risk that enhancement through cyber-technology may lead to the presentation of an idealized self-as-object at the expense of the marginalization of one's offline self-as-object, which, in turn, may impact negatively on one's embodied identity. With regard to the phenomenal self, the line between the authentic and inauthentic is somewhat fuzzy because, in each case, one's embodied experience is a genuine *experience*. In addition, if one's experience is of tool-enhanced embodied prowess then it is *authentic* in that context. However, as became evidenced earlier, when presenting a self-as-object that lacks transcendent authenticity, the continued presentation of such a context-authentic, supermorphic persona is difficult to sustain and is often revealed as ultimately inauthentic by those seeking parity across domains. Likewise, if the experience of the phenomenal self is context dependent and therefore cannot transcend domains, then there is a danger that, like the self-as-object, one's experience of interactions in the form of this supermorphic phenomenal self will be favoured to the detriment of one's non-virtual experience of embodiment.

If the ultimate purpose of employing cyber-technology as a tool in the realization of one's ideal body-image is to transfer this body-image into the offline world, then transcendent authenticity must be sought, otherwise one must remain trapped (in the guise of one's supermorphic persona) within the confines of one's own 'cyber-reality'. Likewise, if the purpose of, say, the karate simulation is to train an individual in the use of this particular martial art then an enhanced version complete with idealized 'moves' would fail, and achieve little beyond gameplay (it would lack transcendent authenticity) – although, for many, being limited to gameplay may be perfectly acceptable. In the absence of enhancement, however, if/when technology makes available a tighter isomorphism between objective and virtual bodies, the simulation would facilitate the emergence of the ideal phenomenal self and, if successful, contribute to the individual achieving their potential.

In summary, throughout Part 2 we discussed how the altered contingencies constitutive of cyberspace could impact on an individual's sense of self, either by affording disembodiment (which we rejected) or by providing fresh arenas for the staging of the body (to borrow Balsamo's (1993) metaphor one more time). By accepting that cyberspace enables the user to transcend the physical body, but not embodiment, we explored the notions of somatic flexibility and progressive embodiment. We did this in order to support the case for the importance of developing a psychological understanding of the effects of space, representation and engagement on the individual who transcends the offline world. By considering how the self presented within these divergent spaces might vary with regard to its authenticity, we concluded that in the absence of transcendent authenticity, although the expression of supermorphia is authentic within the confines and context of one's *virtual* world, we nevertheless anticipate that problems will arise when users find themselves seeking parity across domains and measuring their authenticity by the standards of the virtual world, particularly if, within this virtual world, their self-image is enhanced; and, even more pertinent to this book, if this enhanced self-image is the result of enactments that are taboo offline.

In Part 3, we discuss what the potential detrimental effects of cyberspace might be on the individual's sense of self. And although we accept that these detrimental effects should form the basis for legitimate moral concern, we nevertheless maintain that, ultimately, judgements regarding the *permissibility* of virtual content should be informed by psychology. In the final part, then, we conclude our case for promoting psychological understanding as a more valid measure of STA permissibility.

Part 3

Psychological parity and changes to the self

13 Violent games

Where's the harm in playing?

In Part 1, we presented a series of arguments supporting the conclusion that questions regarding the morality of *acts* with a purely virtual genesis (e.g. video game interactions) are the wrong sorts of questions to ask. In effect, when it comes to the virtual act itself, there is no moral issue to consider, no rightness or wrongness to debate. Klimmt *et al.* (2006, p. 313) appear to share this view:

> Obviously, in violent video games no living creatures are harmed and no real objects are damaged. Dead bodies, blood, and injuries are nothing more than pixels. The non-reality status of video games can therefore be used to explain why moral concerns are not 'necessary', applicable, or rational in their context; there simply seems nothing to be 'real' in a game that moral concerns could arise from. Consequently, players are not required to cope with moral ruminations.

That said, it seems fair to say that those who *do* wish to question the morality of such (violent) games do not limit their moralizing to the virtual act itself. We have already noted objections to violent acts committed within games based on what these acts represent – their *socially significant expression* – or their corrupting influence on the gamer's virtue or even rationality (Chapters 8 and 9). However, by far the most extensive research has focused on the behavioural consequences of playing these games (and, related to this, affective and cognitive changes within the gamer), and the extent to which this behaviour is said to be aggressive or otherwise anti-social.

A comprehensive understanding of whether violent video games breed violence is of course important empirical research that ought to be undertaken. To date, however, research findings on the effects of video game violence on offline behaviour are far from unambiguous; although, in a comprehensive review of the literature, and based on weight of evidence, Barlett *et al.* (2009) attempted to categorize video game effects as either confirmed, suspected or speculative.

Even taking such a review into account, any attempt to posit a direct causal link between game content and violent offline behaviour should be regarded as overly simplistic, largely uncorroborated and ultimately contentious. Instead, it is our view that underlying *much* of the cognitive, affective or behavioural changes measured in gamers offline, and perhaps to some degree online, are more basic and fundamental processes involving gamer identification and the need to maintain psychological parity across spaces.[1] Discussion on what this entails, and the potential positive and negative impact of these processes on the gamer, is postponed until the next chapter. In the meantime, let us consider research that has been conducted and explanations that have been forwarded with regard to the effects of video game content. Within this chapter, we present an overview of key research into the effects of playing (mostly violent) video games in both single-player and MMORPG formats. In addition, we critically examine some of the models and theories created to explain more general aggressive behaviour, which have then been applied to video game violence.

AGGRESSION AS A CONSEQUENCE OF VIOLENT GAMES

The literature on the transferral of negative behaviours played within a game to *actual* behaviours has mainly focused on aggression (Anderson *et al.*, 2004; Anderson and Dill, 2000; Barlett *et al.*, 2007; Bartholow *et al.*, 2005, 2006; Bushman and Anderson, 2009; Carnagey and Anderson, 2005; Carnagey *et al.*, 2007; Lemmens, 2006; Staude-Müller *et al.*, 2008). The media, especially, have concerned themselves with stories that place the blame for atrocities such as the shootings at Columbine high school squarely at the feet of violent video game content. And ironically a game exists (*Super Columbine Massacre RPG*, 2005) where players relive the day through the lens of those responsible for the shootings. However, we should also be mindful that the press have given similar attention to other media, such as music, films and television. Ferguson (2010) reminds us that concerns about violent media have been around for a long time. Plato, he says, cautioned that plays and poetry might have a negative impact on the youth. Similarly, early Christian philosophers, such as Augustine, were concerned with the detrimental moral effects of the Roman Games (which featured public executions and gladiatorial combats) on the spectator. In addition, the issue of 'video game violence' often garners much attention as politicians and public health policy makers grasp for evidence in order to make important decisions about how to rate games, and even which games ought to be censored (see Byron, 2008).

When it comes to academic research on the topic, there is still no agreement among researchers as to whether playing violent video games leads to aggressive behaviour. In a review, Anderson *et al.* (2003) (see also Anderson, 2004) report that many studies have found short-term effects of playing video games, including the increased likelihood of physically and verbally aggressive behaviour, aggressive thoughts and emotions. However, in his meta-analytic review on video game violence, Ferguson (2007a) warns us to treat many of the findings with caution, arguing that the measures of aggression lack validity and that often the effect sizes are close to zero. He also suggests that there is a bias in the academic literature towards papers that report significant differences (see also Ferguson, 2007b).

Based on a cursory treatment of the literature, at least, it would appear that the jury is still out on this issue.

In addition, several theories have driven research into the impact of media violence on behaviour. Social learning theory (SLT) really started to push the notion that there is a link between aggressive media and aggressive behaviour. Other theories have been offered as an alternative to SLT (e.g. script theory and the Cognitive Neoassociation Model), although perhaps the most currently cited theory is the General Aggression Model, which incorporates numerous mini-theories on aggression.

In the sections to follow, we briefly examine each of these theories in terms of their contribution to our understanding of violent video content and real-world aggression, and consider in more detail the seemingly contradictory findings regarding the effects of violent gameplay on actual behaviour.

THEORIES AND MODELS OF AGGRESSION

Research looking at violent video games was prompted by earlier research on children watching violent television (Bandura *et al.*, 1963; see Gunter, 2008, for a detailed review of empirical research relating to media violence). Theorists utilize Bandura's social learning theory – which posits that we learn by observing others – to explain behaviour. In Bandura's early work, he argued that individuals acquire attitudes, emotional responses and new styles of behaviour by modelling and imitating others' behaviours – that is, we are not passive observers or recipients of external stimuli; therefore, watching violent cartoons or other forms of media leads to aggressive behaviour (Bandura *et al.*, 1963). The view that individuals are not passive observers is arguably even more relevant with regard to the playing of video games. In such a context, one might contend that hitting or shooting another character is (or is held to be) an appropriate response in a conflict situation, and therefore this type of aggression is likely to be reinforced. This is also arguably the case with verbal aggression. Ivory *et al.* (2009), for example, found that profanity was included within the dialogue of about 20 per cent of video games; and those games that did contain profanity tended to express it frequently. Moreover, games often give explicit rewards (e.g. points) for engaging in symbolic violent acts, which then might be transferred to real-life behaviours.

Much of the research that has applied SLT to video games has focused on children. Researchers often create similar experimental conditions to the ones that Bandura originally employed – asking children to play an aggressive video game and then subsequently watching them at play with objects such as a Bobo doll (e.g. Silvern and Williamson, 1987). Critiques of this type of research, however, contend that the 'aggression' witnessed might be better understood as play fighting rather than 'authentic' aggression, and that such experiments appear very artificial (Cumberbatch *et al.*, 1988). Cumberbatch (2010) argues that there is in fact little else to do with a Bobo doll besides hitting it. Borden (1975) has likewise criticized these sorts of experiments, saying that results are an artefact of demand characteristics whereby the children have an idea of what the researcher is expecting and are aiming to please. Ferguson (2010) argues that any modelling effects from these experiments appear to be small and short lasting. Importantly, he notes that it is not clear whether the children are mimicking specific aggressive acts as opposed to being motivated to engage in aggression *per se*. Equally, some researchers have argued that modelling is something that individuals *can* do rather than something they *necessarily* do (Ferguson, 2010; Huesmann and Taylor, 2003).

Alternatively, script theory purports that behaviours fall into certain patterns known as 'scripts'. Scripts are learned interactions that serve as social functions. From the culture they are living in, individuals learn appropriate ways to behave and the meanings ascribed to certain behaviours. Huesmann (1988) was one of the first to apply script theory to explain aggressive behaviour. Along with a colleague, he argued:

> Aggressive behavior is controlled to a great extent by scripts that are encoded, rehearsed, stored, and retrieved in much the same way as are scripts for intellectual behavior. The constancy of such scripts once encoded, accounts to a great extent for the stability of aggression across time and situations.
>
> (Huesmann and Guerra, 1997, pp. 408–409)

Drawing from script theory, Huesmann (1988) posits that scripts are filtered through self-regulating beliefs; something Huesmann and Guerra (1997) refer to as *normative beliefs*, which they argue filter out inappropriate behaviours. Moreover, normative beliefs can affect an individual's emotional reaction to others' behaviours and thereby stimulate the use of appropriate scripts. They further contend that normative beliefs may or may not be consistent with the prevailing social norms, although there is typically much overlap. According to script theory, then, individuals who are more aggressive should hold normative beliefs that approve of aggressive behaviour; and, with regard to children, Huesmann and Guerra contend that engaging in aggressive behaviour promotes the development of normative beliefs that approve of aggressive behaviour. Importantly, the theory has been applied to aggressive behaviour in children, generally, but not in its own right to examine the effects of playing video games. Instead, it has been considered together with other theories (see the discussion on the General Aggression Model below).

The Cognitive Neoassociation Model (Berkowitz, 1984) subsumes the earlier well-known frustration-aggression hypothesis (Dollard *et al.*, 1939). The frustration-aggression hypothesis suggests that frustration develops when an individual is unable to achieve a particular goal. The build-up of this frustration then leads to aggressive behaviour. Social learning theorists criticized this model, arguing that frustrations typically only create a general emotional arousal and that it is important instead to examine how individuals respond to this arousal (Bandura, 1973).

The Cognitive Neoassociation Model, however, also grew out of dissatisfaction with SLT's ability to explain certain behaviours; the criticism being that learning does not necessarily take place from observing an event. Berkowitz (1984, p. 414) writes:

> I do not want to deny or even minimize the importance of learning. Nevertheless, it is apparent that media influences do not operate through observational learning only, if this concept is understood to refer to a relatively long-lasting acquisition of new knowledge or the adoption of a novel form of behavior. Some media effects are fairly transient . . . as if the observed event had activated reactions or thoughts only for a relatively brief period.

Berkowitz also states that it is problematic to argue that individuals imitate media given that, typically, there is no opportunity to act out a similar physical act, and that most studies that use aggressive measures consider acts that are physically different.

Proponents of the Cognitive Neoassociation Model argue that thoughts, feelings and action tendencies are linked together in a person's memory, which form an *associative network* (Collins and Loftus, 1975). Concepts that are primed are more accessible in memory. The model posits that individuals repeatedly exposed to particular stimuli start to link and activate other similar thoughts (Berkowitz, 1984, 1990). This approach has been applied to explain both pro-social and aggressive behaviour. With regard to aggressive behaviour, Berkowitz (1990, p. 494) states:

> [F]oul odors, high temperatures, exposure to painfully cold water, and even disgusting scenes can also heighten the hostility displayed, or the aggression that is directed toward another person, even when that individual cannot possibly be blamed for the unpleasantness and the aggression cannot alleviate the negative state of affairs.

Applying this theory to media, Berkowitz (1984) argues that media do not necessarily produce a persistent learning outcome but, rather, the effects of media tend to be short-lived. Media, instead, spur individuals into action. Therefore, watching a violent film can prime other semantically related thoughts, which increase the chances that the spectator will have other aggressive notions during this period (see also Anderson and Ford, 1986). All this can occur automatically without conscious awareness. Hence, exposure to any form of aggressive media can trigger aggressive feelings and bring to mind aggressive memories, beliefs and aggression-related skills. Giumetti and Markey (2007) give the example that one might be exposed to an image of a gun, which then evokes ideas with similar meanings (e.g. shooting, bullets), which, in turn, activates other semantically associated ideas (e.g. to kill or murder). Repetition of the aggressive media (i.e. the continual playing of an aggressive video game) could, according to this theory, lead to an increase in the tendency of a person to behave aggressively. This theory would predict that individuals who regularly play violent video games are more likely to be aggressive individuals.

Critics of the Cognitive Neoassociation Model argue that even if an individual's emotional responses to watching violence are enhanced, it does not necessarily follow that individuals will act more aggressively (Sherry, 2001). To illustrate, Bryant and Linz (2008) set out to test an assumptions made by the US government in defence of the Child Pornography Protection Act 1996 (CPPA): 'that virtual child pornography stimulates and whets adults' appetites for sex with children and that such content can result in the sexual abuse or exploitation of minors becoming acceptable to and even preferred by the viewer' (p. 35). After exposing adults to 'barely legal'[2] pornography, Bryant and Linz concluded that although those who viewed the material were more likely to cognitively associate sexual activity to non-sexual images of minors (based on response latency), there was no evidence that exposure caused participants to be more accepting of child pornography or paedophilia.

Rather than criticizing the Cognitive Neoassociation Model *per se*, scholars have tended to add to it. Bushman (1995, 1996), for example, extended the model by arguing that individuals with certain dispositions are more prone to the effects of priming than others. An individual who is more dispositionally angry, for example, might possess a more developed cognitive-associative network of semantically related ideas about anger than those who are not. When this person is exposed to violent media, they will be more likely to become primed to act in a more aggressive manner compared with someone who does not have an angry disposition (or so the argument goes). Bushman (1996) did in fact find that individuals who scored high on trait aggressiveness had more extensive aggressive cognitive-associative networks compared with those who scored low on trait aggressiveness.

The General Aggression Model (GAM), previously referred to as the General Affective Aggression Model (GAAM), was developed because it was believed that no single theory of aggression is adequate enough to competently predict aggressive behaviour. The model is a theoretical framework that integrates a conglomeration of mini-theories (Anderson and Bushman, 2002). A number of versions of the theory have been developed over the years (e.g. Anderson, 1997, 2004; Anderson and Bushman, 2002; Anderson and Dill, 2000; Bushman and Anderson, 2001). The model is, in the main, based on social learning and social-cognitive theories (as described above). In addition, the GAM draws from research that examines the development and use of knowledge structures that guide perception, interpretation, decision making and action. According to the model, both situational and person variables interact to affect a person's internal state. The internal state contains cognitions, affects and arousals, which all influence each other and have an effect on an individual's appraisal of an aggressive act. Once appraised, the individual then decides how to act next.

RESEARCH FINDINGS

According to the GAM, violent video games have both short- and long-term effects. As noted earlier, in a review of the literature, Anderson *et al.* (2003) found that many studies reported a number of short-term negative effects of playing video games. Sherry's (2001) meta-analysis likewise found that games had some kind of effect on aggression; *however*, the effect was smaller than that produced by watching television. Moreover, the treatment time in the studies she considered varied from five to 75 minutes, making it difficult to determine precisely how long the effect actually lasted. In addition, Giumetti and Markey (2007) found that *only* those with higher levels of anger prior to playing the game were adversely affected, whereas, in Markey and Scherer's (2009) study, a negative effect occurred only in those with elevated levels of psychoticism. Unsworth and Devilly (2007) also reported that levels of aggression were mediated by the player's feelings immediately prior to playing the game, along with their temperament (disposition towards aggression). Polman *et al.* (2008), for their part, found that actively engaging in a violent video game produced higher levels of aggression than passively watching the same game (in boys but not girls). Similarly, Ivory and Kalyanaraman (2007) found that the more immersed an individual was in a game the greater their physiological and self-reported levels of arousal and aggression. Related to this, Konijn and Bushman (2007) found that boys who felt more immersed in the game, and identified more with the protagonist, exhibited more aggressive behaviour.

There is currently very little literature available on the long-term effects of playing violent video games. Möller and Krahé (2009), however, recently conducted a 30-month longitudinal study in which they found links to aggressive behaviour. Likewise, few studies have focused on *online* games (compared to more traditional single-player video games). Having said that, Williams and Skoric's (2005) longitudinal study of MMORPG players found no evidence for the claim that online violent games cause substantial increases in real-world aggression; neither did playing online violent games result in more accepting beliefs about violent behaviours. Nevertheless, any firm conclusions remain speculative.

DESENSITIZATION

Some writers have suggested that violent video games, such as shooter games, might explain previous school shootings, given that these games lead to strong desensitization effects (Grossman and DeGaetano, 1999). Currently, however, there is no hard evidence to support this claim. Nonetheless, there is research to support the view that playing violent video games can lead to desensitization. As Carnagey *et al.* (2007, p. 490) point out:

> [T]he term 'desensitization' has been used by scholars, public policy analysts, politicians, and the lay public to mean effects as varied as: (a) an increase in aggressive behavior; (b) a reduction in physiological arousal to real-life violence; (c) a flattening of affective reactions to violence; (d) a reduction in likelihood of helping a violence victim; (e) a reduction in sympathy for a violence victim; (f) a reduction in the sentence for a convicted violent

offender; (g) a reduction in the perceived guilt of a violence perpetrator; and (h) a reduction in judged severity of a violence victim's injuries.

They propose that a clearer definition of desensitization to violence is 'a reduction in emotion-related physiological reactivity to real violence' (p. 490). They argue that their definition fits well with cognitive-behavioural treatment of phobias, where the point of therapy is to reduce unwanted negative emotional reactions to stimuli. Others too have used this definition when studying desensitization to violence (e.g. Bartholow *et al.*, 2006).

It has been found that media violence initially produces emotions such as fear and disgust (Cantor, 2000). With increased play, these emotions have been found to decrease and eventually there is an increase in aggressive approach-related motivational states (Bartholow *et al.*, 2006). In fact, Bartholow *et al.* argue that the reason why studies find that playing violent video games leads to increased aggressive behaviour and a decrease in helping behaviour is because players become desensitized to violence (see, for example, Anderson, 2004; Anderson and Bushman, 2001; Silvern and Williamson, 1987). In their research, Bartholow *et al.* found that, compared with gamers who did not play violent video games, gamers who did play such games showed reduced P300 amplitude and increased P300 latency to violent images but not to other equally negative non-violent images.[3]

Others, too, have argued that repeated exposure makes individuals less physiologically responsive to the pain and suffering experienced by victims of violence (Carnagey *et al.*, 2007; Funk *et al.*, 2004). Carnagey *et al.* (2007) found that participants who played a violent video game for 20 minutes compared with those who played non-violent games were less likely to be physiologically aroused by watching real violence. Moreover, participants playing violent video games were more likely than those who played non-violent games to have lower heart rates and galvanic skin responses whilst watching actual footage of people being beaten, stabbed and shot. It is important to note, however, that whilst the study found evidence for physiological desensitization, it did not then go on to test whether participants were more likely to actually be aggressive or less likely to engage in helping behaviours. Related to this point, one might conjecture that police officers (and suchlike) who are regularly exposed to violence are likely to exhibit signs of desensitization without suggesting that they are more likely to be aggressive or less likely to help those in need. Indeed, Hinte (1971) asks us to consider whether techniques for desensitization ought to be part of police recruitment training.

CRITIQUING THE LITERATURE ON THE EFFECTS OF VIOLENT VIDEO GAMES

Cumberbatch (2004, 2010) has strongly criticized researchers who claim that watching violent media or playing violent video games leads to aggressive acts. He states (2004, p. 34; emphasis in original):

The real puzzle is that anyone looking at the research evidence in this field could draw any conclusions about the pattern, let alone argue with such confidence and even passion that it demonstrates the harm of violence on television, in film and in video games. While tests of statistical significance are a vital tool of the social sciences, they seem to have been used more often in this field as instruments of torture on the data until it confesses something to justify a publication in a scientific journal. If one conclusion is possible, it is that *the jury is not still out. It's never been in.* Media violence has been subjected to lynch mob mentality with almost any evidence used to prove guilt.

To date, meta-analyses conducted on studies drawing from the GAM have found only weak effects (Ferguson, 2007a, 2007b; Sherry, 2001). Recall how Sherry (2001) found that the effects of violent video games were weaker than for television. Ferguson and Kilburn (2009), for their part, found that the better-validated measures of aggression produced the weakest results. Moreover, they found no evidence for the claim that video games produce stronger effects owing to their interactive nature (unlike Polman *et al.*, 2008, noted above). In fact, Ferguson and Rueda (2009) claim the opposite: that playing violent video games can *decrease* hostile feelings and depression. To understand why such contradictory conclusions might be drawn, consider the work of Schmierbach (2010), who found that game characteristics had an important mediating effect on violent content. Schmierbach studied the extent to which game mode – cooperative, competitive or solo – shaped aggressive cognition. He found that solo players exhibited the most frustration and anger (aggressive affect) when playing against computer-generated opponents, or when having to navigate through difficult parts of the gameplay. In contrast, in competitive gameplay, when combat was against a fellow gamer, task difficulty varied depending on the skill of the opponent, and so frustration diminished and was replaced by aggressive cognition. In contrast, those engaged in cooperative strategies exhibited less aggressive cognition (as perhaps one might expect), although they did show an increase in frustration and aggressive affect. Schmierbach attributed the increase in aggressive cognition shown by those employing competitive strategies to social learning, suggesting that players (particularly men) 'feel more rewarded for aggressive play in competitive situations, and that these rewards – rather than frustration – account for increases in violent cognition' (p. 270).

Ferguson (2007a) likewise critiqued advocates of the GAM, suggesting that a close reading of these researchers' papers revealed questionable and inconsistent evidence, and that some of the measures of aggression used in previous studies, such as the Taylor Competitive Reaction Time Test, lacked external validity (e.g. Anderson and Dill, 2000). He also claimed that there is a publication bias towards positive results in this area. In his analysis of the 'third' era of video games, he contended that there is no compelling evidence to support the existence of either a correlational or a causal relationship between violent gameplay and actual aggressive behaviour. In fact, as intimated earlier, Ferguson (2010, p. 74) went so far as to state that estimates for the size of the effect of violent video game content on aggressive behaviour 'range from (using $r^2 \times 100$) effectively zero through 2.5%'. However, he did maintain that research on aggressive thoughts provides the strongest evidence for a link, although the question still remains as to whether these aggressive thoughts transfer into aggressive behaviours.

In a similar vein, Olson (2004) concluded that, overall, there is little evidence for any link between exposure to violent interactive games and serious real-life violence or crime. Instead, she argued that the strongest childhood predictors of youth violence were involvement in crime, male gender, illegal substance use, physical aggressiveness, family poverty and anti-social parents. Olson also pointed out that, for adolescents, peer relationships became more important predictors. What is perhaps more interesting is her argument that most aggressive children do not grow up to be violent adolescents or adults. Conversely, most violent adolescents were not aggressive children. In fact, arguably the most important point made by Olson, which seems to have been ignored within the literature, is her suggestion that violent gameplay may disproportionately affect more vulnerable children – that is, those who lack protective factors such as a nurturing relationship.

In a well-considered literature review of the effects of media on children, Livingstone (2007) argues that culturally oriented developmental theories by Vygotsky (1986 [1934]) and Bronfenbrenner (1980) might be useful to consider in research on media effects. She argues that work by cultural critics who contend that regulatory moves towards censorship might lead to constraints on freedom of expression has its virtues. Media, for example, can provide children with the opportunity to experiment with identity. However, she also questions what the limit is to this position. She writes (2007, p. 9):

> In short, it seems wise to frame the question differently, eschewing the bald question – do the media have harmful effects or not, and instead insisting on a more complex formulation of the question, namely – in what way and to what extent do the media contribute, if at all, as one among several identifiable factors that, in combination, account for the social phenomenon under consideration (violence, racism, etc.).

Some scholars warn us of the risk that concerns about the effects of playing violent video games might move beyond objective scientific examination into the realm of moral panic (e.g. Ferguson, 2010). This potential moral panic, Ferguson believes, could be fuelled by the media (where it is often implied that the concern is *fact*), as well as the aforementioned publication bias (i.e. the tendency in psychology to publish papers with a positive statistical result over a null result). Politicians, he suggests, draw from these media reports, which yet again perpetuates the moral panic wheel. Instead of considering the potential vices of video games, Ferguson encourages researchers to consider what individuals might learn from playing them. He argues that it is plausible to maintain that individuals can learn visuospatial cognitions, and information about maths, science and medical diseases, from such games. This is because this type of learning does not require internal shifts in personality characteristics. He further states (2010, p. 76) that 'video games may be effective in communicating raw data or information, but they aren't effective in transmitting moral beliefs, personality traits, and so forth. Information transfers but personality traits such as aggressiveness do not'. (We will have more to say on the effectiveness of transmitting moral beliefs in Chapter 14.)

In sum: if the conclusions of Ferguson are to be adopted, in conjunction with the lack of clear evidence for a link between violent video game content and actual aggressive behaviour or otherwise detrimental effects, then it would seem that there are no grounds for condemning violent video game content beyond the offence it causes some, or general issues to do with taste. If this is the case, then reasons for distinguishing between permitted content involving killings, mutilations, torture and murder and other STAs such as rape and paedophilia appear, on the face of it, to be arbitrary because they are equally related to offence caused and questions of taste. Or is there something different about rape and paedophilia, along with other STAs such as necrophilia, incest, bestiality and cannibalism, that would lead to psychological harm? If so, what is this difference and what do we mean by psychological harm anyway?

In Chapter 15, we begin to address these questions. Before that, we wish to explore the issue of psychological parity. Towards the end of Part 1, we argued that in cases of interactions involving acts with a purely virtual genesis, STAs or other acts were not in and of themselves of moral concern. Instead, we claimed, decisions about the permissibility of virtual content, including certain sorts of representation and interaction within a given virtual space, would be better informed by understanding the impact such altered contingencies might have on the individual. In Part 2, we began to lay the foundation for why psychological parity potentially becomes an issue whenever an individual is able to transcend spaces with divergent contingencies; and although not unique to cyberspace, the possibility of virtual immediacy means that the discrepancy between representations of self (supermorphic personas) and others and interactions within these spaces is potentially more diverse (therefore greater), and certainly more immediate. The discrepancy is no more evident, we contend, than in spaces in which offline taboos are permitted.

In the next chapter, we consider the issue of psychological parity in more detail, particularly in relation to spaces in which STAs are permitted. We look at ways in which individuals who engage within these spaces are able to (a) manage the types of engagements constitutive of STAs and (b) maintain psychological parity across domains. We also begin to consider the potential benefits and pitfalls of this process.

14 Psychological parity

Coping with altered contingencies

It may be that to murder, rape, torture or even eat another virtual character is deemed unlawful or taboo within a given virtual space, but if so then this is in line with certain status functions established within the virtual community by those who occupy that space (see Chapter 9), or is constitutive of a particular feature of the game design (see below). Either way, it is not unlawful or taboo *per se*. To say that such virtual actions *should* be judged wrong, because they are wrong offline, is to import a system of morality from our offline world into a given virtual space; but such heterogeneous spaces are by definition constituted from different contingency relations and, as such, are governed (potentially at least) by different moral codes. Consequently, it would be inappropriate, we contend, for a moral system built on different contingency relations to transcend these spaces. Sicart (2009, p. 199) recognizes this point when he states: 'There is nothing essentially wrong in games with unethical content . . ... But this does not mean that computer games can use unethical content and expect their users not to be affected'.

Sicart seems to share our view that there is nothing wrong *per se* with games that include STAs (recall a similar view expressed by Klimmt *et al.* (2006) at the start of the last chapter). We understand him to mean by this that there is nothing ethically contentious with virtual murder, rape, torture, cannibalism (etc.) when considering the virtual *act* itself. However, Sicart does offer a caveat: that one should not expect the players of such unethical content (unethical by the standards of our offline world) to be unaffected by this content and their engagement with it. For this reason, Sicart insists, the game's content has ethical ramifications, and so should be looked on as an ethical object in and of itself.

In this chapter, we consider the means by which individuals cope with and manage the representations they are exposed to and the activities they engage in within virtual space, particularly when they constitute objects/events prohibited offline (Sicart's unethical content). We also discuss in more detail the process of maintaining psychological parity in light of these altered moral freedoms, as well as some of the problems that may arise from this.

MORAL MANAGEMENT

As stated in Chapter 8, it is our view that we are affected by all our interactions, however trivial they may seem, even if negligibly so. We take this as a given. Moreover, in the last chapter we discussed ways in which one might be affected by violent content, particularly in terms of behavioural consequences. The issue, then, is not whether we are affected by virtual interactions involving violent or otherwise taboo activities; rather, it is in the manner and the extent to which we are affected by them and how we cope with this that is of interest. The way in which gamers cope with violent gameplay is referred to by Klimmt *et al.* (2008) as *moral management*. Moral management, in part, involves cognitively managing the conflict that potentially arises within the gamer between enjoying the gameplay and any aversion they may have towards the violence represented and even virtually engaged in. According to Klimmt *et al.* (2006, p. 325):

> [F]indings support the proposition that dealing with moral issues is a cognitive task that players of violent video games have to resolve in order to maintain or enhance their entertainment experience. Therefore, the players' ways to deal with game violence display some similarities to individuals who perform aggressive behavior in real life.

Klimmt *et al.* (2006) argue that the same mechanisms of *moral disengagement* (Bandura, 2002) found within perpetrators of real-life violence are often found at work within many individuals who play violent video games. For some, the disengagement is relatively easy, as the moral concern is low – 'it's just a game'. For others, however, the means of disengaging may take the form of the strategies found in Box 14.1.

In support of moral management, Klimmt *et al.* (2006) interviewed ten players of violent video games, asking them to discuss their thoughts and feelings about playing their favourite games, particularly with a mind to the types of strategies used to cope with the violent behaviour and any moral concerns they may have with this. Klimmt *et al.* identified a number of themes that link to the mechanisms of moral disengagement listed in Box 14.1 – for example, the dehumanization of game characters and the use of euphemistic labelling. Of particular interest, here, is their identification of the themes '*Game violence as self-defence*' (in which gamers justify their actions in terms of 'kill or be killed') and '*Fighting evil: Narrative-normative justification of game violence*' (whereby the game narrative positions them as fighting evil). Each of these themes, we contend, is compatible with the principle of sanctioned equivalence introduced in Chapter 8.

To maintain an identity as 'morally virtuous' or as simply 'one of the good guys', the gamer may seek to justify their violent acts within the context of the game's pre-determined narrative. The principle of sanctioned equivalence holds that this is much easier to do when violent acts have sanctioned equivalents such as legitimate killing of the enemy or in self-defence, or even if cannibalism is equated with the restoration of health. In the case of torture, again, this may be

---

Box 14.1 Cognitive strategies identified by Bandura (2002) to aid moral management

- Moral justification (e.g. committing violence to fight for social values such as freedom).
- Euphemistic labelling (e.g. describing violent acts using non-violent words such as 'neutralising' instead of 'killing').
- Advantageous comparison (i.e. one's own behaviour is justified by comparing it with more condemnable actions of others).
- Displacement or diffusion of responsibility (i.e. the individual responsibility for violence is transferred to others, e.g. 'commanders').
- Disregard or distortion of consequences (i.e. downplaying the consequences of violence).
- Dehumanization (targets of violent actions are declared to lack human dignity and/or quality, which makes them seemingly ineligible for moral concern about their faith).
- Attribution of blame (justifies violence by arguing that the target of violent action deserves nothing but violence).

Source: Taken from Klimmt *et al.* (2006, p. 312)

---

legitimized as self-defence (of a nation) – extracting information by any means necessary will save lives in a ticking bomb scenario, for example. In fact, more recently, Hartmann and Vorderer (2010) have argued that violent games often provide moral disengagement cues, which enable the gamer to automatically separate their violent actions from their own internalized moral standards. Such cues are often compatible with the principle of sanctioned equivalence. If these disengagement cues fail, however, Hartmann and Vorderer tell us, then it may be that the gamer has to adopt a more reflective strategy of moral management (as described above) in order to continue enjoying the game.

Where there is no sanctioned equivalence (e.g. rape, paedophilia, necrophilia or incest), identifying oneself as virtuous is likely to be much harder to justify (see Hartmann *et al.*, 2010). For some, this may be reason enough not to engage in the activity, either by simply not playing the game or by choosing to avoid that particular possibility within the gameplay (should the game mechanics allow for other options, of course – see below). For others, however, moral management may simply involve other ways of coping, which, by not adhering to the principle of sanctioned equivalence, allows for more 'moral flexibility'. Klimmt *et al.* (2006) identified further themes that give some insight into what these other coping strategies may be – namely *Game-reality distinction* ('it's just a game and therefore not real') and *Game violence as necessary part of (sports-like) performance* (the nature of the game is such that aggressive action is necessary to win). Gamers who justified their actions within the game with reference to these strategies reported thinking of game violence as morally irrelevant or, because it is just a game, as not having any *real* consequences. Within the game, however, such violence was often thought of as a necessary part of winning. Whang and Chang (2004, p. 595) categorized gamers who adopted this type of approach as *off-real world players*. These players are said to 'use every possible means to achieve personal success inside the game world', including harming other players, even though they would not do this offline. Related to this point, Shibuya *et al.* (2008, p. 536) state that '[p]layers in video games may have few chances to be sympathetic toward victims because players need to win the battle and continue the game'.

In a similar vein, Glock and Kneer (2009, p. 153), when commenting on the findings of a study by Ladas (2003), note how gamers seemed 'to focus on competition, success, thrill, and the virtual simulation of power and control rather than damaging other persons'. Glock and Kneer consider this way of thinking about the game (notably, *not* in saliently aggressive terms) to be suggestive of the existence of *differentiated knowledge structures* in those with prolonged violent game exposure when compared to novice gamers. It may be, they surmise, that novice players associate violent video games with aggression because of media coverage to that effect; however, through 'repeated exposure to violent digital games, links to game-specific concepts are strengthened, thereby overrunning [media-related] associations to aggression' (p. 153). For De Vane and Squire (2008, p. 267), the idea that prolonged engagement with video game violence may actually lead to less aggression (see Sherry, 2001) suggests that experienced players 'develop metacognitive understandings of how violence is represented' within the game – namely, as instrumental to the success of the game, or even as immersed within a narrative that extols the principle of sanctioned equivalence (for example). De Vane and Squire go on to note that the meaning that players derived from interaction with various media (such as violent video games) must be contextualized. In other words, for researchers to understand the meaning of seemingly or symbolically violent interaction, they must understand what these interactions are taken to mean by those engaged in them within the context in which they occur (this point will be discussed further in Chapter 15).

The meaning 'behind' the action, and the potential for ambiguity and misconstruing the intention of another within the gamespace, were discussed earlier in relation to status functions (see Chapter 9). If these status functions are not clearly delineated then there is the potential for grievance and perhaps even psychological harm. Wolfendale (2007) discusses just such a possibility, even when the insult is directed towards one's avatar. Wolfendale evidences the occurrence of strong avatar identification through the gamer's use of language. Within the context of *EverQuest*, she notes how gamers may say things like '*I* was ignored' or '*I* never let anyone talk to *me* like that again' (p. 114; emphasis in original). Wolfendale goes on to state: '[t]his identification with the avatar means that harm to avatar is felt as harm to the individual' (ibid.). She therefore considers unsolicited aggression or other violations directed towards avatars to be constitutive of real moral harm. Consequently, she rejects the view that the fault is with the gamer who may have too much psychological investment in the avatar. Equally, she rejects as inappropriate the argument that gamers should avoid harm by psychologically distancing themselves from their virtual personas.

Wolfendale compares avatar attachment to the attachment one might feel towards certain possessions, and states that one would not consider it inappropriate for an individual to feel upset or otherwise aggrieved if their car had been stolen or their house burgled. Likewise, it would not be appropriate to advise the victim to distance themselves from such possessions in the future so as to avoid feeling similarly upset if such an incident were to occur again. Such a position has a certain appeal; however, on closer inspection, does the analogy of attachment to personal possessions transfer so readily to one's avatar? After all, avatars are commonly found within *game*space. Suppose, then, that as part of an offline trip away I decided to spend time in an unlicensed casino (a gamespace broadly construed). During my gambling spree, I wager my car and house, and lose. I may no doubt feel upset, but I wonder whether others would be as consoling towards a gambler who had risked so much on the roll of the dice as they would to someone in Wolfendale's example who had had their possessions stolen. Even if I do not consider that, *qua* my avatar, I am playing a game, I am still entering a different space where there may be the potential for 'avatar harm', and must accept this; much as the professional gambler may not consider what they are doing is 'playing', but nevertheless accepts the potential risk involved.

In addition, there does seem to be something different about the possessive quality we are able (in some cases) to feel towards our avatar compared to our house or car, which entails a strong element of identification. This difference is not lost on Wolfendale. However, we postpone discussion on avatar identification until the next chapter. The point we are making here is that, within gamespace, there is the potential for moral ambiguity (first noted in Chapter 2). There may be spaces where the status functions are much more clearly prescribed; however, in others, this may not be the case. When one freely enters such a space, much as the gambler entering the casino, one may come out of it harmed: psychologically scarred, perhaps (I've lost everything!). But does the interaction itself, which brought about this response in one particular individual, constitute a moral harm *per se*, as Wolfendale would have us believe? The answer is not as clear cut as it is in the case of having one's car stolen or house burgled, we would argue, even if the identification with the object (the avatar) is stronger. After all, it is not the level of identification that is important, here, but the context in which the alleged moral harm occurred.

In short, it is not so clear how much one needs to solicit directly a particular response from within a given space before it is considered appropriate, particularly when others may perceive one's presence within that space as consent enough. Put differently, if one causes by one's actions (as an avatar towards another avatar) someone to feel aggrieved, upset or in any way harmed, then should one be adjudged to have inflicted a *moral* harm on another, especially when it may not be at all evident within that space that one's actions are not in fact permissible? It is perhaps easier to accept that one may have offended the other, but offence is not the same as moral harm. Moreover, one might wish to argue that the other person does not have the right to feel offended in this space – a space where X counts as Y (in context C) or at least where some (perhaps many) assume that this is the case. The matter seems to rest, then, as noted earlier, on the prescriptive strength and clarity of the status functions constitutive of a given space – namely, whether we are all agreed, or at least understand, that X counts as Y (in context C).

A RETURN TO VIRTUE

Without wishing to overstate the obvious, it is understood that virtual killing does not result in any actual harm to the avatar killed or the avatar doing the killing. As is often the retort of gamers, we are talking about pixels here! The act is mere simulation. However, and unlike other moral theories that focus on the morality of the act itself (e.g. Kant and utilitarianism), virtue ethics focuses on the subject engaged in the alleged immoral activity. It is for this reason that virtue theory is considered by some to be more applicable to the unique qualities of (violent) gameplay: for, in such a context, where the act is by its very nature (and design) context specific, it is the subject alone who transcends spaces. In being able to transcend the divergent spaces of the virtual and non-virtual, the subject, by their very nature, is *not* context specific (however, see discussion on the player-subject, below, for a development of this view). Moral harm may therefore be (self-) inflicted on the subject because the moral freedoms that they are potentially able to indulge within one space are likely to be incongruent with a different (offline) space. It is the contamination of the subject who transcends these spaces with moral practices frowned on or even outlawed offline that is the concern of virtue ethics.

We have already encountered virtue ethics (however briefly) in Chapter 8. Recall how McCormick (2001) argued that STAs are harmful because they have the potential to morally corrupt those who engage in them. Sicart (2009, p. 194) describes the position of virtue ethics in a similar way:

> Virtue ethics would argue that computer games with unethical content actually reinforce practices and habits that ought not to be present in the virtuous human being, and that to commit an act of unethical meaning within a game world is to practice the wrong habits that will lead to a nonvirtuous life.

However, Sicart considers the gamer (or *player-subject*, to use his terminology) to be created at the point of entering the gamespace and engaging with the game. The gamer, *qua* player-subject, is that component of the person that occupies the online world, and is created in the act of immersion within the gamespace. (At this point, the reader might wish to pause to consider the extent to which Sicart's player-subject constitutes a kind of supermorphic persona, as discussed in Chapter 12, and therefore whether or to what extent characteristics of the player-subject amount to ideal or idealized representations of the gamer's self-image. This issue will be discussed further below.) Once created, the gamer (*qua* player-subject) can continue to exist even when not playing the game. He/she (again, *qua* player-subject) is still part of a particular gaming community when engaged in discussions on the site forum, for example. As McDonald and Kim (2001, p. 255) note: 'In all probability, one of the chief joys of being a successful gamer is being able to discuss strategy, episodes, or techniques with other gamers'. Moreover, for Sicart, the player-subject is a moral agent because he/she (*qua* player-subject) is a component of the person who is a moral agent offline. However, Sicart accepts that what is deemed morally acceptable within a given space is dependent on a number of interactive factors. First, the game is itself a moral object; its design – including constraints and affordances – can shape the moral choices available and the consequences of those choices (see Pohl, 2008; Zagal, 2009; recall also Hartmann and Vorderer's, 2010, research on moral disengagement cues as a feature of the game design). Second, as just noted, the person playing the game is a moral agent offline, from which is derived the morals of the player-subject created online. The application of these moral components will also impact on the gamer's experience of the game – whether they will feel morally compromised owing to the moral constraints of the game design or, instead, feel they have the opportunity to reflect on certain moral choices and consequences.

What this means, for Sicart, is that the online practice of what would otherwise be non-virtuous activities offline does not, in and of itself, lead to the moral corruption of the individual. The gamer's experience of the game should be understood within the context of game design (game as moral object) and person as moral agent. It may be that the game *requires* the gamer to engage in a particular STA (e.g. commit rape in the game), which the person as a moral agent is not prepared to do because it violates their offline moral code; in which case, according to Sicart, the process of *subjectivization* – what the gamer experiences within the game – will cease, because they will disengage from the game. On the other hand, the moral agent, *qua* player-subject, may be prepared to engage in certain activities that would be illegal, immoral, even taboo offline, because they are *a*, or possibly even *the* only, means of playing the game, in which case the subjectivization process would include reflecting on the action in relation to the moral agent's own set of offline values.

For Sicart, the player-subject is a moral being because the person out of whom the player-subject emerges is a moral being. The moral being, *qua* player-subject, may engage in STAs, but this takes place within the context of the game and therefore reflects the constraints set by the game as a moral object – what Ducheneaut (2010, p. 137) refers to as 'the "laws" of the game embedded in its design'. According to Sicart, in the case of the *mature* moral being, there would be no moral corruption, no transfer of values from those evident in the game to the offline world because the mature moral being is able to understand that the values and unethical content espoused by the gameplay are part of the experience (the subjectivization) of playing the game. A view endorsed by Simkins and Steinkuehler (2008, p. 352) when they state:

> [W]e find it worth noting that players of RPGs [role-playing games] engage in ethical decision making as part of their game play and that games, under the right set of conditions, have at least the potential to foster critical ethical

reasoning through their ability to provide individuals spaces in which they can make significant decisions of situated (albeit in-game) import. They can also experience and reflect on the effects of those decisions. RPGs, even violent games with dark and transgressive themes such as vampires and assassins, provide us simulated social spaces in which we can play through various ways of being in the world.

Aristotle called such moral wisdom (such knowledge of how to act morally) *phronesis*; and in striving for phronesis, Schulzke (2009) considers certain video games a beneficial tool. Video games that include moral choices as an integral part of their gameplay (he uses *Fallout 3* as an example) can act as useful moral training grounds: not by teaching morality *per se* – or distinguishing the moral from the immoral – but by affording the opportunity for players to practise making moral decisions, whether for 'good' or 'bad'. Importantly, though, Sicart (2009, p. 197) concludes that computer games 'with unethical content should only be marketed to and consumed by virtuous players, those player-subjects who have actually developed their ethical reasoning'. Perhaps Klimmt *et al.* (2006, 2008) would similarly conclude that we should only encourage those who have a developed means of moral management to play these games. So, whether in the guise of developed moral reasoning or moral management, it would seem that the mature moral being, *qua* player-subject, is able to engage in STAs because they know that such provocative content 'is only meaningful within the game, because it is related to the game system' (Sicart, 2009, p. 197); that, or they will abstain from playing the game altogether. Either way, the moral corruption feared by proponents of virtue theory will be negated. Sicart further suggests that moral maturity is arrived at through a process of understanding – namely, that the provocative content is only meaningful, or should only be construed as meaningful, within the gamespace itself.

The contingent relation between the moral system and the space it governs is implicit within Sicart's views. The moral being who understands this contingency relation is free to experience the gamespace (the particular subjectivization) without the threat of this practice leading to a detrimental change in virtuousness. The player-subject derived from the mature moral being is also able to terminate any engagement judged to violate a personal taboo, should they choose to exercise their right to veto. However, if no alternative course of action is available within the game (owing to game mechanic constraints) then the gamer may be forced to withdraw altogether. We saw in Chapter 9, with the torture example from *World of Warcraft*, how some objections to the torture were based on a lack of alternative ways of progressing, rather than to the torture itself, thus supporting the argument that, in this space, torture is tacitly accepted as a permissible practice even by those who may not wish to engage in it.

In short, Sicart argues that only those gamers who have developed their ethical reasoning sufficiently will be able to resist the alleged corrupting influence of the unethical practices evident in some gameplays, which are feared by virtue theorists to lead to a non-virtuous life. However, is an understanding of the contingent relation between a particular moral system and a particular means of interacting and representing enough to avoid the potential detrimental effect of these altered contingencies on the individual who transcends spaces? In contrast to Sicart, despite this understanding, might there be a further, more fundamental, psychological process at play that is affected by the types of interactions afforded by gameplays, not least unethical gameplays, and therefore by the potential discrepancy between moral freedoms in offline and online spaces? And might this psychological process better explain how one copes (or not) – or even the type of moral management strategies one employs – when moving from one space to another? Further, might it explain the potentially positive or negative effects of morally neutral discrepancies between spaces (e.g. being able to fly or change form) as well as those brought about as a result of moral extremes such as STAs? The psychological process we are proposing is morally neutral, but has implications for moral systems such as virtue ethics and the development of the virtuous being (to borrow Sicart's phrase) or moral management (Klimmt *et al.*). The process involves achieving or maintaining *psychological parity*.

PSYCHOLOGICAL PARITY

Ducheneaut (2010, p. 144) has this to say about what he considers to be typical of cyberspace:

> Virtual worlds and online games are not exotic environments dedicated to the 'identity play' of a few, but instead spaces that users move in and out of fluidly, which in turn leads to the construction of a 'synthetic' identity that remains fairly stable online and off.

For the sake of argument, even if we concede this point, we are confident that Ducheneaut and proponents of this view would likewise concede that virtual worlds can be, and certainly cyberspace has the potential to be, a place for exotic 'identity play', particularly if one considers the possibility of using such a space to engage in STAs. In such an environment, would one's identity remain, as Ducheneaut would have us believe, 'fairly stable' online and off?

Again, we find Turkle (1995, p. 258) broaching essentially the same issue when, in the context of self and identity, she asks: 'How can we be multiple and coherent at the same time?'. In response, and borrowing from Lifton (1993), she considers whether a self that transcends these spaces would be fragmented and lacking moral content, or be a kind of *Protean Self*: coherent and integrated with a moral outlook. Turkle and Lifton seem to accept that there is a clear association between the nature of the self and one's moral tendency. Psychological parity should therefore be seen as a development of Turkle's reference to the possible fragmentation or coherence and integration of the self across divergent spaces. However, and importantly, it is our contention that an individual who seeks parity of self (that is, who seeks integration of previously disparate selves) by favouring a self realized within cyberspace would *potentially* have a moral outlook incongruent with their offline world, especially if that self is *defined* by the characteristics and actions of someone who engages in STAs. So, it is not necessarily the case that the person would have a fragmented self lacking in moral content, but the 'wrong' sort of integration – that is, seeking parity that favours the altered contingencies of a given virtual world – may bring its own moral problems. The remaining chapters aim to delineate what some of these problems might be and the factors that feature in enabling us to cope with them, or identifying those who are more susceptible to the effects of STAs and other moral freedoms, or more general discrepancies across these spaces.

Psychological parity amounts to one's sense of continuity of self across spaces. As was discussed in Part 2, cyberspace (including gamespace) affords the potential for progressive embodiment, in terms of both the supermorphic self-as-object and the supermorphic phenomenal self. When discussing one's sense of continuity of self, the further issue of authenticity arises (as discussed in Chapters 11 and 12). Boellstorff (2008, p. 129) argues that avatars 'make virtual worlds real, not actual: they are a position from which the self encounters the virtual'. For Boellstorff, then, the virtual world is as real as the actual world; it just so happens that one's access to this reality is mediated by one's avatar. In fact, one might say that it is through one's avatar that Sicart's player-subject is created and experiences subjectivization. This mediated reality, along with the virtual immediacy discussed in Parts 1 and 2, enables the potential for alterations to how one presents oneself (supermorphic self-as-object) and how one experiences oneself (supermorphic phenomenal self) to occur on a scale difficult to accomplish in the actual (offline) world – all of which forms part of the gamer's subjectivization. The extent to which one's supermorphic self-as-object and phenomenal self are authentic is measured by the extent to which these components of the self are able to transcend spaces. On such occasions, the supermorphic persona is said to have transcendent authenticity. However, if those components of the self, as represented and experienced through one's avatar, are restricted to context authenticity, then a discrepancy will exist between the self as presented and experienced across spaces. Allison *et al.* (2006, p. 384) illustrate the potential starkness of this discrepancy when discussing their patient, Mr A:

> [T]he games allowed Mr. A to express aspects of himself that served a compensatory function psychologically. In other words, he could put on a new identity like a new suit of clothes, becoming someone who walked on water, healed others, and cast lightning bolts, in stark contrast to his daily experience of himself as inadequate.

Recall also Bessière *et al.*'s (2007) findings (Chapter 11): that players with lower levels of psychological well-being (e.g. lower self-esteem) tended to rate their avatar more favourably than they did themselves, something that was not found in players with higher rated self-esteem. In addition, identification with one's avatar was found to be more pronounced in those under the age of 27 (Smahel *et al.*, 2008).[1] For certain types of player, then, the realization of one's supermorphic persona through one's avatar has the potential to create a large discrepancy between one's perceived identity status and social prowess in this world and that attainable in cyberspace (see Klimmt *et al.*, 2010). Moreover, Gonzales and Hancock (2008) found that repeated *public* presentation of a particular self – say, presenting oneself as extroverted – produced gradual, but long-term shifts in one's self-concept. However, in MMORPGs, the public presentation of one's self is, as already noted, context specific. Typically, the virtual and social environments are vastly different within the gamespace compared to the gamer's offline world (which may be socially impoverished). As such, it may be extremely difficult to demonstrate one's ideal (supermorphic) character traits of strength, courage and honour (for example), which are normally demonstrated through one's virtual persona – the dragonslayer – in an offline context. If one is able to do this, then one's altered self-image ceases to be context specific, and instead transcends domains. If one cannot, then the psychological discrepancy between offline self and avatar is made salient every time the gamer leaves the gamespace.

Any discrepancy that exists need not be morally charged, of course, or reflect one's virtuousness (or lack thereof). It may be that in a particular virtual space one has the ability to fly at will, or has an extended social circle. On leaving the space, one can no longer fly at will and, let us say, one's social circle diminishes. How one experiences oneself will therefore change. As noted in Chapter 12, there will not simply be a *lack* of *x* (be it flying ability or social extension); rather, the lack of *x* will be made salient as a *loss* – as something that is now missing. In those individuals who identify much less with their avatar (we are certainly not denying that for some there is no strong avatar identification) or whose avatar and offline self are much more congruent, the discrepancy, in terms of a *psychological* disparity between the two, is smaller. For these players, there is a much less severe sense of loss (if any) when they return to the offline world: for whilst the environment in which they socialize may be different in gamespace (or whichever space it occurs), the *extent* to which they socialize may not be so vastly different. As such, their prowess as a social being is not experienced as diminished outside of the virtual arena.

These examples illustrate morally neutral ways in which someone may be affected by differences in the components of their self across spaces. But, to reiterate, the issue is not whether one is affected by these differences, but how one copes with them. How does one integrate this loss within one's continuity of self? Does one compartmentalize different selves such that some form of discontinuity or 'double life' is created? After all, one cannot be at the same time one's virtual and non-virtual embodiment. Might there occur, then, a separation of selves, which coincides with the dichotomy of corporeal and virtual? Alternatively, perhaps one seeks some form of reconciliation or integration such that one does not lead a 'double life' (as it were) but, rather, extends one's self into each respective space by virtue of each respective form of embodiment (corporeal and virtual), thereby maintaining parity of *selfhood*. Either way, what are the psychological implications of each possibility? This is something we will begin to consider below and continue to examine in the following chapter.

To summarize the argument so far, the process of striving to maintain psychological parity underlies the virtuousness of which Sicart (2009) and even McCormick (2001) speak. To illustrate, suppose that within a given gamespace I, *qua* player-subject, am a brutal torturer, rapist and murderer. Offline, I am none of these things. Yet, knowing that *these* acts of torture, rape and murder are only meaningful within the gameplay, as Sicart would have it, and therefore a product of the game system (something that does not carry the same meaning offline), does not eliminate the sense of loss of moral freedom I experience when leaving the gamespace. When transcending spaces, being virtuous does not negate the sense of loss or the general discrepancy I encounter between both my self-as-object and phenomenal self as they occur online compared to offline. This is something that is present irrespective of the morality of the activity engaged in; it underlies both morally charged and morally neutral activities, although it may be particularly pronounced when engaging in STAs because of the fact that they are *taboo* activities offline, perhaps even accompanied by a sense of disgust.

PROBLEMATIC INTERNET USE

The potential for disparity between those aspects of oneself presented online compared to offline is implicated within a more general cognitive-behavioural model of *problematic Internet use* (PIU) proposed by Davis (2001).[2] According to Davis (2001, p. 191), psychosocial problems (such as depression or loneliness) may make an individual vulnerable to certain maladaptive thoughts about the self – such as 'I am only good on the Internet' or 'I am worthless offline, but online I am someone' or even 'I am a failure when I am offline' (see also Montag *et al.*, 2010, for a discussion on 'self-directedness' as a predictor of PIU). The resulting need for the kind of 'social contact and reinforcement obtained online results in an increased desire to remain in a virtual social life' (Davis, 2001, p. 188). Such maladaptive, Internet-biased, thoughts and behaviours are deemed by Davis to be a necessary, proximate cause of PIU.

By way of an amendment to Davis's model, Caplan (2003, 2005) proposed that the likelihood of PIU was further mediated by *a preference for online socializing*. As Caplan (2003, p. 629) explains:

[P]reference for online social interaction is a cognitive individual-difference construct characterized by beliefs that one is safer, more efficacious, more confident, and more comfortable with online interpersonal interactions and relationships than with traditional FtF [face-to-face] social activities.

For Caplan, then, it is not just that those vulnerable to PIU hold more positive views of themselves when interacting in an online environment, or that they enjoy being in that environment because of its perceived personal and social benefits; more than this, they *prefer* interacting online. In other words, the individual's desire to be online, as noted by Davis, quickly turns into a preference to be online, which comes at a cost of relegating their offline social engagements to a lower level of personal importance – in some cases, perhaps even discarding them altogether.

Caplan *et al.* (2009) note how relatively little attention has been given to MMORPGs in relation to PIU (some exceptions being Meerkerk *et al.*, 2006; Morahan-Martin and Schumacher, 2000; Ng and Wiemer-Hastings, 2005). Yet these games are of relevance to the study of PIU not only because they are an increasingly popular form of Internet activity but, equally (perhaps even because of this), they promote interpersonal engagement and potentially complex forms of social interaction, which are an established and even sought-after feature of the gaming experience. According to Liu and Peng (2009), PIU produces *negative life consequences*. Based on prior research on MMORPGs (see Charlton and Danforth, 2007; Chen *et al.*, 2003; Suhail and Bargees, 2006; Young, 2004), these negative life consequences have been categorized into the following three types:

- *physical problems* (such as fatigue, physical pain, reduced sleep and missing meals);
- *personal life problems* (such as conflicts with friends or family, generally low social engagement and decreased time management skills);
- *professional/academic problems* (such as missing work or school and a deterioration in one's performance) (adapted from Liu and Peng, 2009, p. 1306).

Liu and Peng also integrated Davis's 'maladaptive cognitions' and Caplan's 'preference for online socializing' within their own hypothesized construct, which they call *preference for virtual life* (PVL), defined as: 'one's cognitions or beliefs that one will perform better, feel better about oneself, and perceive [oneself] to be better treated by others in the online virtual game world than in offline or real life' (2009, p. 1307).

Liu and Peng found that those scoring high(er) on PVL were more likely to experience psychological dependency on MMORPG playing. Caplan *et al.* (2009) likewise found strong predictive associations between PIU and online social behaviour. This, Caplan anticipated, was owed to MMORPGs' high degree of social engagement. Stetina *et al.* (2011) found that MMORPG users showed more problematic gaming behaviour, symptoms of depression and lower levels of self-esteem than gamers who played online shooter games or real-time strategy games.[3] In fact, Ng and Wiemer-Hastings (2005) argued that it is the increased social element associated with *online* multiplayer games that attracts the more 'hard core' player, such that players of these games are more likely to develop symptoms characteristic of negative life consequences (noted above) than offline players.

In a longitudinal study, Lemmens *et al.* (2011) found that social competence, self-esteem and loneliness were significant predictors of pathological gaming (even six months after the initial trial began), but that loneliness was also a *consequence* of the pathology. They surmised that '[a]lthough playing online games may temporarily reduce negative feelings associated with social deficiencies, pathological gaming does little to facilitate the development or maintenance of real-life contacts' (p. 150). Thus, even if pathological gaming requires an antecedent detriment in one's psychosocial competence, an unfortunate consequence of the pathology is likely to be the further deterioration, if not complete abandonment, of one's offline relationships; what Putnam (2000) referred to as *social capital*.

Despite the above research providing some insight into the potential negative impact and moral ramifications of prolonged engagement in certain types of VE for certain types of people, to date, and by comparison, research looking specifically at the experiences of gamers who engage in or witness STAs is somewhat scarce. This means that we are in the unfortunate position of only being able to speculate, based on what we do know, on what the effects of STAs might be and how this is underscored by the need to maintain psychological parity. Nevertheless, in the next chapter, we consider further the significance of gamer identification with the avatar on how individuals interpret virtual content and interactions, and present informed speculation (based partly on the limited reported experiences of gamers engaged in STAs) on the role played by psychological parity, as well as the types of coping strategies employed by gamers: the latter lending some weight to the principle of sanctioned equivalence and other means of moral management.

15 Identity and interpretation
Repercussion for parity and potential harm

In this chapter we are interested in the role that identity plays in how one might *interpret* media content, and the significance of embodied identity to the interactive nature of video game violence and other STAs. We also discuss in detail the findings of a study that looked at how gamers experience or believe they would experience STAs.

A QUESTION OF IDENTIFICATION

If, as Sicart (2009) maintains, the player-subject is created at the point of first playing the game, then typically one's embodied form is represented by one's avatar (potentially, one's supermorphic persona). Now, depending on the game mechanics, this avatar may be more developed, more entrenched within the pre-determined narrative, in some games than others; or, conversely, it may not be part of conventional gameplay at all (instead, being part of a sandbox environment like *Second Life*, for example). The degree to which one is free to express oneself within the gamespace will therefore always be, to a greater or lesser extent, constrained by the game mechanics: this is no more evident than in terms of how much one can 'customize' one's avatar, or the choices and types of engagement available. Arguably, the most restrictive game mechanics are to be found in single-player games, although such games may still offer considerable scope (e.g. *Heavy Rain*), and so are likely to include 'events' that may impact on one's psychological parity, particularly when played in their most extreme and violent form.

In Chapter 6, we discussed how genuine emotions can be elicited from acts of fiction. Traditionally, this has taken the form of books and plays and, more recently, films and television. With each of these mediums, the relationship between audience and characters/events has been understood to be largely passive and *dyadic* – in so far as 'viewers or media users perceive a social distinction between themselves (the observers) and the media characters' (Klimmt *et al.*, 2009, p. 352). With the advent of video game technology, not only has the relationship between audience (or gamer) and media become more (inter)active but the distinction between gamer and character (protagonist) reduced, perhaps even eliminated. Consequently, comprehending the character's goals should be easier to manage when the character's goals are the gamer's goals. In the words of Klimmt *et al.* (2009, p. 354; emphasis in original):

> Instead of providing opportunities to follow autonomous characters' actions, playing video games simulates the circumstances of *being* a media character (or holding a social role), for instance, of being a war hero or a police officer. Video games thus seem to facilitate a nondyadic or *monadic* user–character relationship in the sense that players do not perceive the game (main) character as a social entity distinct from themselves, but experience a merging of their own self and the game protagonist. This understanding of a monadic user–character relationship converges with the concept of *identification*.

Identification is expressed by Klimmt *et al.* as a set of increased associations between the gamer's self-concept and certain selective concepts, which contingently characterize the online protagonist (e.g. courage, agility, honour, charisma, social status and physical and sexual prowess). In addition, identification is typically defined as a *temporary* state of emotional and cognitive connection with the character (Oatley, 1999a). As Klimmt *et al.* (2009, p. 356) explain:

> For most people, their image of themselves under the condition of identification with James Bond [for example] would differ substantially from their usual self-image. After game exposure, internal processes (e.g., cognitions about the working day) and external cues (e.g., friends addressing the media user by his/her real name instead of saying '007') will quickly realter the situational self-concept toward the original configuration.

Typically, one's self-image (self-as-object and phenomenal self) differs substantially from the protagonist featured in video games, especially violent ones; and, typically, on exiting the game, one's original self-image is restored and is no longer aligned with, say, '007'. Nevertheless, it is our view that for those whose identity merges strongly with their gameworld character, the restoration of their original self-image, which includes their self-as-object and phenomenal self (what Klimmt *et al.* seem to allude to by virtue of a 'situational self-concept'), makes salient to them the very discrepancies that mark out the protagonist from themselves. As noted earlier, discrepancies that exist between one's self offline and one's self *qua* online character, especially in relation to those characteristics that may be valued – strength, honour, courage etc. – are made salient as a *loss*: one experiences a loss of strength, a loss of honour, a loss of courage, etc.

If this discrepancy is salient when leaving the gaming environment of single-player games, where often one is the sole gamer, and therefore socially isolated, then how much more, we contend, is there scope for a salient discrepancy between one's online and offline self when engaged in social games constitutive of MMORPGs. Liu and Peng (2009, p. 1307) offer commentary to that effect:

[B]y identifying with game characters who can achieve various unusual goals in MMOGs [massively multiplayer online games], gamers may regard themselves as more valuable and successful people in the game world than in the offline real world, and this may lead to unpleasant feelings or withdrawal symptoms when MMOG playing is suddenly unavailable.

Hsu *et al.* (2009) reported that MMORPG addiction is associated with the player's motivation to develop their character (in order to progress within the game). If I identify strongly with my avatar then the avatar's progression and increased status become my progression and increased status (unless my aim is *solely* to win the game; in which case, avatar progression and status may be viewed as instrumental to that goal and nothing more). Hsu *et al.* also found MMORPG addiction to be associated with emotional attachment to one's avatar and, on a more communal level, to a strong sense of belonging and obligation to the virtual group.

The gamer, in identifying with the gaming avatar, recognizes or accepts aspects of the avatar's features as representative of their own self-as-object, including aspects of the self-concept. This is particularly so when game mechanics allow for the *extensive customization* of one's default avatar: for, as Boellstorff (2008, p. 129) notes (in the context of *Second Life*), very little is left to chance or randomization; instead, one can assume 'near-total intentionality with regard to virtual embodiment'. Boellstorff further states that such intentional (sometimes time-consuming) customization makes one's (supermorphic) self-as-object transparent to others; for as a participant in his research commented: 'I've come to observe that the outward appearance really does communicate a lot about who you are, because it is made up of conscious choices about how you want to present yourself' (p. 130). By way of a caveat, however, it may also be the case that the avatar is understood simply as an object one controls within the particular space – instrumental to one's being there, as it were. So, whilst there may exist valid cases of, for example, online gender swapping occurring so that players can explore different genders (Hussain and Griffiths, 2008), we must also accept that, for some, this may not be the case.[1] As Huh and Williams (2010, p. 170) note: 'many male players have quipped that they play a female avatar because it is a pleasing visual object, not a source of identification'. Whilst accepting the validity of this last point, we nevertheless seek to pursue further the significance of identification with the avatar to how one interprets the virtual content.

THE ROLE OF IDENTITY IN INTERPRETATION

According to Liebes and Katz (1990), dyadic identification operates on three levels, each, it would seem, further blurring the distinction between self and other. One may simply *like* the fictional character, finding certain characteristics appealing, one may see oneself as *being like* (similar to) the character or one may desire *to be like* (to model oneself on) the person from fiction. According to Cohen (2001), these varying levels of identification manifest perhaps the extent to which one is willing to replace one's own perspective with another's, and in the process forget, however temporarily, oneself. Hoffner and Buchanan (2005; following the work of von Feilitzen and Linne, 1975; and Hoffner, 1996) refer to this as *wishful identification*, which they define as 'the desire to become like a media character' (p. 327). As an expression of wishful identification, Hoffner and Buchanan describe how the viewer may alter their appearance to more closely match the fictional other, as well as adopt his/her attitudes and values (see also, Caughey, 1986; Leckenby, 1978; Schreiber, 1979). Moreover, for Oatley (1994), an important antecedent for identification is that the individual understands the intentions of the character – his/her goals within the context of the unfolding drama – and can experience something of what the character feels when these goals/intentions succeed or are quashed. Cohen (2001) thought this type of identification constitutive of a more proximate mode of reception – and antecedent to the effects of media – whereby the psychological distance between self and other is reduced.

An important distinction between wishful identification as it occurs in relation to media characters (such as those in television dramas, for example) and MMORPG avatars is that, in the latter case, one does not have to, nor does one tend to, lose one's original identity in order to assume the identity of *another* (it may be, of course, that one does not assume the identity of the character at all when playing the game – see below). That said, the term 'wishful identification' may still serve a useful function here. The desire to act and look a certain way does not require us to take on the identity of another at the expense of our own. Instead, and as we discussed in Chapters 11 and 12, it may be that a given virtual space affords the opportunity for us to try out or even bring forth certain characteristics in an attempt to express a desired way of being *ourselves*, not somebody else; or at least explore this possibility. As Turkle (1995, p. 192) noted in the early days of multi-user domains, 'people don't just become who they play, they play who they are or who they want to be or who they don't want to be'. And, again, as discussed in Chapters 11 and 12, such exploration has potential benefits. In accordance with this view, Simkins and Steinkuehler (2008, p. 352) have this to say:

> It may very well be that playing through such roles, including those we would never consider taking up in the real world, has the potential not only to foster greater empathy, tolerance, and understanding for others but [also] to help us critically reflect on who we want to be for others and how we have both power and responsibility in all of the roles we inhabit in our lives.

In Chapter 12 we presented the exploration of one's embodied self within virtual space as an expression of one's supermorphic persona, and also claimed that whether the supermorphic persona is able to transcend spaces will have repercussions for one's psychological parity and whether one experiences psychological harm. In addition, in Chapter 7, we discussed the issue of play and cyberspace as a virtual playground, and how play occurs in a separate space, but not *too* separate. The necessary sense of connectedness of the potential space of play to oneself outside of this space, we would argue, has clear implications for the issue of

Exposure factors ──────────→ Mediating factors ──────────→ Evidence of effect

Figure 15.1 A simple model indicating the role of exposure and mediating factors in accounting for the effects of media violence.

Source: Taken from Potter and Tomasello (2003, p. 315).

psychological parity, as well as how one *interprets* a given interaction within a given space.

With this in mind, let us consider the link between interpretation of game content and identity. According to Potter and Tomasello (2003), research into the effects of viewing more traditional media violence (television/films) has tended to concentrate on exposure factors such as whether the perpetrator of the violence was rewarded or punished (Bryant *et al.*, 1981), or whether the violent act was depicted realistically (Cantor, 1994), graphically (Ogles and Hoffner, 1987) or even in a humorous way (Gunter, 1985). In addition, mediating factors have concerned gender and age differences (Eron *et al.*, 1972), other demographics such as social class (Huesmann *et al.*, 1984) and ethnicity (Greenberg, 1988), traits such as aggression (Lagerspetz and Engblom, 1979) and frustration (Geen, 1975) and states of arousal (Zillmann, 1971). Such research, Potter and Tomasello (2003) assert, typically adheres to the model presented in Figure 15.1.

Absent from Figure 15.1, Potter and Tomasello point out, is how the viewer *interprets* the violence, which may account for the variation found within the same experimental condition – that is, differences found between participants with similar mediating factors who are assigned to the same task and therefore exposed to the same act of violence presented in the same way. Williams *et al.* (2008) similarly criticize the General Aggression Model (GAM) and GAM-based research (see Chapter 13) because, in their view, it does not distinguish between those who seek to be competitive within a game, for example, and achieve personal success, and those who might be playing in order to socialize with a friend. Similarly, Shibuya *et al.* (2008, p. 537), after conducting a longitudinal study (involving 10- to 11-year-old children in Japan), concluded that 'quality and context of video game violence can be more important than the presence and quantity of violence in the long term'. They also recognized that how these children interpreted the violent content had not been fully investigated in their study. In fact, the switch in emphasis from the effects of video content on the individual to how the individual extracts from it meaning within a given context is, according to Williams (2005), symptomatic of differences between more traditional social scientists who adopt a quantitative approach and humanists who endorse a more qualitative methodology.

To be clear, Potter and Tomasello (2003) are not claiming that exposure/mediating factors have no part to play in the effect that viewing violence has on the individual; rather, they argue that it is our interpretation of the act, which may be shaped by the aforementioned factors in terms of meaning and personal significance, that ultimately determines how we react to what we are witnessing. As they explain (p. 316; emphasis added):

Whereas demographics, traits, and states all potentially influence how a person interprets the *meaning* of elements in a media portrayal, it is the set of receiver interpretations that most likely influences the probability of an *effect*. Therefore, if we want to explain better the differences in effects, we need to improve our understanding about the interpretive elements that influence participants' reactions to the treatment materials.

Potter and Tomasello discuss the explanatory significance of 'receiver interpretations' within the context of film and television; yet we see no reason why this additional factor cannot be incorporated within theories and models looking at the effects of video game violence. In Chapter 14, we discussed Sicart's (2009) morally mature player-subject and the work of Klimmt *et al.* on moral management. For Sicart, the morally mature player-subject is one who understands that the meaning of game violence is meaningful only within the context of that game. Likewise, Klimmt *et al.* identified a number of strategies used by gamers to manage the freedom they have within games to engage in activities (including STAs) that are morally proscribed offline. Part of the maturity Sicart requires of his player-subject, it would seem, is the ability to *interpret* the violence within the game as context dependent, and consequently not to imbue it with meaning beyond this. So too might a gamer, adopting a strategy of moral management, *interpret* the violence as instrumental to their success at the game, and no more than this, or as having no real-world consequences. Alternatively, the personal meaning the STA is imbued with may be such as to prevent one from either taking part in the specific activity (e.g. torture or rape) or continuing with the gameplay at all (recall Power's (2003) *socially significant expression*).

How one interprets and interacts with such content has led Juul (2005) to think of video games as '*half-real*': for the way we interact with the game provides some indication of our relation to the game 'in reality'. (This is akin to the notion raised in Chapter 7 of 'potential space' – somewhere between reality and fantasy.) In such cases, the separation of spaces and, with it, the fiction–reality divide may be blurred. As we have already noted, some players may consider the video game to be just that – a game – and separate more or less completely the online action and representation from offline reality, even in cases of extreme violence and other STAs. However, for some, the half-reality noted by Juul (or the 'potential space' of play) may mean that the space does provide a means of exploring one's self – how one thinks, feels and wishes to behave in various contexts; and as we saw in Chapter 12, it may even be a space where one can develop one's supermorphic persona and, if authentic, successfully transfer it (those aspects of selfhood) to the offline world.

Of course, a difference between traditional media violence and video game violence (as has been noted many times already) is the level of interaction available to the gamer compared to the viewer of television or film. Hamlen (2011), for example, found that a large (unspecified) percentage of children in her study were motivated to play certain video games because they get to 'punch and kill people' (p. 537). Hamlen asks us to consider why this is so appealing for some children (a large percentage, apparently), and, based on sales figures, adults as well (it would seem). Of course, it would be a bold claim to say that it is because such gamers (young or old) actually wish to punch and kill people offline. Nevertheless, it is an important question because the personal meaning integral to the interpretation of the violence, as noted by Potter and Tomasello (2003), is likely to be the personal meaning given to a violent act, or other STA, that *I* am engaged in through my avatar (*qua* player-subject). Thus, the interpretation of the act will be influenced by the identity of my character within the game – this is what a soldier, a dragon-slayer or a serial killer is supposed to do in this situation or even this game (or not, as the case may be). Or this is what even an ordinary citizen can be driven to do when protecting their family.

Krcmar *et al.* (2011) found that strength of identification with the character correlated with level of aggression shown whilst playing the video game *Doom 3*. Similarly, Eastin (2006) found that aggression in females increased when identifying with a female character in the first-person shooter game *Unreal Tournament: Game of the Year Edition*. Hefner *et al.* (2007), for their part, argued that identification with the character is 'an essential element of game enjoyment' (p. 40), describing identification 'as "feeling like" or as creating the illusion to "become" a key person within a computer game's universe' (pp. 39–40) – a statement compatible with the idea of supermorphic identification posited in Chapter 12, we contend.

According to Pohl (2008), although emotional involvement is a characteristic of video games, we must differentiate between two types. One, she tells us:

> [I]s instantaneous and spontaneous: We play a game, because we want to win a game. . . . [But we are also] concerned about the avatar's fate, not only because the avatar is our representative in the fictional world and the instrument we need in order to actually play and win the game, but because we feel for him, we identify with his concerns and want to know how the story turns out for him and for us.
>
> (pp. 100–101)

Thus, with monadic identification, when we feel for him, we feel ourselves. Hefner *et al.* (2007) further state that part of the enjoyment experienced through identification is when one finds certain attributes or characteristics of the fictional character appealing – perhaps because they match attributes and characteristics one wishes to possess or at least try out. In the former case, by identifying with the object of fiction, even temporarily, one reduces the discrepancy between how one typically perceives oneself and how one wishes to be perceived; and according to Hefner *et al.*, this discrepancy reduction creates an enjoyable experience.

THE SIGNIFICANCE OF IDENTITY TO INTERPRETATION

In order to foster monadic identification, the fictional character must possess a degree of attractiveness and personal desirability, including what he/she does or what the game mechanics afford the character (oneself, in effect). We are reminded of Turkle's (1995) comment (above): when one plays, one may play who one wants to be or even who one does not want to be. It may be, then, that by way of exploration, I am attracted to the character and narrative of a particular game, even in cases of STAs, or precisely because the game involves STAs. I may find a certain appeal in being the architect of my own disgust (see Chapter 8). Conversely, identity-based interpretation may cause me to question whether it is what any of these characters *should* do (and therefore what *I* should do in this context). Depending, then, on the situation I find myself in, the narrative, and whether the principle of sanctioned equivalence is being adhered to (for example), normative consideration may increase my enjoyment of the game – this is precisely how a highly skilled special operative would engage the 'enemy' and even inter-rogate them – or it may *decrease* it: after all, I may not like the idea of having to torture, even 'in character'. This last point illustrates the heightened complexity of identification with a video game character – namely, the extent to which I identify not only with the character but also with the *activity* I am undertaking or being asked to undertake.

To illustrate the significance of this, consider a study by Bösche (2009), who recruited participants inexperienced at playing violent video games to test two 'paradigmatically opposite perspectives' (p. 145) on the effects of such games on performance (habitual players were not selected, nor anyone who had played within a week of the study). Bösche was interested in whether playing a violent video game would, because of one's normal aversive reaction to even virtual violence, inhibit task performance compared to an equivalent task in a non-violent game (one perspective), or whether the virtual violence would be perceived as harmless, fun and exciting, thereby enhancing performance compared to the non-virtual equivalent (alternative perspective). What he found was that performance was enhanced in the 'extremely violent' condition (compared to non-violent or moderately violent conditions). From this, he tentatively concluded that violent video games 'are perceived as an essentially harmless acting-out of playful fighting behaviour' (p. 149).

The idea that virtual violence is essentially mock violence, what Bösche refers to as a kind of digitized *rough-and-tumble play*, seems to accord well with reports on the attitude of a number of players of such games, some of which we have already discussed (and certainly seems compatible with the discussion in Chapter 7 on play). We have seen how Klimmt *et al.* (2006) identified the view held by some gamers that violence is 'just part of the game' or 'necessary for successful performance' as a strategy of moral management. It may therefore be the case that, in certain violent games, the violence *is* typically perceived to be a kind of digitized rough-and-tumble play, easily distinguished from real violence.

The 'extreme violence' depicted by Bösche in his study was of a cartoon rabbit being hit over the head with a hammer (see Figure 15.2). Contact with the head produced sounds of pain and the head was dismembered. Such an act, or similar, could easily feature in violent video games. However, it also seems quite simplistic compared to the sorts of violence depicted in many modern video games: compare

Figure 15.2 Target objects and gadgets used in Bösche's three conditions.

Note: Each image was displayed in colour against a green background. From left to right, the three conditions are: non-violent, moderately violent and extremely violent game visuals. In addition, the upper row illustrates the state of the rabbit before the violence occurs; the bottom row illustrates a successful outcome.

Source: Adapted from Bösche (2009, p. 147). Used by permission from *Journal of Media Psychology*, *21* (4), 145–150 © 2009 Hogrefe Publishing.

the fate of Bösche's rabbit to victims in *Manhunt* (for example) who may be 'dispatched' by being bludgeoned to death with a baton, baseball bat or hammer, or stabbed through the neck with a crowbar or more conventionally with a hunting knife. Missing from Bösche's example, we contend, is both narrative and a virtual agent to carry out the violence.

In Bösche's study, the participant simply activated the virtual hammer; there was no avatar in place to wield it. These differences are important, we maintain, because they increase (potentially facilitate) the possibility for gamer identification with the character. To illustrate, consider the description by Crick (2011, p. 250):

> [W]hen playing in first-person mode . . ., the player might notice a shadow that follows the avatar's movements, and they will also see the avatar's reflection when looking through a mirror. Such details . . . reinforce the player's sense of being inside the game world and not merely acting on it.

As we have stated throughout, it is not so much what the game content is doing to us but what we are doing to ourselves through the process of striving for psychological parity that is of concern (or should be). An important factor that contributes to the issue of psychological parity is identification. For some gamers, this identification may be minimal; its purpose being to function purely as a point of agency within the space – what Newman (2002) refers to as *vehicular embodiment*. Similarly, Fuller and Jenkins (1995, p. 61) describe avatars as offering 'traits that are largely capacities for action, fighting skills, modes of transportation, preestablished goals . . . [in effect,] little more than a cursor which mediates the player's relationship to the story' (cited in Crick, 2011, p. 250). On the other hand, and as Crick points out, 'the stylized designs of iconic avatars, such as Lara Croft in the third-person game Tomb Raider or player-customized designs . . . may play an important role in helping the player to identify with the avatar, heightening their affective response to the game' (p. 250).

Wissmath *et al.* (2009), by drawing on the work of Green and Brock (2000; see also Gerrig, 1993), refer to this transition as *transportation* – a term used to describe how the media user is drawn away from their own physical location into the narrative of the fictional (or virtual) world. Transportation theory, they maintain, promotes the idea that the reader/viewer/gamer 'plunges in the world of a narrative by suspending real-world facts' (p. 117). Moreover, an important antecedent to experiencing transportation, they suggest, is identification with characters immersed within the narrative. Cohen (2001), however, offers a caveat to this heightened enjoyment through identification – namely, that it may reduce one's ability to adopt a critical stance towards (in this context) what is being represented and what one is doing within the gamespace. However, in response, we would argue that whatever critical stance (or lack thereof) is adopted, one must understand it not only within the context of the game, but also in relation to how the gamer interprets the representation and action.

In a somewhat bizarre twist on the notion of transportation or immersion, Wilson and Sicart (2010) discuss 'abusive games', which, in the context of a Scandinavian style of role-play known as *Jeepform*, are designed to elicit 'bleed' – that is, the blurring of the border between character and player. To illustrate, Wilson and Sicart describe the multiplayer game *Fat Man Down*. In *Fat Man Down*, the largest (*qua* fattest) male player from the group has to play Fat Man. The function of the other players is to torment Fat Man by ridiculing him about his weight. Often, we are told, the level of abuse the other players have to inflict is too much for them to bear, and hence 'bleed' is achieved – the border between the game characters and those playing the game has been blurred, to the point where gamers wish to stop and retreat from the gamespace. Similarly, Wilson and Sicart discuss *Dark Room Sex Game*, played using wii motes. The game was designed, again we are told, to elicit embarrassment and awkwardness by playing on social taboos surrounding intimacy and sexuality. In both these cases, aspects of the gamer's offline attitude or 'baggage' are carried over into the gamespace, creating discomfort, which is the deliberate intent of the *Jeepform* creators because of the incongruence (for some, perhaps many) of what is occurring or required within the gamespace with social norms.

Returning to the Bösche study, it is interesting to note that habitual players were not included. This could be for a number of methodological reasons, of course. However, it is worth considering the fact that as the participants were not regular gamers they would not have had the opportunity to identify (even potentially) with characters (had there been any), or become accustomed to the association. In addition, Bösche focused on what might be described as more conventional video game violence. Might he consider STAs such as rape, paedophilia (etc.) to be examples of digitalized rough-and-tumble play?

WHAT DO GAMERS EXPERIENCE WHEN
ENGAGED IN STAs?

In order to examine how gamers experience or anticipate that they might experience less typical STAs such as rape, Whitty *et al.* (2011) interviewed five hard-core gamers: players of either *World of Warcraft* (WoW) or *Sociolotron*. They were interested in the perceived psychological impact on these gamers of actually or hypothetically engaging in or witnessing STAs within MMORPGs. The use of semi-structured interviews allowed the gamers to reflect on not only how they experienced playing the game, but also how interacting within the game and the nature of this interaction impacted on their experience of themselves and their everyday lives. Owing to the current paucity of this type of research (see Hartmann *et al.*, 2010, for a recent exception), we will discuss their findings in detail.

Whitty *et al.* found that not everyone experienced playing MMORPGs in the same way. Some participants' experiences were more positive than others and, importantly, there was no clear agreement on which aspects of the game individuals could, or believed they would be able to, cope with regarding the enactment of STAs. Some of the participants interviewed felt that they could easily separate gamespace from the real world, and that playing the game provided them with some escape from ordinary life. They discussed how liberating this felt for them. This is in line with previous work, which has argued that virtual worlds can be liberating for individuals (Whitty and Carr, 2006a). Other forms of moral management consisted in participants reporting that they believed that the unrealistic look of the game (with respect to graphics, in the case of *Sociolotron*, and the characters and virtual world of WoW) assisted them in separating the two spaces. This might be important for game designers to consider, especially given that games are beginning to appear more life-like and gaming narratives are increasingly based on real-world events (e.g. *Call of Duty, Modern Warfare 2*). A possible link between aggression and more realistic representations of real-world violence was suggested by Bensley and van Eenwyk (2001); however, Ivory and Kalyanaraman (2007) found that although technological advancement within video games was linked with an increased sense of presence, this did not increase hostile thoughts or aggression, even when games were more graphic in their portrayal of realistic violence. In keeping with these findings, a few of Whitty *et al.*'s participants did believe that they would be able to separate the game from the real world even if the graphics were improved. In fact, Steuer (1992) found that technological advancement creates increased vividness and a greater potential for involvement (Lombard and Diton, 1997; Witmer and Singer, 1998), and that these factors contribute to a greater sense of presence, but not, importantly, aggression. Interestingly, through the advent of increasingly sophisticated technology – the use of digital photographs and face modelling software – it is possible to create a virtual doppelgänger, which can 'be designed to look strikingly similar to the self' (Bailenson and Segovia, 2010, p. 176). In the case of such a striking virtual doppelgänger, perhaps the separation of self from other, particularly in the case of STAs, would become increasingly difficult.

Irrespective of the virtual doppelgänger, some theorists are unconvinced by the idea that individuals can easily separate VR and the real world (Turkle, 1995; Whitty, 2003a; Whitty and Carr, 2006a). They have insisted that individuals still import part of themselves into this space. Moreover, they believe that engaging in play in these spaces provokes real emotional responses. In Whitty *et al.*'s (2011) study, participants reported an array of positive and negative emotions. Of particular interest are the emotions of shame and anger. Two of the participants reported feeling anger at the thought of witnessing rape in the game, despite also talking about MMORPGs as just games, which they believed they could easily separate from real life. Another participant felt shame at the thought of family members learning about her playing *Sociolotron*: much the same, perhaps, as someone might feel about being caught viewing pornography (Linton, 1979).

In addition to the emotions reported by the participants, Whitty *et al.* found that even those who felt they could separate the real world and gamespace noted some important exceptions to this rule. One participant, for example, initially said he would engage in any STA within the game, because it is just a game; however, later he discussed how his gameplay is constrained because (in the context of WoW) it is quite possible that he is playing with and even against children. Another participant discussed in detail how easily he could separate gamespace and the real world, but when asked to consider enacting rape within the game he claimed he could not envisage doing this because it would feel too real to him. In fact, he said the very idea of it was abhorrent – recall the similar reaction of participants asked to comment on a hypothetical act of brother–sister incest in Chapter 3.

Recall also, from Chapter 6, how, for Kreitman (2006), emotional responses to fiction are only able to occur, and are therefore only able to bridge the gulf, between fictional and real worlds if the novel characteristics and constructs applied to works of fiction are derived from actual experience. Fiction presents us with an 'unreal entity with real characteristics' (p. 616). The commitment we demand of fictional objects is not, therefore, existential (we do not require that they actual exist); rather, we seek authenticity. Real-world authenticity is measured by the number of *attributes* of a certain kind possessed by the object of fiction. Consequently, as previously discussed, for Powers (2003), what the gamer is communicating, even through the *virtual* nature of their action, is socially significant expression, which in the absence of sanctioned equivalence (for example) may appear gratuitous.

The principle of sanctioned equivalence therefore provides some explanation for why certain aspects of the game were easier to separate from the real world and real emotions, and why, where there was no clear real-world sanctioned equivalence, participants were more likely to have difficulty accepting activities within the game. This was especially the case for rape. Yet, within *Sociolotron*, those opposed to rape nevertheless accepted its *permissibility* within the gameplay. One participant talked about how she initially coped well with rape in the game, but then went on to state that it is something she now finds difficult to handle, and watching it makes her angry. Yet she still believes that, in principle, it should exist, and despite her change in feeling – somewhat curiously, perhaps

– does not think any less of those who engage in rape within the game. Irrespective of personal opposition and unwillingness to engage in certain STAs, then, the players of *Sociolotron* who were interviewed nevertheless accepted that such activity is a legitimate part of the game (recall discussion on this point in Chapter 9, mainly within the context of torture in WoW). Such reluctance to take part was not the case for all participants, however. One individual expressed great conviction about rape being something he felt very comfortable role-playing, and that it did not affect him outside of the game.

Within the Whitty *et al.* study, reference to the extent to which a gamer identifies with their character might also shed some light on the extent to which that individual can cope with engaging in STAs. One participant was adamant about his ability to separate real-world moral codes from the game as well as being *nothing like* his game character. Notably, he engaged in more STAs than any of the other participants (this included activities that had no sanctioned equivalence). In contrast, another participant stated that he separated his real self from his gaming character and that it was important, psychologically, to do so. Nevertheless, Whitty *et al.* noted, he still felt anger at the thought of engaging in symbolic rape in the game; and so separation between one's gaming character and offline self is possibly not enough.

With regard to transcendent qualities of the self, Whitty *et al.* found that one of their participants learned something new about herself from engaging in certain sexual activities within *Sociolotron* – something she transferred to the real world. She discovered that she is bisexual. This participant described her new-found identity in a positive way; it was something she wanted to share when being interviewed. Previously, it has been argued that cyberspace is potentially a safe space to learn about and experience sexuality (Whitty, 2003a, 2008a). Perhaps engaging in this type of sexual play within *Sociolotron* afforded this gamer other *ways of being* that are typically shunned in the real world. Whilst one cannot rule out that some of the behaviours learned in this way could be negative (e.g. aggression), Whitty *et al.* nevertheless found that perceived positive aspects about oneself can be learned in MMORPGs and transferred into the real world.

To summarize, Whitty *et al.* found that not all individuals' experiences of STAs or even more conventional gameplay were the same. It seems, then, that future researchers should consider individual differences. Understanding how individuals experience STAs would provide important information for game designers and those bodies responsible for rating and censoring games. Moreover, it is important for psychologists to learn more about how individuals transfer their experience in MMORPGs to the offline world and whether they can cope psychologically with engaging in certain activities in these environments

THE PARITY ISSUE

Research into STAs is still in its infancy. The aim of this book is to provide a conceptual framework for future study. Psychological parity is an important mechanism, we contend. In the absence of detailed evidence (at this stage, at least), we are left to fall back on related findings or more anecdotal evidence as a means of justifying further research in this area. In support of the role of psychological parity, consider Meadows' (2008) anecdote concerning his own experience of VR engagement and transcending worlds. According to Meadows (p. 95), many hard-core users of *Second Life*[2] (the twenty million plus who spend more than nine hours a day as their character) have 'gone native' and 'crossed an important line'. As a former 'native', Meadows comments on how at one time he experienced a certain shift in his own 'psychology'. As he recalls (p. 95):

> Not only would I walk around seeing things in the world that reminded me of Second Life, I caught myself thinking at times that I could affect objects in the same way that I was able to affect objects as my avatar . . . when I was away from the machine, I felt as though I had undergone a kind of terminal amputation. With this ability to dislocate functions of my body, with the mediation of my senses, and with this new prosthetic that allowed me to move to another place, I had stepped across a mysterious and fateful line.

Meadows' description reveals two important points. The first is his salient experience of the loss of embodied prowess when removed from the VE – he felt as though he had undergone a certain 'terminal amputation'. Second is the interrelatedness of both components of his body-image. He started to think about how he could affect states of the offline world in the same way as his avatar (or supermorphic persona) affects states of the virtual world. The way he begins to conceive of himself – his self-as-object – is (a) congruent with his experience of embodiment in *Second Life* and (b) beginning to transcend domains. But as we argued in Chapter 12, even if we permit the *Second Life* avatar a degree of context authenticity, in terms of both self-as-object and phenomenal self, if one's supermorphia is based on computer-mediated enhancement then the authenticity cannot transcend domains. The psychological risk lies in the tendency, for some users, to seek parity across these domains and, importantly, between what are incommensurable body-images, leading to PIU.

The problem for Meadows, of course, is precisely that his self as *experienced* in *Second Life* could not transcend domains because he could not exact the same sorts of actions offline as he could online, hence the salient *loss* of prowess. What was affecting Meadows was his need to close the discrepancy gap evident whenever he moved back across that 'fateful line'. During certain moments, he caught himself identifying with his avatar whilst offline – seeking psychological parity and a unified identity across the divide, we contend. A critical aspect of any prolonged engagement within a virtual world in which one's persona is somehow altered should therefore centre on the individual's need to maintain psychological parity. Large discrepancies between the offline body-image and one's supermorphic persona may lead some individuals to favour and even fixate on their supermorphic self, resulting in the psychological dominance of the virtual over the non-virtual, which, in turn, may result in individuals spending more and more time in a space where one's self is perceived to be enhanced (again, leading potentially to PIU). Importantly, then, it is our contention that underlying any changes to an individual's thoughts, feelings and behaviours is the drive to maintain psychological parity across domains. This principle applies to any two spaces in which there is a (large) disparity between the personas presented therein, but is particularly pronounced in virtual spaces where one can engage in taboo violations, precisely because they involve taboos. Those who engage in STAs as a means of identity enhancement or even consider what they do as identity defining will experience the most salient sense of loss when removed from the VE (again, we contend). We hypothesize that such individuals are the most at risk from engaging in STAs.

16 Transcending taboos
The way forward

As noted in previous chapters, there is a paucity of research on the effect of STAs on those who play video games or otherwise engage in non-gaming online VEs (e.g. *Second Life* and *Sociolotron*). The limited research that has been undertaken on, for example, identification with the virtual character is certainly an important area for continued investigation: for it is our contention that such identification is necessarily antecedent to an individual seeking psychological parity across domains, particularly when they identify with characters or characteristics that are *uncharacteristic* of their offline self. To date, it is not clear what factors affect how well an individual is able to transcend domains after identifying with a character within a space with such potentially different freedoms as discussed here – certainly these factors have not been empirically tested. Moreover, we are still in need of a fuller understanding of how an individual might cope with the disparity between selves when identification in each space is strong and representation and action across spaces incongruent. Neither can we, at this time, fully explain or predict when STAs might become a mark of that which is identity enhancing or even identity defining for a given individual within a given space of altered contingences.

Incorporating what we do know, however, and in accordance with discussion and argument set forth in Part 2, one might wish to ask: Is the individual's self-as-object, as (intentionally) manifest through their avatar, an authentic or inauthentic (super-morphic) expression of their self-image, based on excogitations that are ideal or idealized? Moreover, might identification with the avatar be enhanced if one has more freedom to customize the avatar (as noted by Boellstorff, 2008), and also more freedom of expression, as is arguably the case in sandbox VEs that are not so obviously game based, like *Second Life* or even *Sociolotron*? How might the fact that one's avatar is/is not an authentic expression of one's self-as-object impact on one's psychological parity? We argued in Chapter 12 that authenticity would make transcendence easier, but what if authenticity is based on representation and action that is taboo offline? In addition, recall Liu and Peng's (2009) statement: that for those with high PVL (preference for virtual life), leaving the gamespace may lead to unpleasant feelings or withdrawal symptoms. Therefore, as well as issues relating to the authenticity of the self-as-object, one is left to consider how that other important component of one's self-image – the phenomenal self – is *experienced*. To what extent is the phenomenal self as experienced in virtual space authentic in those with high PVL, and how might this contribute to their high PVL?

In Part 2 we also discussed how research already suggests that those who develop avatars with which they strongly identify, experience games and VR differently. Given this, it seems reasonable to conjecture that these individuals will engage with, and emotionally experience, STAs differently from those who do not identify with their virtual character. The former, one might further conjecture, will be more likely to avoid engaging in STAs, or enjoy engaging in them less, and feel more distress and disgusted by the thought of engaging in them, unless they find a particular STA identity enhancing or defining.

Understanding virtual immediacy, the potential for progressive embodiment and one's supermorphic persona as well as the freedoms afforded by altered contingences within cyberspace – particularly regarding STAs – goes some way towards delineating a new theoretical framework for engagement within VEs. From this, we hope to derive testable hypotheses, which will further contribute to our understanding of how people cope with the potential for change available to them through cyberspace: but we are not there yet. There is much that we still do not know about the types of STAs individuals are prepared to engage in and their emotional responses to such interactions – for example: Which STAs are more likely to elicit enjoyment or distress, and why?

Recall how Whitty *et al.*'s (2011) study (Chapter 15) indicated that some individuals made a clear distinction between the types of STAs they were prepared to engage in and those they were not; some even appeared quite distressed at the thought of the latter. The distinction they most clearly made seemed to have been between those STAs for which there was a sanctioned equivalence, particularly when individuals were playing against real people as opposed to a computer, and those for which no form of sanctioned equivalence was apparent. These individuals also suggested that if the game appeared more real, then they might choose not to engage with some STAs. Whitty *et al.*'s findings are suggestive of differences between individuals and STAs; however, it seems fair to say that this research is still clearly in its infancy.

In Part 1, we saw how research has examined the sorts of individuals who are more likely to experience disgust towards certain real-world activities. In Chapter 3, we theorized that, given the strong visceral responses that accompany disgust, we would expect similar responses to STAs. It would therefore seem important to examine this empirically to see whether individuals who score high on disgust sensitivity also score high on disgust sensitivity to STAs. In addition, researchers have identified relationships between personality characteristics and disgust sensitivity. Druschel and Sherman (1999), for instance, found positive relationships between neuroticism, agreeableness, conscientiousness and disgust sensitivity, and a negative relationship between openness to experience and disgust sensitivity. We would therefore expect similar relationships between personality characteristics and disgust sensitivity when engaging in STAs.

Recall also (from Chapter 14), when discussing moral management, how achievement-oriented players play the game with the intention of developing their character's ability (so as to win the game). In contrast, social types are motivated by a desire to get to know others and be part of a team; while immersion types fully immerse themselves into the game and play in order to escape the real world (Yee, 2007). It is reasonable to surmise that these different categories of player might experience STAs differently. It is difficult, however, to hypothesize exactly how those with differing underlying motivations will experience STAs, and so any hypotheses would need to be exploratory at this stage, we feel.

Learning about the types of individuals who are more likely to engage in certain STAs and how they emote to them can reveal some important information about how people psychologically experience cyberspace (particularly gamespace). Our aim in this book has been to shift the focus of inquiry away from questions regarding the morality of the virtual act towards furthering our understanding of the psychological impact of virtual encounters on the individual, owing to their inherent differences. To focus on the psychology underlying STAs is not to deny that there are (potentially, at least) moral ramifications; rather, it is to allow moral questions to be informed by a greater understanding of how individuals experience and cope with the freedoms – moral or other – afforded by cyberspace. Initial research suggests that there is much to learn. As well as those questions already suggested above, possible future research might also wish to consider the following:

- What are the STAs that individuals most frequently engage in? What STAs would they be prepared to engage in that they do not at present engage in?
- How do individuals feel about engaging in these activities, and do they (or would they) feel different when engaging in single- rather than multiplayer games and why?
- What are the defining personality traits and characteristics of individuals who are more likely to enjoy engaging in certain STAs and how do these differ from those who are more likely to be distressed or even disgusted?
- Do individuals feel that MMORPGs provide them with opportunities to reflect on their 'real-world' identity and morals? If so, which aspects of identity and morality do they reflect on, and does this lead to further development or simply a strengthening of their original view? If it does not lead to reflection, why is it that they feel able to completely separate these spaces?

Finally, it might be that understanding more about how people respond to, for example, MMORPGs could assist in the design of such games in order to achieve the desired psychological effect. It could be, for instance, that some actions need to appear more or less real, or that avatars need to resemble the participant in order to enable close identification with their gaming character. The extent to which identification with the character is achieved may need to be weighed against the types of STAs permitted by the gameplay.

References

Adams, H.E. (2000). Voyeurism. In A.E. Kazdin (Ed.) *Encyclopedia of psychology* (pp. 216–218). Washington, DC: American Psychological Association.

Adler, A. (1996). Photography on trial. *Index on Censorship*, *25*, 141–146.

Aitken, S.C., and Herman, T. (1997). Gender, power and crib geography: Transitional spaces and potential places. *Gender, Place and Culture*, *4*, 63–88.

Ajana, B. (2005). Disembodiment and cyberspace: A phenomenological approach. *Electronic Journal of Sociology*, *7*, 1–10.

Alexander, M.J., and Higgins, E.T. (1993). Emotional trade-offs of becoming a parent: How social roles influence self-discrepancy effects. *Journal of Personality and Social Psychology*, *65*, 1259–1269.

Allison, S.E., von Wahlde, L., Shockley, T., and Gabbard, G.O. (2006). The development of the self in the era of the Internet and role-playing fantasy games. *American Journal of Psychiatry*, *163*, 381–385.

Anderson, C.A. (1997). Effects of violent movies and trait irritability on hostile feelings and aggressive thoughts. *Journal of Personality and Social Psychology*, *45*, 293–305.

Anderson, C.A. (2004). An update on the effects of violent video games. *Journal of Adolescence*, *27*, 113–122.

Anderson, C.A., and Bushman, B.J. (2001). Effects of violent video games on aggressive behavior, aggressive cognition, aggressive affect, physiological arousal, and prosocial behavior: A meta-analytic review of the scientific literature. *Psychological Science*, *12*, 353–359.

Anderson, C.A., and Bushman, B.J. (2002). Human aggression. *Annual Review of Psychology*, *53*, 27–51.

Anderson, C.A., and Dill, K.E. (2000). Video games and aggressive thoughts, feelings, and behavior in the laboratory and in life. *Journal of Personality and Social Psychology*, *78*, 772–790.

Anderson, C.A., and Ford, C.M. (1986). Affect of the game player: Short-term effects of highly and mildly aggressive video games. *Personality and Social Psychology Bulletin*, *12*, 390–402.

Anderson, C.A., Berkowitz, L., Donnerstein, E., Huesmann, L.R., Johnson, J.D., Linz, D., Malamuth, N.M., and Wartella, E. (2003). The influence of media violence on youth. *Psychological Science in the Public Interest*, *4*, 81–110.

Anderson, C.A., Carnagey, N.L., Flanagan, M., Benjamin, A.J., Eubanks, J., and Valentine, J.C. (2004). Violent video games: Specific effects of violent content on aggressive thoughts and behaviour. *Advances in Experimental Social Psychology*, *36*, 199–249.

Andrejevic, M. (2004). *Reality TV: The work of being watched.* Lanham, MD: Rowman & Littlefield Publishers.

Andrejevic, M. (2007). *iSpy: Surveillance and power in the interactive era.* Lawrence, KS: University Press of Kansas.

Angyal, A. (1941). Disgust and related aversions. *Journal of Abnormal and Social Psychology, 36,* 393–412.

Arneson, R.J. (2007). Shame, stigma, and disgust in the decent society. *Journal of Ethics, 11,* 31–63.

Arnold, M.B. (1960). *Emotion and personality (vol. 1): Psychological aspects.* New York: Columbia University Press.

Arnold, P., and Farrell, M.J. (2002). Can virtual reality be used to measure and train surgical skills? *Ergonomics, 45,* 362–379.

Arthur, C. (2009). 'Baby Shaker' game pulled from Apple's iPhone App Store. *The Guardian,* 22 April. Retrieved 5 May 2009 from: http://www.guardian.co.uk/technology/2009/apr/23/apple-iphone-baby-shaker

Back, M.D., Stopfer, J.M., Vazire, S., Gaddis, S., Schmukle, S.C., Egloff, B., and Gosling, S.D. (2009). Facebook profiles reflect actual personality, not self-idealization. *Psychological Science, 21,* 372–374. Retrieved 12 May from: http://www.simine.com/docs/Back_et_al_PSYCHSCIENCE_2010.pdf

Bailenson, J.N., and Segovia, K.Y. (2010). Virtual doppelgangers: Psychological effects of avatars who ignore their owners. In W.S. Bainbridge (Ed.) *Online worlds: Convergence of the real and the virtual* (pp. 175–186). London: Springer.

Ballon, B., and Leszcz, M. (2007). Horror films: Tales to master terror or shapers of trauma? *American Journal of Psychotherapy, 61,* 211–230.

Balsamo, A. (1993). The virtual body in cyberspace. *Research in Philosophy and Technology, 13,* 119–139.

Bandura, A. (1973). *Aggression: A social learning analysis.* Englewood Cliffs, NJ: Prentice-Hall.

Bandura, A. (2002). Selective moral disengagement in the exercise of moral agency. *Journal of Moral Education, 31,* 101–119.

Bandura, A., Ross, D., and Ross, S.A. (1963). Imitation of film-mediated aggressive models. *Journal of Abnormal and Social Psychology, 66,* 3–11.

Bargh, J.A., McKenna, K.Y.A., and Fitzsimons, G.M. (2002). Can you see the real me? Activation and expression of the 'true self' on the Internet. *Journal of Social Issues, 58,* 33–48.

Barlett, C.P., Anderson, C.A., and Swing, E.L. (2009). Video game effects – confirmed, suspected, and speculative: A review of the evidence. *Simulation & Gaming, 40,* 377–403.

Barlett, C.P., Harris, R.J., and Baldassaro, R. (2007). Longer you play, the more hostile you feel: Examination of first person shooter video games and aggression during video play. *Aggressive Behavior, 33,* 486–497.

Bartholow, B.D., Bushman, B.J., and Sestir, M.A. (2006). Chronic violent video game exposure and desensitization to violence: Behavioural and event-related brain potential data. *Journal of Experimental Social Psychology, 42,* 532–539.

Bartholow, B.D., Sestir, M.A., and Davis, E.B. (2005). Correlates and consequences of exposure to video game violence: Hostile personality, empathy, and aggressive behaviour. *Personality and Social Psychology Bulletin, 31,* 1573–1586.

Bartle, R. (2008). Torture. *The everyday blog of Richard Bartle,* 19 November 2008. Retrieved 3 June 2009 from: http://www.youhaventlived.com/qblog/2008/QBlog191108A.html

Bartsch, A., Appel, M., and Storch, D. (2010). Predicting emotions and meta-emotions at the movies: The role of the need for affect in audiences' experience of horror and drama. *Communication Research, 37*, 167–190.

Baruh, L. (2009). Publicized intimacies on reality television: An analysis of voyeuristic content and its contribution to the appeal of reality programming. *Journal of Broadcasting & Electronic Media, 53*, 190–210.

Baruh, L. (2010). Mediated voyeurism and the guilty pleasure of consuming reality television. *Media Psychology, 13*, 201–221.

Bateson, G. (1955). A theory of play and fantasy. *Psychiatric Research Reports, 2*, 39–51.

Bateson, G. (1972). *Steps to an ecology of mind*. New York: Ballantine Books.

Baudrillard, J. (1983). *Simulations*. New York: Semiotext(e).

BBC News (2007). Banned video game is 'fine art'. 21 June 2007. Retrieved 5 May 2009 from: http://news.bbc.co.uk/1/hi/technology/6225286.stm

Bensley, L., and van Eenwyk, J. (2001). Video games and real-life aggression: Review of the literature. *Journal of Adolescent Health, 29*, 244–257.

Berkowitz, L. (1984). Some effects of thoughts on anti- and prosocial media events: A cognitive neoassociation analysis. *Psychological Bulletin, 95*, 410–427.

Berkowitz, L. (1990). On the formation and regulation of anger and aggression. *American Psychologist, 45*, 494–503.

Bessière, K. Seay, A.F., and Kiesler, S. (2007). The ideal elf: Identity exploration in World of Warcraft. *CyberPsychology & Behavior, 10*, 530–535.

Bilton, N. (2010). The surreal world of Chatroulette. *The New York Times*, 20 February 2010. Retrieved 18 September 2010 from: http://www.nytimes.com/2010/02/21/weekinreview/21bilton.html

Biocca, F. (1997). The cyborg's dilemma: Progressive embodiment in virtual environments. *Journal of Computer-Mediated Communication, 3*, 1–31.

Blinka, L. (2008). The relationship of players to their avatars in MMORPGs: Differences between adolescents, emerging adults and adults. *Cyberpsychology: Journal of Psychosocial Research on Cyberspace, 2*, article 1, http://cyberpsychology.eu/view.php?cisloclanku=2008060901&article=1

Bloom, P. (2004). *Descartes' baby*. New York: Basic Books.

Boellstorff, T. (2008). *Coming of age in second life: An anthropologist explores the virtually human*. Princeton, NJ: Princeton University Press.

Boler, M. (2007). Hypes, hopes and actualities: New digital Cartesianism and bodies in cyberspace. *New Media and Society, 9*, 139–168.

Bollas, C. (1987). *The shadow of the object: Psychoanalysis of the unthought known*. London: Free Association.

Bollas, C. (1992). *Being a character: Psychoanalysis and self experience*. New York: Hill and Wang.

Booth, W.C. (1988). *The company we keep: An ethics of fiction*. Berkeley, CA: University of California Press.

Borden, R.J. (1975). Witnesses aggression: Influence of an observer's sex and values on aggressive responding. *Journal of Personality and Social Psychology, 31*, 567–573.

Borg, J.S., Lieberman, D., and Kieh, K.A. (2008). Infection, incest, and iniquity: Investigating the neural correlates of disgust and morality. *Journal of Cognitive Neuroscience, 20*, 1529–1546.

Bösche, W. (2009). Violent content enhances video game performance. *Journal of Media Psychology, 21*, 145–150.

Bourke, M.L., and Hernandez, A.E. (2009). The 'Butner Study' redux: A report of the incidence of hands-on child victimization by child pornography offenders. *Journal of Family Violence, 24*, 183–191.

Brecher, B. (2007). *Torture and the ticking bomb*. Malden, MA: Blackwell.

Bredemeier, B., and Shields, D. (1986). Athletic aggression: An issue of contextual morality. *Sociology of Sport Journal, 3*, 15–28.

Brey, P. (1999). The ethics of representation and action in virtual reality. *Ethics and Information Technology, 1*, 5–14.

Brey, P. (2003). The social ontology of virtual environments. *American Journal of Economics and Sociology, 62*, 269–281.

Brock, S. (2007). Fictions, feelings, and emotions. *Philosophical Studies, 132*, 211–242.

Brody, R. (1987). *Stories of sickness*. New Haven, CT: Yale University Press.

Bronfenbrenner, U. (1980). Ecology of childhood. *Social Psychology Review, 9*, 294–297.

Bryant, J., and Davies, J. (2006). Selective exposure to video games. In E. Vorderer and J. Bryant (Eds) *Playing video games: Motives, responses, and consequences* (pp. 181–194). Mahwah, NJ: Lawrence Erlbaum Associates, Inc.

Bryant. P., and Linz, D.G. (2008). The effects of exposure to virtual child pornography on viewer cognition and attitudes toward deviant sexual behavior. *Communication Research, 35*, 3–38.

Bryant, J., Carveth, R.A., and Brown, D. (1981). Television viewing and anxiety: An experimental examination. *Journal of Communication, 31*, 106–119.

Burwood, S. (2008). The apparent truth of dualism and the uncanny body. *Phenomenology and the Cognitive Sciences, 7*, 263–278.

Bushman, B.J. (1995). Moderating role of trait aggressiveness in the effects of violent media on aggression. *Journal of Personality and Social Psychology, 69*, 950–960.

Bushman, B.J. (1996). Individual differences in the extent and development of aggressive cognitive-associative networks. *Personality and Social Psychology Bulletin, 22*, 811–819.

Bushman, B.J., and Anderson, C.A. (2001). Is it time to pull the plug on the hostile versus instrumental aggression dichotomy? *Psychological Review, 108*, 273–279.

Bushman, B.J., and Anderson, G.A. (2009). Comfortably numb: Desensitizing effects of violent media on helping others. *Psychological Science, 20*, 273–277.

Busselle, R., and Bilandzic, H. (2008) Fictionality and perceived realism in experiencing stories: A model of narrative comprehension and engagement. *Communication Theory, 18*, 255–280.

Byron, T. (2008). *Safer children in a digital world: The report of the Byron Review*. London: Department for Children, Schools and Families and Department for Culture, Media and Sport. Retrieved 3 August 2010 from: http://publications.education.gov.uk/eOrderingDownload/DCSF-00334-2008.pdf

Caillois, R. (1961). *Man, play and games*. New York: Free Press.

Caillois, R., and Mehlman, J. (1968). Riddles and images. *Yale French Studies, 41*, 148–158.

Calleja, G. (2010). Digital games and escapism. *Games and Culture, 5*, 335–353.

Calvert, C. (2002). Violence, video games, and the voice of reason: Judge Posner to the defense of kids' culture and the first amendment. *San Diego Law Review, 39*, 1–30.

Cantor, J. (1994). Fright reactions to mass media. In J. Bryant and D. Zillman (Eds) *Media effects: Advances in theory and research* (pp. 213–245). Hillsdale, NJ: Lawrence Erlbaum Associates, Inc.

Cantor, J. (2000). Media violence. *Journal of Adolescent Health, 27*, 30–34.

Caplan, S., Williams, D., and Yee, N. (2009). Problematic Internet use and psychosocial well-being among MMO players. *Computers in Human Behavior, 25*, 1312–1319.

Caplan, S.E. (2002). Problematic Internet use and psychosocial well-being: Development of a theory-based cognitive-behavioral measure. *Computers in Human Behavior, 18*, 533–575.

Caplan, S.E. (2003). Preference for online social interaction: A theory of problematic Internet use and psychosocial well-being. *Communication Research, 30*, 625–648.

Caplan, S.E. (2005). A social skill account of problematic internet use. *Journal of Communication, 55*, 721–736.

Caplan, S.E. (2010). Theory and measurement of generalized problematic Internet use: A two-step approach. *Computers in Human Behavior, 26*, 1089–1097.

Carnagey, N.L., and Anderson, C.A. (2005). The effects of reward and punishment in violent video games on aggressive affect, cognition and behavior. *Psychological Science, 16*, 882–889.

Carnagey, N.L., Anderson, C.A., and Bushman, B.J. (2007). The effects of video game violence on physiological desensitization to real-life violence. *Journal of Experimental Social Psychology, 43*, 489–496.

Carr, A. (2001). Organisational and administrative play: The potential of magic realism, surrealism and postmodernist forms of play. In J. Biberman and A. Alkhafaji (Eds) *Business research yearbook: Global business perspectives* (pp. 543–547). Saline, MI: McNaughton & Gunn.

Carr, A. (2003). Organizational discourse as a creative space for play: The potential of postmodernist and surrealist forms of play. *Human Resource Developmental International, 6*, 197–217.

Carroll, N. (1990). *The philosophy of horror*. New York: Routledge.

Carter, D. (2005). Living in virtual communities: An ethnography of human relationships in cyberspace. *Information, Communication and Society, 8*, 148–167.

Case, T.I., Repacholi, B.M., and Stevenson, R.J. (2006). My baby doesn't smell as bad as yours: The plasticity of disgust. *Evolution and Human Behavior, 27*, 357–365.

Castronova, E. (2006). Virtual worlds: A first-hand account of market and society on the cyberian frontier. In K. Salen and E. Zimmermann (Eds) *The game design reader: A rule of play anthology* (pp. 814–863). Cambridge, MA: MIT Press.

Castronova, E., Williams, D., Shen, C., Ratan, R., Xiong, L. Huang, Y., and Keegan, B. (2009). As real as real? Macroeconomic behavior in a large-scale virtual world. *New Media Society, 11*, 685–707.

Caughey, J.L. (1986). Social relations with media figures. In G. Gumpert and R. Cathcart (Eds) *Inter/media* (pp. 219–252). New York: Oxford University Press.

Cenite, M. (2004). Federalizing or eliminating online obscenity law as an alternative to contemporary community standards. *Communication Law and Policy, 9*, 25–71.

Champoux, J.E. (2006). At the cinema: Aspiring to a higher ethical standard. *Academy of Management Learning & Education, 5*, 386–390.

Charlton, J.P., and Danforth, I.D.W. (2007). Distinguishing addiction and high engagement in the context of online game playing. *Computers in Human Behavior, 23*, 1531–1548.

Chen, S.H., Weng, L.Z., Su, Y.R., Wu, H.M., and Yang, P.F. (2003). Development of a Chinese Internet addiction scale and its psychometric study. *Chinese Journal of Psychology, 45*, 279–294.

Chouliaraki, L. (2006). *The spectatorship of suffering*. London: Sage Publications.

Chumbley, R. (1979). Introductory remarks toward a 'ploylogue' on play. *SubStance, 8*, 7–10.

Coeckelbergh, M. (2007). Violent computer games, empathy, and cosmopolitanism. *Ethics and Information Technology, 9*, 219–231.

Cohen, J. (2001). Defining identification: A theoretical look at the identification of audiences with media characters. *Mass Communication and Society, 4*, 245–264.

Cole, H., and Griffiths, M.D. (2007). Social interactions in massively multiplayer online role-playing gamers. *CyberPsychology & Behavior, 10*, 575–583.

Collins, A.M., and Loftus, E.F. (1975). A spreading activation theory of semantic processing. *Psychological Review, 82*, 407–428.

Comello, M.L.G. (2009). William James on 'possible selves': Implications for studying identity in communication contexts. *Communication Theory, 19*, 337–350.

Costanzo, M., Gerrity, E., and Brinton Lykes, M. (2007). Psychologists and the use of torture in interrogations. *Analysis of Social Issues and Public Policy, 7*, 7–20.

Coyne, R. (1994). Heidegger and virtual reality: The implications of Heidegger's thinking for computer representations. *Leonardo, 27*, 65–73.

Crawford, G. and Gosling, V.K. (2009). More than a game: Sports-themed video games and player narratives. *Sociology of Sport Journal, 26*, 50–66.

Crick, T. (2011). The game body: Toward a phenomenology of contemporary video gaming. *Games and Culture, 6*, 245–258.

Cumberbatch, G. (2004). *Video violence: Villain or victim? A review of the research evidence concerning media violence and its effects in the real world with additional reference to video games: A report prepared for The Video Standards Council.* Retrieved 14 September 2010 from: http://www.xlq50.dial.pipex.com/sections/downloads/pdfs/Video%20Violence%202004.pdf

Cumberbatch, G. (2010). Effects. In D. Albertazzi and P. Cobley (Eds) *The media: An introduction* (3 edn, pp. 354–368). Harlow: Pearson.

Cumberbatch, G., Jones, I., and Lee, M. (1988). Measuring violence on television. *Current Psychology, 7*, 10–25.

Damasio, A.R. (1994). *Descartes' error: Emotion, reason, and the human brain.* New York: Avon.

Danet, B., Ruedenberg, L., and Rosenbaum-Tamari, Y. (1998). 'Hmmm . . . where's that smoke coming from?': Writing, play and performance on Internet relay chat. In F. Sudweeks, M. McLaughlin, and S. Rafaeli (Eds) *Network and netplay: Virtual groups on the Internet* (pp. 47–85). Cambridge, MA: MIT Press.

Danovitch, J., and Bloom, P. (2009). Children's extension of disgust to physical and moral events. *Emotion, 9*, 107–112.

Davis, R.A. (2001). A cognitive-behavioral model of pathological Internet use. *Computers in Human Behavior, 17*, 187–195.

De Vane, B., and Squire, K.D. (2008). The meaning of race and violence in Grand Theft Auto: San Andreas. *Games and Culture, 3*, 264–285.

Deigh, J. (1994). Cognitivism in the theory of emotions. *Ethics, 104*, 824–854.

Dery, M. (1994). *Flame wars: The discourse of cyberculture.* Durham, NC: Duke University Press.

Descartes, R. (1997a). Discourse on method. In E. Chavez-Arvizo (Ed.) *Descartes: Key philosophical writings.* Ware: Wordsworth Editions Limited. (Original work published 1637.)

Descartes, R. (1997b). Meditations. In E. Chavez-Arvizo (Ed.) *Descartes: Key philosophical writings.* Ware: Wordsworth Editions Limited. (Original work published 1647.)

Di Muzio, G. (2006). The immorality of horror films. *International Journal of Applied Philosophy*, *20*, 277–294.

Dibbel, J. (1993). A rape in cyberspace. *The Village Voice*, *38*, 26–42.

Dillon, M.C. (1982). The phenomenon of obscenity in literature: The specification of a value. *Journal of Value Inquiry*, *16*, 259–274.

Dixon, T.L., and Linz, D.G. (1997). Obscenity law and sexually explicit rap music: Understanding the effects of sex, attitudes, and beliefs. *Journal of Applied Communication Research*, *25*, 217–241.

Dollard, J., Doob, L., Miller, N., Mowrer, O., and Sears, R. (1939). *Frustration and aggression*. New Haven, CT: Yale University Press.

Dooley, S. (1995). Obscene material on the Internet. *Solicitors Journal*, 8 September, 866–868.

Druschel, B.A. and Sherman, M.F. (1999). Disgust sensitivity as a function of the Big Five and gender. *Personality and Individual Differences*, *26*, 739–748.

Ducheneaut, N. (2010). Massively multiplayer online games as living laboratories: Opportunities and pitfalls. In W.S. Bainbridge (Ed.) *Online worlds: Convergence of the real and the virtual* (pp. 135–145). London: Springer.

Eastin, M. (2006). Video game violence and the female game player: Self- and opponent-gender effects on presence and aggressive thoughts. *Human Communication Research*, *32*, 351–372.

Edelstein, D. (2006). Now playing at your local multiplex: Torture porn. *NewYork Movies*, 28 January. Retrieved 17 March 2010 from: http://nymag.com/movies/features/15622/

Ehrmann, J. (1968). Homo Ludens revisited. *Yale French Studies*, *41*, 31–57.

Ekman, P. (1980). Biological and cultural contributions to body and facial movements in the expression of emotions. In A.O. Rorty (Ed.) *Explaining emotions* (pp. 73–101). Berkeley, CA: University of California Press.

Ellen, B. (2009). Vanessa George case shows armchair paedophiles are just as guilty. *The Observer*, 4 October. Retrieved 21 April 2010 from: http://www.guardian.co.uk/commentisfree/2009/oct/04/vanessa-george-paedophiles-barbara-ellen

Ellis, M.J., and Scholtz, G. (1978). *Activity and play in children*. Englewood Cliffs, NJ: Prentice-Hall.

Ellison, N., Heino, R., and Gibbs, J. (2006). Managing impression online: Self-presentation processes in the online dating environment. *Journal of Computer-Mediated Communication*, *11*, 415–441.

Elwood, L.S., and Olatunji, B.O. (2008). A cross-cultural perspective on disgust. In B.O. Olatunji and D. Mckay (Eds) *Disgust and its disorders: Theory, assessment, and treatment implications* (pp. 99–122). Washington, DC: American Psychological Association.

Erikson, M.G. (2007). The meaning of the future: Toward a more specific definition of possible selves. *Review of General Psychology*, *11*, 348–358.

Eron, L.D., Huesmann, L.R., Lefkowitz, M.M., and Walder, L.D. (1972). Does television violence cause aggression? *American Psychologist*, *27*, 253–263.

Fairweather, N.B. (2002). Disembodied sport: Ethical issues of virtual sport, electronic games and virtual leisure. *Sport Technology: History, Philosophy and Policy*, *21*, 235–249.

Featherstone, M., and Burrows, R. (1995). *Cyberspace/cyberbodies/cyberpunk: Cultures of technological embodiment*. London: Sage Publications.

Feinberg, J. (1988). *The moral limits of criminal law, volume 2: Offense to others*. Oxford: Oxford University Press.

Ferguson, C.J. (2007a). Evidence for publication bias in video game violence effects literature: A meta-analytic review. *Aggression and Violent Behavior*, *12*, 470–482.

Ferguson, C.J. (2007b). The good, the bad and the ugly: A meta-analytic review of positive and negative effects of violent video games. *Psychiatric Quarterly*, *78*, 309–316.

Ferguson, C.J. (2010). Blazing angels or resident evil? Can violent video games be a force for good? *Review of General Psychology*, *14*, 68–81.

Ferguson, C.J., and Kilburn, J. (2009). The public health risks of media violence: A meta-analytic review. *Journal of Pediatrics*, *154*, 759–763.

Ferguson, C.J., and Rueda, S. M. (2009). The Hitman Study: Violent video game exposure effects on aggressive behavior, hostile feelings and depression. *European Psychologist*, *15*, 99–108.

Fineman, S., Maitlis, S., and Panteli, N. (2007). Virtuality and emotion. *Human Relations*, *60*, 555–560.

Fink, E. (1968). The oasis of happiness: Toward an ontology of play. *Yale French Studies*, *41*, 19–30.

Fisher, S. (1991). Virtual environments: Personal simulations and telepresence. In K. Helsel and J.P. Roth (Eds) *Virtual reality: Theory, practice, and promise* (pp. 101–110). Westport, CT: Meckler.

Fitzgerald, D.A., Posse, S., Moore, G.J., Tancer, M.E., Nathan, P.J., and Phan, K.L. (2004). Neural correlates of internally generated disgust via autobiographical recall: A functional magnetic resonance imaging investigation. *Neuroscience Letters*, *370*, 91–96.

Fodor, J. (1983). *The modularity of mind*. Cambridge, MA: MIT Press.

Ford, P.J. (2001). Paralysis lost: Impacts of virtual worlds on those with paralysis. *Social Theory and Practice*, *27*, 661–680.

Forsyth, C.J. (1996). The structuring of vicarious sex. *Deviant Behavior: An Interdisciplinary Journal*, *17*, 279–295.

Freud, S. (1950). *Totem and taboo: Some point of agreement between the mental lives of savages and neurotics* (J. Strachey, Trans.). London: Routledge & Kegan Paul. (Original work published 1913.)

Freud, S. (1985). Creative writers and day-dreaming. In J. Strachey (Ed. and Trans.) *Art and literature* (vol. 14, pp. 129–141). Harmondsworth: Penguin Freud Library. (Original work published 1908.)

Fuller, L. (1949). The case of the Speluncean Explorers. *Harvard Law Review*, *62*, 616–645.

Fuller, M., and Jenkins, H. (1995). Nintendo and new world travel writing: A dialogue. In S.G. Jones (Ed.) *Cybersociety: Computer-mediated communication and community* (pp. 57–72). London: Sage Publications.

Funk, J.B., Bechtoldt-Baldacci, H., Pasold, T., and Baumgartner, J. (2004). Violence exposure in real-life, video games, television, movies, and the Internet: Is there desensitisation? *Journal of Adolescence*, *27*, 23–39.

Gallagher, S. (2005a). *How the body shapes the mind*. Oxford: Clarendon Press.

Gallagher, S. (2005b). Metzinger's matrix: Living the virtual life with real body. *Psyche*, *11*, 1–9. Retrieved 1 February 2008 from: http://psyche.cs.monash.edu.au/

Galloway, A.R. (2004). Social realism in gaming. *Game Studies*, *4*. Retrieved 8 December 2010 from: http://gamestudies.org/1001/archive

Gardner, S. (1994). Other minds and embodiment. *Proceedings of the Aristotelian Society*, XCIV, 35–52.

Gaut, B. (1993). The paradox of horror. *British Journal of Aesthetics*, *33*, 333–345.

Gee, J.P. (2006). Why game studies now? Video games: A new art form. *Games and Culture: A Journal of Interactive Media, 1*, 58–61.

Geen, R.G. (1975). The meaning of observed violence: Real vs fictional violence and consequent effects on aggression and emotional arousal. *Journal of Research in Personality, 9*, 270–281.

Gentile, D.A., and Anderson, C.A. (2003). Violent video games: The newest media violence hazard. In D.A. Gentile (Ed.) *Media violence and children* (pp. 131–152). Westport, CT: Praeger Publishing.

Gergen, K.J. (1991) *The saturated self.* New York: Basic Books.

Gerrig, R.J. (1993). *Experiencing narrative worlds.* New Haven, CT: Yale University Press.

Gert, J. (2005). Neo-sentimentalism and disgust. *The Journal of Value Inquiry, 39*, 345–352.

Gibbard, A. (1990). *Wise choices, apt feelings: A theory of normative judgment.* Cambridge, MA: Harvard University Press.

Gibson, W. (1984). *Neuromancer.* New York: Ace Books.

Giumetti, G.W., and Markey, P.M. (2007). Violent video games and anger as predictors of aggression. *Journal of Research in Personality, 41*(6), 1234–1243.

Glock, S., and Kneer, J. (2009). Game over? The impact of knowledge about violent digital games on the activation of aggression-related concepts. *Journal of Media Psychology, 21*, 151–160.

Goffman, E. (1974). *An essay on the organization of experience.* New York: Harper & Row.

Gonzales, A.L., and Hancock, J.T. (2008). Identity shift in computer-mediated environments. *Media Psychology, 11*, 167–185.

Gough, B. (2006). Try to be healthy, but don't forgo your masculinity: Deconstructing men's health discourse in the media. *Social Science & Medicine, 63*, 2476–2488.

Granberg, E. (2006). Is that all there is? Possible selves, self-change, and weight loss. *Social Psychology Quarterly, 69*, 109–126.

Green, M.C., and Brock, T.C. (2000). The role of transportation in the persuasiveness of public narratives. *Journal of Personality and Social Psychology, 79*, 701–721.

Greenberg, B.S. (1988). Some uncommon television images and the drenched hypothesis. In S. Oskamp (Ed.) *Applied social psychology annual, vol. 8: Television as a social issue* (pp. 88–102). Beverley Hills, CA: Sage Publications.

Greenberg, B.S., Sherry, J., Lachlan, K., Lucas, K., and Holmstrom, A. (2010). Orientations to video games among gender and age groups. *Simulation & Gaming, 41*, 238–259.

Greene, J.D., Sommerville, R.B., Nyystrom, L.E., Darley, J.M., and Cohen, J. (2001). An fMRI investigation of emotional engagement in moral judgment. *Science, 293*, 2105–2108.

Griffiths, M.D., Davies, M.N.O., and Chappell, D. (2003). Breaking the stereotype: The case of online gaming. *CyberPsychology & Behavior, 6*, 81–91.

Griffiths, P.E. (1990). Modularity, and the psychoevolutionary theory of emotion. *Biology and Philosophy, 5*, 175–196.

Griffiths, P.E. (1997). *What emotions really are.* Chicago, IL: University of Chicago Press.

Grossman, D., and DeGaetano, G. (1999). *Stop teaching our kids to kill: A call to action against TV, movie & video game violence.* New York: Crown.

Grusser, S.M., Thalemann, R., and Griffiths, M.D. (2007). Excessive computer game playing: Evidence for addiction and aggression? *CyberPsychology & Behavior, 10*, 290–292.

Gunkel, D.J (1998). Virtual transcendent: Cyberculture and the body. *Journal of Mass Media Ethics*, *13*, 111–123.

Gunter, B. (1985). *Dimensions of television violence*. Aldershot: Gower.

Gunter, B. (2008). Media violence: Is there a case for causality? *American Behavioral Scientist*, *51*, 1061–1122.

Gurak, L.J. (1997). Utopian visions of cyberspace. *Computer Mediated Communications*, pp. 1–2. Retrieved 30 March 2007 from: http://www.december.com/cmc/mag/1997/may/last.html

Gutierrez, R., and Giner-Sorolla, R. (2007). Anger, disgust, and presumption of harm as reactions to taboo-breaking behaviors. *Emotion*, *7*, 853–868.

Gwinnell, E. (1998). *Online seductions: Falling in love with strangers on the Internet*. New York: Kodansha International.

Haidt, J. (2001). The emotional dog and its rational tail: A social intuitionist approach to moral judgment. *Psychological Review*, *108*, 814–834.

Haidt, J., and Hersh, M.A. (2001). Sexual morality: The cultures and emotions of conservatives and liberals. *Journal of Applied Social Psychology*, *31*, 191–221.

Haidt, J., Koller, S.H., and Dias, M.G. (1993). Affect, culture, and morality, or is it wrong to eat your dog? *Journal of Personality and Social Psychology*, *65*, 613–628.

Hamlen, K.R. (2011). Children's choices and strategies in video games. *Computers in Human Behavior*, *27*, 532–539.

Haraway, D. (1991). *Symians, cyborgs and women: The reinvention of nature*. London: Free Association Books.

Hardey, M. (2002). Life beyond the screen: Embodiment and identity through the Internet. *The Sociological Review*, *50*, 570–585.

Hartmann, T., and Vorderer, P. (2010). It's okay to shoot a character: Moral disengagement in violent video games. *Journal of Communication*, 60, 94–119.

Hartmann, T., Toz, E., and Brandon, M. (2010) Just a game? Unjustified virtual violence produces guilt in empathetic players. *Media Psychology*, *13*, 339–363.

Hartz, G.A. (1999). How we can be moved by Anna Karenina, Green Slime, and a red pony. *Philosophy*, *74*, 557–578.

Haugeland, J. (1995). Mind embodied and embedded. *Acta Philosophica Fennica*, 58, 233–266.

Hefner, D., Klimmt, C., and Vorderer, P. (2007). Identification with the player character as determinant of video game enjoyment. In L. Ma, R. Nakatsu and M. Rauterberg (Eds) *Entertainment Computing – ICEC 2007: 6th International Conference* (pp. 39–48). New York: Springer.

Heim, M. (1993). *The metaphysics of virtual reality*. New York: Oxford University Press.

Hemenover, S.H., and Schimmack, U. (2007). That's disgusting! . . ., but very amusing: Mixed feelings of amusement and disgust. *Cognition and Emotion*, *21*, 1102–1113

Henderson, S., and Gilding, M. (2004). 'I've never clicked this much with anyone in my life': Trust and hyperpersonal communication in online friendships. *New Media and Society*, *6*, 487–506.

Henricks, T.S. (2006). *Play reconsidered: Sociological perspectives on human expression*. Urbana, IL: University of Illinois Press.

Herring, S.C. (1993). Gender and democracy in computer-mediated communication. *Electronic Journal of Communication*, *3*. Retrieved 7 February 2005 from: http://ella.slis.indiana.edu/~herring/ejc.txt

Herschovitch, P. (2003). 'Rest in Plastic': Review of the London Body Worlds exhibition of Gunther von Hagens. *Science*, *299*: 828.

Higgins, E.T. (1987). Self-discrepancy theory. *Psychological Review, 94,* 319–340.

Hinte, F. (1971). Should desensitization techniques be part of police recruit training? *Group Psychotherapy and Psychodrama, 24,* 107–110.

Hoffman, H. (1998). Virtual reality: A new tool for interdisciplinary psychology research. *CyberPsychology & Behavior, 1,* 195–200.

Hoffner, C. (1996). Children's wishful identification and parasocial interaction with favorite television characters. *Journal of Broadcasting & Electronic Media, 40,* 389–402.

Hoffner, C., and Buchanan, M. (2005). Young adults' wishful identification with television characters: The role of perceived similarity and character attributes. *Media Psychology, 7,* 325–351.

Horberg, E.J., Oveis, C., Keltner, D., and Cohen, A.B. (2009). Disgust and the moralization of purity. *Journal of Personality and Social Psychology, 97,* 963–976.

Hsu, S.H., Wen, M.H., and Wu, M.C. (2009). Exploring user experiences as predictors of MMORPG addiction. *Computers and Education, 53,* 990–998.

Huesmann, L.R. (1988). An information processing model for the development of aggression. *Aggressive Behavior, 14,* 13–24.

Huesmann, L.R., and Guerra, N.G. (1997). Children's normative beliefs about aggression and aggressive behavior. *Journal of Personality and Social Psychology, 72,* 408–419.

Huesmann, L.R., and Taylor, L.D. (2003). The case against the case against media violence. In D. Gentile (Ed.) *Media violence and children* (pp. 107–130). Westport, CT: Greenwood Press.

Huesmann, L.R., Lagerspetz, K., and Eron, L.D. (1984). Intervening variables in the TV violence-aggression relation: Evidence from two countries. *Developmental Psychology, 20,* 746–777.

Hugh-Jones, S., Gough, B., and Littlewood, A. (2005). Sexual exhibitionism can be good for you: Critique of psycho-medical discourse from the perspectives of women who exhibit. *Sexualities, 8,* 259–281.

Huh, S., and Williams, D. (2010). Dude looks like a lady: Gender swapping in an online game. In W.S. Bainbridge (Ed.) *Online worlds: Convergence of the real and the virtual* (pp. 161–174). London: Springer.

Huizinga, J. (1992). *Homo ludens: The study of the play-element in culture.* Boston, MA: The Beacon Press. (Original work published 1950.)

Hume, D. (1978). *A treatise of human nature.* L. Selby-Bigge (Ed.) (2nd edn). Oxford: Oxford University Press. (Original work published 1739.)

Hunter, I., Saunders, D., and Williamson, D. (1993). *On pornography: Literature, sexuality and obscenity law.* London: Macmillan.

Hussain, Z., and Griffiths, M.D. (2008). Gender swapping and socializing in cyberspace: An exploratory study. *CyberPsychology & Behavior, 11,* 47–53.

Ilyenkov, E.V. (1977). *Dialectical logic: Essays in its history and theory* (H. Campbell Creighton, trans.). Moscow: Progress. (Original work published 1974.)

Ivory, J.D., and Kalyanaraman, S. (2007). The effects of technological advancement and violent content in video games on players' feelings of presence, involvement, physiological arousal, and aggression. *Journal of Communication, 57,* 532–555.

Ivory, J.D., Williams, D., Martins, N., and Consalvo, M. (2009). Good clean fun? A content analysis of profanity in video games and its prevalence across game systems and ratings. *CyberPsychology & Behavior, 12,* 1–4.

James, W. (1981). *The principles of psychology* (vol. 1) (8th edn). Cambridge, MA: Harvard University Press. (Original work published 1890.)

Jansz, J. (2005). The emotional appeal of violent video games for adolescent males. *Communication Theory*, *15*, 219–241.

Jay, T. (2009). Do offensive words harm people? *Psychology, Public Policy, and Law*, *15*, 81–101.

Jenson, J., and de Castell, S. (2010). Gender, simulation, and gaming: Research review and redirections. *Simulation & Gaming*, *41*, 51–71.

Johnston, D.D. (1995). Adolescents' motivations for viewing graphic horror. *Human Communication Research*, *21*, 522–552.

Joinson, A.N. (2001). Self-disclosure in computer-mediated communication: The role of self-awareness and visual anonymity. *European Journal of Social Psychology*, *31*, 177–192.

Jones, A., and Fitness, J. (2008). Moral hypervigilance: The influence of disgust sensitivity in the moral domain. *Emotion*, *8*, 613–627.

Jones, S. (2000). Towards a philosophy of virtual reality: Issues implicit in 'consciousness reframed'. *Leonardo*, *33*, 125–132.

Juul, J. (2005). *Half-real: Video games between real rules and fictional worlds*. Cambridge, MA: MIT Press.

Kaigo, M., and Watanabe, I. (2007). Ethos in chaos? Reaction to video files depicting socially harmful images in the Channel 2 Japanese Internet forum. *Journal of Computer-Mediated Communication*, *12*, 1248–1268.

Kass, L.R. (2002). *Life, liberty, and the defense of dignity: The challenge for bioethics*. San Francisco, CA: Encounter Books.

Kekes, J. (1992). Disgust and moral taboos. *Philosophy*, *67*, 431–446.

Kieran, M. (2002). On obscenity: The thrill and repulsion of the morally prohibited. *Philosophy and Phenomenological Research*, *64*, 31–55.

Kim, E.J., Namkoong, K., Ku, T., and Kim, S.J. (2008). The relationship between online game addiction and aggression, self-control and narcissistic personality traits. *European Psychiatry*, *23*, 212–218.

King, J.A., Blair, R.J.R., Mitchell, D.G.V., Dolan, R.J., and Burgess, N. (2006). Doing the right thing: A common neural circuit for appropriate violent or compassionate behaviour. *NeuroImage*, *30*, 1069–1076.

Kingsepp, E. (2007). Fighting hyperreality with hyperreality: History and death in World War II digital games. *Games and Culture*, *2*, 366–375.

Klein, R. (1999). If I'm a cyborg rather than a goddess will patriarchy go away? In S. Hawthorne and R. Klein. (Eds) *Cyberfeminism: Connectivity, critique and creativity* (pp. 185–212). North Melbourne, Australia: Spinifex Press.

Klimmt, C., Hefner, D., and Vorderer, P. (2009). The video game experience as 'True' identification: A theory of enjoyable alterations of players' self-perception. *Communication Theory*, *19*, 351–373.

Klimmt, C., Hefner, D., Vorderer, P., Roth, C., and Blake, C. (2010). Identification with video game characters as automatic shift of self-perceptions. *Media Psychology*, *13*, 323–338.

Klimmt, C., Schmid, H., Nosper, A., Hartmann, T., and Vorderer, P. (2006). How players manage moral concerns to make video game violence enjoyable. *Communications*, *31*, 309–328.

Klimmt, C., Schmid, H., Nosper, A., Hartmann, T., and Vorderer, P. (2008). 'Moral management': Dealing with moral concerns to maintain enjoyment of violent video games. In A. Sudmann-Jahn and R. Stockmann (Eds) *Computer games as a sociocultural phenomenon: Games without frontiers – wars without tears* (pp. 108–118). Basingstoke: Palgrave.

Knapp, C. (2003). De-moralizing disgustingness. *Philosophy and Phenomenological Research*, *66*, 253–278.

Konijn, E.A., and Bushman, B.J. (2007). I wish I were a warrior: The role of wishful identification on the effects of violent video games on aggression in adolescent boys. *Developmental Psychology*, *43*, 1038–1044.

Koppelman, A. (2005). Does obscenity cause moral harm? *Columbia Law Review*, *105*, 1635–1680.

Kosse, S.H. (2004). Virtual child pornography: A United States update. *Communications Law*, *9*, 39–46.

Krcmar, M., Farrar, K., and McGloin, R. (2011). The effects of video game realism on attention, retention and aggressive outcomes. *Computers in Human Behavior*, *27*, 432–439.

Kreider, S.E. (2008). The virtue of horror films: A response to Di Muzio. *International Journal of Applied Philosophy*, *22*, 149–157.

Kreitman, N. (2006). Fantasy, fiction, and feelings. *Metaphilosophy*, *37*, 605–622.

Kupfer, J.H. (2007). Mobility, portability, and placelessness. *Journal of Aesthetic Education*, *41*, 38–50.

Lack, J. (2008). Censoring provocative art is the worst advert for 2012. *The Guardian*, 26 August 2008. Retrieved 12 April 2010 from: http://www.guardian.co.uk/artanddesign/2008/aug/26/art.olympics2012

Ladas, M. (2003). Eine Befragung von 2141 Computerspielern zuWirkung und Nutzung von Gewalt [A survey of 2,141 computer game players on effect and use of violence]. In F. Rötzer (Ed.) *Virtuelle Welten – reale Gewalt* [Virtual worlds – real violence] (pp. 26–35). Hannover, Germany: Hans Heise Verlag.

Laetz, B. (2008). Two problematic theses in Carroll's account of horror. *Film and Philosophy*, *12*, 67–72.

Lagerspetz, K.M.J., and P. Engblom (1979). Immediate reactions to TV violence by Finnish pre-school children of different personality types. *Scandinavian Journal of Psychology*, *20*, 43–53.

Lakoff, G., and Johnson, M. (1999). *Philosophy in the flesh: The embodied mind and its challenge to Western thought*. New York: Basic Books.

Laurenson, L. (2005). The inevitably-named 'Rape in RPGs'. *Gamegrene*, 22 March 2005. Retrieved 12 June 2009, from: http://www.gamegrene.com/node/447

Lazarus, R.S. (1991). Progress on the cognitive-motivational-relational theory of emotion. *American Psychologist*, *46*, 819–834.

Lea, M., and Spears, R. (1995). Love at first byte? Building personal relationships over computer networks. In J.T. Wood and S.W. Duck (Eds) *Understudied relationships: Off the beaten track* (pp. 197–233). Newbury Park, CA: Sage Publications.

Leckenby, J.D. (1978). Attributions to TV characters and opinion change. *Journalism Quarterly*, *55*, 241–247.

Legrand, D. (2007). Subjectivity and the body: Introducing basic forms of self-consciousness. *Consciousness and Cognition*, *16*, 577–582.

Lehdonvirta, V. (2010). Virtual worlds don't exist: Questioning the dichotomous approach in MMO studies. *Game Studies*, *10*. Retrieved 8 December 2010 from: http://gamestudies.org/1001/archive

Leiberich, P., Loew, T., Tritt, K., Lahmann, C., and Nickel, M. (2006). Body Worlds exhibition: Visitor attitudes and emotions. *Annals of Anatomy*, *188*, 567–573.

Lemmens, J.S. (2006). The appeal of violent video games to lower educated aggressive adolescent boys from two countries. *CyberPsychology & Behavior*, *9*, 638–641.

Lemmens, J.S., Valkenburg, P.M., and Peter, J. (2011). Psychosocial causes and consequences of pathological gaming. *Computers in Human Behavior, 27*, 144–152.

Lenggenhager, B., Tadi, T., Metzinger, T., and Blanke, O. (2007). Video ergo sum: Manipulating bodily self-consciousness. *Science, 317*, 1096–1099.

Lennon, J., and Foley, M. (1996) JFK and dark tourism: A fascination with assassination. *International Journal of Heritage Studies, 2*, 198–211.

Levine, D. (2000). Virtual attraction: What rocks your boat. *CyberPsychology & Behavior, 3*, 565–573.

Levine, M. (2001). Depraved spectators and impossible audiences. *Film and Philosophy, 5/6*, 63–71.

Levy, N. (2002). Virtual child pornography: The eroticization of inequality. *Ethics in Information Technology, 4*, 319–323.

Levy, N. (2003). What (if anything) is wrong with bestiality? *Journal of Social Philosophy, 34*, 444–456.

Lichtenstein, S., Gregory, R., and Irwin, J. (2007). What's bad is easy: Taboo values, affect and cognition. *Judgment and Decision Making, 2*, 169–188.

Liebes, T., and Katz, E. (1990). *The export of meaning: Cross-cultural readings of* 'Dallas'. New York: Oxford University Press.

Lifton, R.J. (1993). *The protean self: Human resilience in an age of fragmentation*. New York: Basic Books.

Linsley, W. (1998). The case against censorship of pornography. In R. Baird (Ed.) *Pornography: Private rights or public menace?* (pp. 176–190). Amherst, NY: Prometheus.

Linton, D. (1979). Why is pornography offensive? *Journal of Value Inquiry, 13*, 57–62.

Lisewski, A.M. (2006). The concept of strong and weak virtual reality. *Minds and machines, 16*, 201–219.

Liu, M., and Peng, W. (2009). Cognitive and psychological predictors of the negative outcomes associated with playing MMOGs (massively multiplayer online games). *Computers in Human Behavior, 25*, 1306–1311.

Livingstone, S. (2007). Do the media harm children? Reflections on new approaches to an old problem. *Journal of Children and Media, 1*, 5–14.

Lo, S. (2008). The impact of online game character's outward attractiveness and social status on interpersonal attraction. *Computers in Human Behavior, 24*, 1947–1958.

Lombard, M., and Ditton, T.B. (1997). At the heart of it all: The concept of presence. *Journal of Computer-Mediated Communication, 3*. Retrieved 13 December 2010 from: http://jcmc.indiana.edu/vol3/issue2/

Luck, M. (2009). The gamer's dilemma: An analysis of the arguments for the moral distinction between virtual murder and virtual paedophilia. *Ethics and Information Technology, 11*, 31–36.

Manago, A.M., Graham, M.B., Greenfield, P.M., and Salimkhan, G. (2008). Self-presentation and gender on MySpace. *Journal of Applied Developmental Psychology, 29*, 446–458.

Manning, R.C. (1988). Redefining obscenity. *Journal of Value Inquiry, 22*, 193–205.

Mannison, D. (1985). On being moved by fiction. *Philosophy, 60*, 71–87.

Manovich, L. (2001). *The language of new media*. Cambridge, MA: MIT Press.

Mantovani, G. (1995). Hallucination, fiction, and possible selves: Virtual reality as a communication environment: Consensual. *Human Relations, 48*, 669–683.

Mar, R.A., and Oatley, K. (2008). The function of fiction is the abstraction and simulation of social experience. *Perspectives on Psychological Science, 3*, 173–192.

Marcuse, H. (2005). *Eros and civilization: A philosophical inquiry into Freud.* Oxford: Routledge & Kegan Paul. (Original work published 1956.)

Markey, P.M., and Scherer, K. (2009). An examination of psychoticism and motion capture controls as moderators of the effect of violent video games. *Computers in Human Behavior, 25,* 407–411.

Markus, H., and Nurius, P. (1986). Possible selves. *American Psychologist, 41,* 954–969.

Markus, H., and Ruvolo, A. (1989). Possible selves: Personalized representations of goals. In L.A. Pervin (Ed.), *Goal concepts in personality and social psychology* (pp. 211–241). Hillsdale, NJ: Lawrence Erlbaum Associates, Inc.

McAdams, D.P. (1985). The 'imago': A key narrative component of identity. In P. Shaver (Ed.) *Self, situation, and social behaviour: vol. 6. Review of personality and social psychology* (pp. 115–141). Beverley Hills, CA: Sage Publications.

McAllister, M. (2006). Irreversible movie review. *Future Movies,* 13 December 2006. Retrieved 8 March 2010 from: http://www.futuremovies.co.uk/review.asp?ID=639

McCabe, J. (2007). Rape in second life. *The f word: Contemporary UK feminism.* 30 April 2007. Retrieved 12 June 2009 from: http://www.thefword.org.uk/blog/2007/04/rape_in_second

McCormick, M. (2001). Is it wrong to play violent video games? *Ethics and Information Technology, 3,* 277–287.

McDonald, D.G., and Kim, H. (2001). When I die, I feel small: Electronic game characters and the social self. *Journal of Broadcasting & Electronic Media, 45,* 241–258.

McKenna, K.Y.A., Green, A.S. and Gleason, M.E.J. (2002). Relationship formation on the Internet: What's the big attraction? *Journal of Social Issues, 58,* 9–31.

Meadows, M.S. (2008). *I, Avatar: The culture and consequences of having a second life.* Berkeley, CA: New Riders.

Meerkerk, G.J., Van Den Eijnden, R.J., and Garretsen, H.F. (2006). Predicting compulsive Internet use: It's all about sex! *CyberPsychology & Behavior, 9,* 95–103.

Mellman, K. (2002). E-motion: Being moved by fiction and media? Notes on fictional worlds, virtual contacts and the reality of emotions. *PsyArt,* 1–13 (online journal). Retrieved 30 October 2008 from: http://www.clas.ufl.edu/ipsa/journal/2002_mellmann01.shtml

Merleau-Ponty, M. (1962). *Phenomenology of perception* (C. Smith, trans.). London: Routledge & Kegan Paul. (Original work published 1945.)

Merleau-Ponty, M. (1968). *The visible and invisible* (A. Lingis, trans.). Evanston, IL: Northwestern University Press. (Original work published 1964.)

Metzinger, T. (2004). *Being no one: The self-model theory of subjectivity.* Cambridge, MA: MIT Press.

Metzl, J.M. (2004). Voyeur nation? Changing definitions of voyeurism, 1950–2004. *Harvard Review of Psychiatry, 12,* 127–131.

Mey, K. (2007). Art & obscenity. New York: Palgrave Macmillan.

Milgram, S. (1974). *Obedience to authority.* New York: Harper & Row.

Miller, M.C. (1988). 'Big Brother is you, watching'. In *Boxed in: The culture of TV.* Evanston, IL: Northwestern University Press.

Miller, W.I. (1998). Sheep, joking, cloning and the uncanny. In M.C. Nussbaum and C.R. Sunstein (Eds) *Clones and clones: Facts and fantasies about human cloning* (pp. 78–87). New York: Norton.

Minsky, M. (1980). Telepresence. *OMNI,* 2, 45–51.

Mitchell, E. (2001). Wife hunting is a sick and frightful business. *The New York Times,* 8 August 2010. Retrieved 17 March 2010 from: http://www.nytimes.com/2001/08/08/movies/08AUDI.html

Mitchell, E. (2003). Rape, violence . . . it's O.K. to look away. *The New York Times*, 7 March 2003. Retrieved 8 March 2010 from: http://movies.nytimes.com/movie/review ?res=9E07EFDD133FF934A35750C0A9659C8B63

Modell, A H. (1996). *Other times, other realities: Toward a theory of psychoanalytic treatment*. Cambridge, MA: Harvard University Press. (Original work published 1990.)

Mohney, C. (2006). Second life: Rape for sale. *Valleywag*, 15 December 2006. Retrieved 12 June 2009 from: http://gawker.com/news/second-life/second-life-rape-for-sale-222099.php

Möller, I., and Krahé, B. (2009). Exposure to violent video games and aggression in German adolescents: A longitudinal analysis. *Aggressive Behavior*, *35*, 75–89.

Montag, C. Jurkiewicz, M., and Reuter, M. (2010). Low-self-directedness is a better predictor for problematic Internet use than high neuroticism. *Computers in Human Behavior*, *26*, 1531–1535.

Mooradian, N. (2006). Virtual reality, ontology, and value. *Metaphilosophy*, *37*, 673–690.

Moore, C.M., and Brown, M. (2007). Experiencing Body Worlds: Voyeurism, education, or enlightenment? *Journal of Medical Humanities*, *28*, 231–254.

Morahan-Martin, J., and Schumacher, P. (2000). Incidence and correlates of pathological Internet use among college students. *Computers in Human Behavior*, *16*, 13–29.

Mos, L.P., and Boodt, C.P. (1991). Friendship and play: An evolutionary developmental view. *Theory & Psychology*, *1*, 132–144.

Mueller, F., Stevens, G., Thorogood, A., O'Brien, S. and Wulf, V. (2007). Sports over a distance. *Personal and Ubiquitous Computing*, *11*, 633–645.

Nabi, R.L. (2002). The theoretical versus the lay meaning of disgust: Implications for emotion research. *Cognition and Emotion*, *16*, 695–703.

Namir, S. (2006). Embodiment and disembodiment: The relation of body modification to two psychoanalytic treatments. *Psychoanalysis, Culture and Society*, *11*, 217–223.

Newman, J. (2002). The myth of the ergodic videogame: Some thoughts on player-character relationships in videogames. *Game Studies* [online], *2*, 1–8.

Ng, B.D., and Wiemer-Hastings, P. (2005). Addiction to the Internet and online gaming. *CyberPsychology & Behavior*, *8*, 110–113.

Nichols, S. (2008). Sentimentalism naturalized. In W. Sinnott-Armstrong (Ed.) *Moral psychology: The evolution of morality, volume 2* (pp. 255–274). Cambridge, MA: MIT Press.

Nichols, S., and Mallon, R. (2005). Moral dilemmas and moral rules. *Cognition*, *100*, 530–542.

Novitz, D. (1980). Fiction, imagination and emotion. *Journal of Aesthetics and Art Criticism*, *38*, 279–288.

Nussbaum, M.C. (1992). *Love's knowledge. Essays on philosophy and literature*. Oxford: Oxford University Press.

Nussbaum, M.C. (2004). *Hiding from humanity: Disgust, shame and the law*. Princeton, NJ: Princeton University Press.

Oaten, M., Stevenson, R.J., and Case, T.I. (2009). Disgust as a disease-avoidance mechanism. *Psychological Bulletin*, *135*, 303–321.

Oatley, K. (1994). A taxonomy of the emotions of literary response and a theory of identification in fictional narrative. *Poetics*, *23*, 53–74.

Oatley, K. (1999a). Meeting of minds: Dialogue, sympathy, and identification in reading fiction. *Poetics*, *26*, 439–454.

Oatley, K. (1999b). Why fiction may be twice as true as fact: Fiction as cognitive and emotional simulation. *Review of General Psychology*, 3, 101–117.

O'Brien, J. (1999). Writing in the body: Gender (re)production in online interaction. In M.A. Smith and P. Kollock (Eds) *Communities in cyberspace* (pp. 76–106). London: Routledge.

Ogden, T.H. (1985). On potential space. *The International Journal of Psychoanalysis*, *66*, 129–141.

Ogles, R.M., and Hoffner, C. (1987). Film violence and perception of crime: The cultivation effect. In M.L. McLaughlin (Ed.) *Communication yearbook 10* (pp. 384–394). Thousand Oaks, CA: Sage Publications.

Ogunyemi, O. (2008). No place for cultural taboos in cyberspace. *In Media res: A commons project*, 17 April. Retrieved 1 November 2011 from: http://mediacommons. futureofthebook.org/imr/2008/04/17/no-place-for-cultural-taboo-in-cyberspace

Olson, C.K. (2004). Media violence research and youth violence data: why do they conflict? *Academic Psychiatry*, *28*, 144–150.

Opotow, S. (2007). Moral exclusion and torture: The ticking bomb scenario and the slippery ethical slope. *Peace and Conflict: Journal of Peace Psychology*, *13*, 457–461.

Parés, N., and Parés, R. (2006). Towards a model of virtual reality experience: The virtual reality subjectiveness. *Presence*, *15*, 524–538.

Patel, N. (2006). Medical Foundation urges retailers to boycott violent video games promoting torture (26 July). Retrieved 5 May 2009 from: http://www.freedomfromtorture.org/node/296

Patterson, J. (2009). Out of bounds. *The Guardian*, 2 May 2009. Retrieved 8 March 2010 from: http://www.guardian.co.uk/film/2009/may/02/incest-film-taboos-delta

Peng, W., Lee, M., and Heeter, C. (2010). The effects of a serious game on role-taking and willingness to help. *Journal of Communication*, *60*, 723–742.

Peters, C.S., and Malesky, Jr., L.A. (2008). Problematic usage among highly-engaged players of massively multiplayer online role playing games. *CyberPsychology & Behavior*, *11*, 481–484.

Phillips, M.L., and Sierra, M. (2003). Depersonalization disorder: A functional neuroanatomical perspective. *Stress*, *6*, 157–165.

Piaget, J. (1951). *Play, dreams and imitation in childhood*. New York: Norton.

Piazza, J. (2010). Audiences experience 'Avatar' blues. *CNN Entertainment*, 11 January 2010. Retrieved 28 January 2010 from: http://www.cnn.com/2010/SHOWBIZ/Movies/01/11/avatar.movie.blues/index.html

Plant, S. (1992). *The most radical gesture: The situationist interactional in a postmodern age*. London: Routledge.

Pohl, K. (2008). Ethical reflection and involvement in computer games. In S. Günzel, M. Liebe and D. Mersch (Eds), *Conference proceedings of the philosophy of computer games*, 2008 (pp. 92–107). Berlin: Potsdam University Press.

Polman, H., Orobio de Castro, B., and van Aken, M.A.G. (2008). Experimental study of the differential effects of playing versus watching violent video games on children's aggressive behaviour. *Aggressive Behavior*, *34*, 256–264.

Poole, H. (1982). Obscenity and censorship. *Ethics*, *93*, 39–44.

Porzig-Drummond, R., Stevenson, R., Case, T., and Oaten, M. (2009). Can the emotion of disgust be harnessed to promote hand hygiene? Experimental and field-based tests. *Social Science & Medicine*, *68*, 1006–1012.

Potter, W.J., and Tomasello, T.K. (2003). Building upon the experimental design in media violence research: The importance of including receiver interpretations. *Journal of Communication*, *53*, 315–329.

Powers, T.M. (2003). Real wrongs in virtual communities. *Ethics in Information Technology*, 5, 191–198.

Prinz, J. (2006). The emotional basis of moral judgment. *Philosophical Explorations*, 9, 29–43.

Prinz, J.J. (2007). *The emotional construction of morals*. Oxford: Oxford University Press.

Putnam, R.D. (2000). *Bowling alone: The collapse and revival of American community*. New York: Simon & Schuster.

Radford, C. (1975). How can we be moved by the fate of Anna Karenina? I. *Proceedings of the Aristotlelian Society (Supplementary)*, 49, 67–80.

Radford, C. (1977). Tears and fiction. *Philosophy*, 52, 208–213.

Radley, A. (1998). Displays and fragments: Embodiment and the configuration of social worlds. In H.J. Stam (Ed.) *The body and psychology* (pp. 13–29). London: Sage Publications.

Raman, L., and Gelman, S.A. (2008). Do children endorse psychosocial factors in the transmission of illness and disgust? *Developmental Psychology*, 44, 801–813.

Rheingold, H. (1993). *The virtual community: Homesteading on the electronic frontier*. Reading, MA: Addison-Wesley.

Rollman, J., Krug, K., and Parente, F. (2000). The chat room phenomenon: Reciprocal communication in cyberspace. *CyberPsychology & Behavior*, 3, 161–166.

Ross, S. (2010). TV Networks give public 'sanitized' war coverage. *OpEdNews.com*, 21 January 2010. Retrieved 1 March 2010 from: http://hwww.opednews.com/articles/TV-Networks-Give-Public-S-by-Sherwood-Ross-100119-423.html

Royzman, E.B., and Sabini, J. (2001). Something it takes to be an emotion: The interesting case of disgust. *Journal for the Theory of Social Behaviour*, 31, 29–59.

Royzman, E.B., Leeman, R.F., and Sabini, J. (2008). 'You make me sick': Moral dyspepsia as a reaction to third-party sibling incest. *Motivation and Emotion*, 32, 100–108.

Rozin, P. (1990). Getting to like the burn of chilli pepper: Biological, psychological and cultural perspectives. In B.G. Green, J.R. Mason and M.R. Kare (Eds) *Chemical senses, Volume 2: Irritation* (pp. 231–269). New York: Marcel Dekker.

Rozin, P., and Fallon, A.E. (1987). A perspective on disgust. *Psychological Review*, 94, 23–41.

Rozin, P., and Nemeroff, C. (1990). The laws of sympathetic magic: A psychological analysis of similarity and contagion. In J.W. Stigler, R.A. Shweder and G. Herdt (Eds) *Cultural psychology: Essays on comparative human development* (pp. 205–232). Cambridge: Cambridge University Press.

Rozin, P., and Singh, L. (1999). The moralization of cigarette smoking in America. *Journal of Consumer Behavior*, 8, 321–337.

Rozin, P., Haidt, J., and McCauley, C.R. (1999). Disgust: The body and soul emotion. In T. Dalgleish and M.J. Power (Eds) The handbook of cognition and emotion (2nd edn, pp. 429–445). Chichester: Wiley.

Rudinow, J. (1979). Representation, voyeurism, and the vacant point of view. *Philosophy and Literature*, 3, 173–186.

Russell, G. (2008). Pedophiles in wonderland: Censoring the sinful in cyberspace. *Journal of Criminal Law and Criminology*, 98, 1467–1499.

Ryan, R.M., Rigby, C.S., and Przybylski, A. (2006). The motivational pull of video games: A self-determination theory approach. *Motivation and Emotion*, 30, 347–363.

Rye, B.J., and Meaney, G.J. (2007). Voyeurism: It is good as long as we do not get caught. *International Journal of Sexual Health*, 19, 47–56.

Ryle, G. (1949). *The concept of mind*. London: Hutchinson.

Säätelä, S. (1994). Fictions, make-believe, and quasi emotions. *British Journal of Aesthetics*, *34*, 25–34.

Salen, K., and Zimmerman, E. (2003). *Rules of play*. Cambridge, MA: MIT Press.

Sample, M.L. (2008). Virtual torture: Videogames and the war on terror. *Game Studies*, *8*. Retrieved 8 December 2010 from: http://gamestudies.org/1001/archive

Sanchez-Vives, M., and Slater, M. (2005). From presence to consciousness through virtual reality. *Nature Reviews Neuroscience*, *6*, 332–339.

Sandler, E.P. (2010). Avatar blues? *Psychology Today*, 13 January 2010. Retrieved 28 January 2010 from: http://www.psychologytoday.com/blog/promoting-hope-preventing-suicide/201001/avatar-blues

Schaefer, C. (1993) *The therapeutic powers of play*. Lanham, MD: Jason Aronson.

Scharlott, B.W., and Christ, W.G. (1995). Overcoming relationship-initiation barriers: The impact of a computer-dating system on sex role, shyness, and appearance inhibitions. *Computers in Human Behavior*, *11*, 191–204.

Schmierbach, M. (2010). 'Killing spree': Exploring the connection between competitive game play and aggressive cognition. *Communication Research*, *37*, 256–274.

Schnall, S., Haidt, J., Clore, G.L., and Jordan, A.H. (2008). Disgust as embodied moral judgment. *Personality and Social Psychology Bulletin*, *34*, 1096–1109.

Schouten, A.P., Valkenburg, P.M., and Peter, J. (2007). Precursors and underlying processes of adolescents' online self-disclosure: Testing an 'internet-attribute-perception' model. *Media Psychology*, *10*, 292–315.

Schouten, A., Valkenburg, P., and Peter, J. (2009). An experimental test of processes underlying self-disclosure in computer-mediated communication. *Cyberpsychology: Journal of Psychosocial Research on Cyberspace*, *3*, article 1. Retrieved 12 May, 2011 from: http://www.cyberpsychology.eu/view.php?cisloclanku=2009111601

Schreiber, E.S. (1979). The effects of sex and age on the perceptions of TV characters: An inter-age comparison. *Journal of Broadcasting*, *23*, 81–93.

Schroeder, R. (2006). Being there together and the future of connected presence. *Presence*, *15*, 438–454.

Schulzke, M. (2009). Moral decision making in fallout. *Games Studies*, *9*. Retrieved 8 December 2010 from: http://gamestudies.org/1001/archive

Scott, J.E. (1991). What is obscene? Social science and the contemporary community standard test of obscenity. *International Journal of Law and Psychiatry*, *14*, 29–45.

Shapiro, M.A., and McDonald, D.G. (1992). I'm not a real doctor, but I play one in virtual reality: Implications of virtual reality for judgments about reality. *Journal of Communication*, *42*, 94–114.

Shapiro, M.A., Barriga, C.A., and Beren, J. (2010) Causal attribution and perceived realism of stories. *Media Psychology*, *13*, 273–300.

Shapiro, M.A., Peña-Herborn, J., and Hancock, J.T. (2006). Realism, imagination, and narrative video games. In P. Vorderer and J. Bryant (Eds) *Playing video games: Motives, responses, and consequences* (pp. 275–289). Mahwah, NJ: Lawrence Erlbaum Associates, Inc.

Sherry, J.L. (2001). The effects of violent video games on aggression: A meta-analysis. *Human Communication Research*, *27*, 409–431.

Shibuya, A., Sakamoto, A., Ihori, N., and Yukawa, S. (2008). The effects of the presence and contexts of video game violence on children: A longitudinal study in Japan. *Simulation & Gaming*, *39*, 528–539.

Sicart, M. (2009). *The ethics of computer games*. Cambridge, MA: MIT Press.

Silvern, S.B., and Williamson, P.A. (1987). The effects of video game play on young children's aggression, fantasy, and prosocial behavior. *Journal of Applied Developmental Psychology, 8*, 453–462.

Simkins, D.W., and Steinkuehler, C. (2008). Critical ethical reasoning and role-play. *Games and Culture, 3*, 333–355.

Simmel, G. (1950). *The sociology of Georg Simmel* (K. Wolff Ed. and Trans.). New York: Free Press.

Sims, A. (1995). *Symptoms in the mind*. London: Saunders.

Singh, A. (2009). Brooke Shields nude photograph causes controversy at Tate exhibition. *The Telegraph*, 29 September 2009. Retrieved 20 April 2010 from: http://www.telegraph. co.uk/news/newstopics/celebritynews/6244330/Brooke-Shields-nude-photograph-causes-controversy-at-Tate-exhibition.html

Sky News (2007). Paedophiles target virtual world. 31 October. Retrieved 12 June 2009 from:http://news.sky.com/skynews/Home/Sky-News-Archive/Article/20080641290719

Sky News (2009). Publisher pulls plug on Iraq war video game. 29 April. Retrieved 5 May 2009 from: http://news.sky.com/skynews/Home/World-News/Iraq-War-Video-Game-Called-Six-Days-In-Fallujah-Is-Withdrawn-After-A-Storm-Of-Protest/Article/2009044 15271595?f=rss

Slater, D. (1998). Trading sexpics on IRC: Embodiment and authenticity on the Internet. *Body and Society, 4*, 91–117.

Slater, M., Antley, A., Davison, A., Swapp, D., Guger, C., Baker, C., Pistrang, N., and Maria, V.S. (2006). A virtual reprise of the Stanley Milgram obedience experiments. PLoS ONE, *1*: e39. doi: 10.1371/journal.pone.0000039.

Slattery, B. (2010). Is Chatroulette cleaning up its x-rated act? *Reuters*, 23 August. Retrieved 30 September 2010 from: http://www.reuters.com/article/idUS8898432320100823

Smahel, D., Blinka, L., and Ledabyl, M.A. (2008). Playing MMORPGs: Connection between addiction and identifying with a character. *CyberPsychology & Behavior, 11*, 715–718.

Smith, B.P. (2006). The (computer) games people play. In P. Vorderer and J. Bryant (Eds) *Playing video games: Motives, responses, and consequences* (pp. 43–56). Mahwah, NJ: Lawrence Erlbaum Associates, Inc.

Smyth, J.M. (2007). Beyond self-selection in video game play: An experimental examination of the consequences of massively multiplayer online role-playing game play. *CyberPsychology & Behavior, 10*, 717–721.

Soldz, S. (2008). Healers and interrogators: Psychology and the United States torture regime. *Psychoanalytic Dialogues, 18*, 592–613.

Solomon, R. (1988). On emotions as judgements. *American Philosophical Quarterly, 25*, 183–191.

Solomon, R. (2004). Emotions, thoughts and feelings: Emotions as engagements with the world. In R. Solomon (Ed.) *Thinking about feeling: Contemporary philosophers on emotion* (pp. 76–88). Oxford: Oxford University Press.

Speisman, J.C., Lazarus, R.S., Mordkoff, A., and Davison, L. (1964). Experimental reduction of stress based on ego-defense theory. *Journal of Abnormal and Social Psychology, 68*, 367–380.

Standage, T. (1998). *The Victorian Internet: The remarkable story of the telegraph and the nineteenth century's on-line pioneers*. New York: Walker Publishing Company.

Staude-Müller, F., Bliesener, T., and Luthman, S. (2008). Hostile and hardened? An experimental study on (de)sensitization to violence and suffering through playing video games. *Swiss Journal of Psychology, 67*, 41–50.

Stefanescu, T. (2006). 2Moons aims to be the most violent game ever: 2Moons MMORPG in development for the US market. *Softpedia*, 9 August. Retrieved 2 June 2009 from http://news.softpedia.com/news/2Moons-aims-to-be-the-most-violent-game-on-the-market-32428.shtml

Sternberg, R.J. (2003). A duplex theory of hate: Development and application to terrorism, massacres, and genocide. *Review of General Psychology*, *7*, 299–328.

Stetina, B.U., Kothgassner, O.D., Lehenbauer, M., and Kryspin-Exner, I. (2011). Beyond the fascination of online-games: Probing addictive behavior and depression in the world of online-gaming. *Computers in Human Behavior*, *27*, 473–479.

Steuer, J. (1992). Defining virtual reality: Dimensions determining telepresence. *Journal of Communication*, *42*, 73–93.

Stevenson, S.J., Oaten, M.J., Case, T.I., Pepacholi, B.M., and Wagland, P. (2010). Children's response to adult disgust elicitors: Development and acquisition. *Developmental Psychology*, *46*, 165–177.

Stone, A. (1992). Will the real body please stand up? Boundary stories about virtual cultures. In M. Benedikt (Ed.) *Cyberspace: First steps* (pp. 81–118). Cambridge, MA: MIT Press.

Stone, A. (1996). *The war on desire and technology at the end of the mechanical age.* Cambridge, MA: MIT Press.

Stone, G.R. (2007). Sex, violence, and the first amendment. *The University of Chicago Law Review*, *74*, 1857–1871.

Stone, P.R. (2006). A dark tourism spectrum: Towards a typology of death and macabre related tourist sites, attractions and exhibitions. *Tourism: An International Interdisciplinary Journal*, *54*, 145–160.

Stone, P.R., and Sharpley, R. (2008). Consuming dark tourism: A thanatological perspective. *Annals of Tourism Research*, *35*, 574–595.

Stratton, J. (1997). Not really desiring bodies: The rise and rise of email affairs. *Media International Australia*, *84*, 28–38.

Strauman, T.J., and Higgins, E.T. (1987). Automatic activation of self-discrepancies and emotional syndromes: Cognitive structures influence affect. *Journal of Personality and Social Psychology*, *53*, 1004–1014.

Suhail, K., and Bargees, Z. (2006). Effects of excessive Internet use on undergraduate students in Pakistan. *CyberPsychology & Behavior*, *9*, 297–307.

Suits, D.B. (2006). Really believing in fiction. *Pacific Philosophy Quarterly*, *87*, 369–386.

Suler, J. (1996). *Life at the palace: A cyberpsychology case study.* Retrieved 12 May 2011 from: http://www-usr.rider.edu/~suler/psycyber/palacestudy.html

Suler, J. (2004). The online disinhibition effect. *CyberPsychology & Behavior*, *7*, 321–326.

Super Columbine Massacre RPG (2005). Retrieved 4 August 2010 from: http://www.columbinegame.com/

Sutton-Smith, B. (2001). *The ambiguity of play.* Cambridge, MA: Harvard University Press.

Switzer, R. (1997). Over-writing the body: Virtual reality and Cartesian metaphysics. *Philosophy Today*, *41*, 507–519.

Tait, S. (2008). Pornographies of violence? Internet spectatorship on body horror. *Critical Studies in Media Communication*, *25*, 91–111.

Takatalo, J., Nyman, G., and Laaksonen, L. (2008). Components of human experience in virtual environments. *Computers in Human Behavior*, *24*, 1–15.

Tan, E.S.-H. (1994). Film-induced affect as a witness emotion. *Poetics*, *23*, 7–32.

Tan, T.M. (2007). Beastiality in second life. *Dorks & Losers*, 25 July 2007. Retrieved 12 June 2009 from: http://www.dorksandlosers.com/2007/07/25/beastiality-in-second-life/

Tavinor, G. (2005). Videogames and interactive fiction. *Philosophy and Literature*, *29*, 24–40.

Taylor, A. (2002). Man's sex with goat. *The Sun*, 31 January. Retrieved 13 April 2010 from: http://www.thesun.co.uk/sol/homepage/news/article145635.ece

Taylor, K. (2007). Disgust is a factor in extreme prejudice. *British Journal of Social Psychology*, *46*, 597–617.

Thompson, D., Baranowski, T., Buday, R., Baranowski, J., Thompson, V., Jago, R., and Griffith, M.J. (2010). Serious video games for health: How behavioral science guided the development of a serious video game. *Simulation & Gaming*, *41*, 587–606.

Thomson, R., and Murachver, T. (2001). Predicting gender from electronic discourse. *British Journal of Social Psychology*, *40*, 193–208.

Tidwell, L.C., and Walther, J.B. (2002). Computer-mediated communication effects on disclosure, impressions, and interpersonal evaluations: Getting to know one another a bit at a time. *Human Communication Research*, *28*, 317–348.

Toronchuck, J.A., and Ellis, G.F.R. (2007). Disgust: Sensory affect or primary emotional system? *Cognition and Emotion*, *21*, 1799–1818.

Toronto, E. (2009). Time out of mind: Dissociation in the virtual world. *Psychoanalytic Psychology*, *26*, 117–133.

Turan, K. (2004) The Passion of the Christ. *Los Angeles Times*, 24 February. Retrieved 8 March 2010 from: http://www.calendarlive.com/movies/reviews/cl-et-turan24feb24,2, 3350498.story

Turkle, S. (1995). *Life on the screen: Identity in the age of the Internet*. Cambridge, MA: MIT Press.

Unsworth, G., and Devilly, G.J. (2007). The effect of playing violent video games on adolescents: Should parents be quaking in their boots? *Psychology, Crime and Law*, *13*, 383–394.

Unz, D., Schwab, F., and Winterhoff-Spurk, P. (2008). TV news – The daily horror? Emotional effects of violent television news. *Journal of Media Psychology*, *20*, 141–155.

vanDellen, M.R., and Hoyle, R.H. (2008). Possible selves as behavioral standards in self-regulation. *Self and Identity*, *7*, 295–304.

Van Loon, J. (2008). *Media technology: Critical perspectives*. New York: McGraw-Hill/ Open University Press.

Vignoles, V.L., Manzi, C., Regalia, C., Jemmolo, S., and Scabini, E. (2008). Identity motives underlying desired and feared possible future selves. *Journal of Personality*, *76*, 1165–1200.

von Feilitzen, C., and Linne, O. (1975). Identifying with television characters. *Journal of Communication*, *25*, 51–55.

Vygotsky, L. S. (1986). *Thought and language*. Cambridge, MA: MIT Press. (Original work published 1934.)

Waddington, D.I. (2007). Locating the wrongness in ultra-violent video games. *Ethics and Information Technology*, *9*, 121–128.

Walton, K.L. (1978). Fearing fictions. *Journal of Philosophy*, *75*, 5–27.

Weisbuch, M., Ivcevic, Z., and Ambady, N. (2009). On being liked on the web and in the 'real world': Consistency in first impressions across personal webpages and spontaneous behaviour. *Journal of Experimental Social Psychology*, *45*, 573–576.

Whang, L.S., and Chang, G. (2004). Lifestyles of virtual world residents: Living in the on-line game 'lineage'. *CyberPsychology & Behavior*, *7*, 592–600.

White, A. (2004). The obscenity of Internet regulation in the United States. *Ethics and Information Technology*, *6*, 111–119.

White, A. (2006). *Virtually obscene: The case for an uncensored Internet*. London: McFarland & Company, Inc.

Whitty, M.T. (2002). Liar, liar! An examination of how open, supportive and honest people are in chat rooms. *Computers in Human Behavior*, *18*, 343–352.

Whitty, M.T. (2003a). Cyber-flirting: Playing at love on the internet. *Theory and Psychology*, *13*, 339–357.

Whitty, M.T. (2003b). Pushing the wrong buttons: Men's and women's attitudes towards online and offline infidelity. *CyberPsychology & Behavior*, *6*, 569–579.

Whitty, M.T. (2005). The 'realness' of cyber-cheating: Men and women's representations of unfaithful Internet relationships. *Social Science Computer Review*, *23*, 57–67.

Whitty, M.T. (2007). The art of selling one's self on an online dating site: The BAR approach. In M.T. Whitty, A.J. Baker and J.A. Inman (Eds) *Online matchmaking* (pp. 57–69). Houndmills: Palgrave Macmillan.

Whitty, M.T. (2008a). Revealing the 'real' me, searching for the 'actual' you: Presentations of self on an internet dating site. *Computers in Human Behavior*, *24*, 1707–1723.

Whitty, M.T. (2008b). The joys of online dating. In E. Konjin, T. Martin, S. Utz and A. Linden (Eds) *Mediated interpersonal communication: How technology affects human interaction* (pp. 234–251). New York: Taylor & Francis/Routledge.

Whitty, M.T. (2008c). Liberating or debilitating? An examination of romantic relationships, sexual relationships and friendships on the Net. *Computers in Human Behavior*, *24*, 1837–1850.

Whitty, M.T. (2010). Internet infidelity: A 'real' problem. In K. Young and C. Nabuco de Abrue (Eds) *Internet addiction: A handbook for evaluation and treatment* (pp. 197–212). Hoboken, NJ: John Wiley.

Whitty, M.T., and Carr, A.N. (2003). Cyberspace as potential space: Considering the web as a playground to cyber-flirt. *Human Relations*, *56*, 861–891.

Whitty, M.T., and Carr, A.N. (2005). Taking the good with the bad: Applying Klein's work to further our understandings of cyber-cheating. *Journal of Couple and Relationship Therapy*, *4*, 103–115.

Whitty, M.T., and Carr, A.N. (2006a). *Cyberspace romance: The psychology of online relationships*. Basingstoke: Palgrave Macmillan.

Whitty, M.T., and Carr, A.N. (2006b). New rules in the workplace: Applying object-relations theory to explain problem Internet and email behavior in the workplace. *Computers in Human Behavior*, *22*, 235–250.

Whitty, M.T., and Gavin, J. (2001). Age/sex/location: Uncovering the social cues in the development of online relationships. *CyberPsychology & Behaviour*, *4*, 623–630.

Whitty, M.T., and Joinson, A. (2009) *Truth, lies and trust on the Internet*. Hove: Routledge.

Whitty, M.T., Young, G., and Goodings, L. (2011). What I won't do in pixels: Examining the limits of taboo violation in MMORPGs. *Computers in Human Behavior*, *27*, 268–275.

Wilkinson, J. (2000). The paradox(es) of pitying and fearing fictions. *South African Journal of Philosophy*, *19*, 8–25.

Williams, D. (2005). Bridging the methodological divide in game research. *Simulation & Gaming*, *36*, 447–463.

Williams, D., and Skoric, M. (2005). Internet fantasy violence: A test of aggression in an online game. *Communication Monographs, 22*, 217–233.

Williams, D., Consalvo, M., Caplan, S., and Yee, N. (2009a). Looking for gender: Gender roles and behaviors among online gamers. *Journal of Communication, 59*, 700–725.

Williams, D., Martins, N., Consalvo, M., and Ivory, J.D. (2009b). The virtual census: Representations of gender, race and age in video games. *New Media and Society, 11*, 815–834.

Williams, D., Yee, N., and Caplan, S.E. (2008). Who plays, how much, and why? Debunking the stereotypical gamer profile. *Journal of Computer-Mediated Communication, 13*, 993–1018.

Wilson, D., and Sicart, M. (2010). Now it's personal: On abusive game design. Paper presented at *FuturePlay*, 6–7 May 2010, Vancouver, Canada. Retrieved 15 December 2010 from: http://www.copenhagengamecollective.org/uploads/On%20Abusive%20 Game%20Design%20(web).pdf

Winnicott, D.W. (1971a). *Playing and reality*. New York: Basic Books.

Winnicott, D. W. (1971b). Transitional objects and transitional phenomena. In D.W. Winnicott, *Playing and reality* (pp. 1–25). New York: Basic Books. (Original work published 1951.)

Winnicott, D.W. (1971c). Dreaming, fantasying and living. In D.W. Winnicott, *Playing and reality* (pp. 26–37). New York: Basic Books.

Winnicott, D.W. (1971d). Playing: A theoretical statement. In D.W. Winnicott, *Playing and reality* (pp. 38–52). New York: Basic Books.

Winnicott, D.W. (1971e). The use of an object and relating through cross identifications. In D.W. Winnicott, *Playing and reality* (pp. 86–94). New York: Basic Books. (Original work published 1968.)

Winnicott, D.W. (1971f). The location of cultural experience. In D.W. Winnicott, *Playing and reality* (pp. 95–103). New York: Basic Books. (Original work published 1967.)

Winnicott, D.W. (1971g). The place where we live. In D.W. Winnicott, *Playing and reality* (pp. 104–110). New York: Basic Books.

Wissmath, B., Weibel, D., and Groner, R. (2009). Dubbing or subtitling? Effects on spatial presence, transportation, flow, and enjoyment. *Journal of Media Psychology, 21*, 114–125.

Witmer, B.G., and Singer, M.J. (1998). Measuring presence in virtual environments: A presence questionnaire. *Presence: Teleoperators and Virtual Environments, 7*, 225–240.

Witmer, D., and Katzman, S. (1997). On-line smiles: Does gender make a difference in the use of graphic accents? *Journal of Computer Mediated Communication, 2*. Retrieved 7 February 2005 from http://ascusc.org/jcmc/vol2/issue4/witmer1.html

Wolfendale, J. (2007). My avatar, my self: Virtual harm and attachment. *Ethics and Information Technology, 9*, 111–119.

Wonderly, M. (2008). A humean approach to assessing the moral significance of ultra-violent video games. *Ethics in Information Technology, 10*, 1–10.

Wood, R.T.A. (2008). Problems with the concept of video game 'Addiction': Some case study examples. *International Journal of Mental Health Addiction, 6*, 169–178.

Woods, S. (2004). Loading the dice: The challenge of serious videogames. *Game Studies, 4*. Retrieved 8 December 2010 from: http://gamestudies.org/1001/archive

Wurf, E., and Markus, H. (1991). Possible selves and the psychology of personal growth. In D.J. Ozer, J.M. Healy and A.J. Stewart (Eds) *Perspectives on personality* (vol. 3, pp. 39–62). London: Jessica Kingsley Publishers.

Yee, N. (2006a). Motivations for play in online games. *CyberPsychology & Behaviour, 9,* 772–775.

Yee, N. (2006b). The demographics, motivations and derived experiences of users of massively-multiuser online graphical environments. *PRESENCE: Teleoperators and Virtual Environments, 15,* 309–329.

Yee, N. (2006c). The psychology of massively multi-user online role-playing games: Motivations, emotional investment, relationships and problematic usage. In R. Schoreder and A. Axelsson (Eds) *Avatars at work and play: Collaboration and interaction in shared virtual environments* (pp. 1431–1496). Dordrecht, the Netherlands: Springer.

Yee, N. (2007). Motivations of play in online games. *CyberPsychology & Behavior, 9,* 772–775.

Yee, N., Bailenson, J.N., and Ducheneaut, N. (2009). The proteus effect: Implications of transformed digital self-representation on online and offline behavior. *Communication Research, 36,* 285–312.

Yee, N., Bailenson, J.N., Urbanek, M., Chang, F., and Merget, D. (2007). The unbearable likeness of being digital: The persistence of nonverbal social norms in online virtual environments. *CyberPsychology & Behavior, 10,* 115–121.

Young, A. (2000). Aesthetic vertigo and the jurisprudence of disgust. *Law and Critique, 11,* 241–265.

Young, G. (2010). Virtually real emotions and the paradox of fiction: Implications for the use of virtual environments in psychological research. *Philosophical Psychology, 23,* 1–21.

Young, G., and Whitty, M.T. (2010a). Games without frontiers: On the moral and psychological implications of violating taboos within multi-player virtual spaces. *Computers in Human Behavior, 26,* 1228–1236.

Young, G., and Whitty, M.T. (2010b). In search of the Cartesian self: An examination of disembodiment within 21st century communication. *Theory and Psychology, 20,* 209–229.

Young, G., and Whitty, M.T. (2011a). Progressive embodiment within cyberspace: Considering the psychological impact of the supermorphic persona. *Philosophical Psychology, 24,* 537–560.

Young, G., and Whitty, M.T. (2011b). Should gamespace be a taboo-free zone? Moral and psychological implications for single-player video games. *Theory and Psychology, 21,* 802–820.

Young, K.S. (2004). Internet addiction: A new clinical phenomenon and its consequences. *American Behavioral Scientist, 48,* 402–415.

Yurchisin, J., Watchravesringkan, K., and McCabe, D.B. (2005). An exploration of identity re-creation in the context of Internet dating. *Social Behavior and Personality, 3,* 735–750.

Zagal, J.P. (2009). Ethically notable videogames: Moral dilemmas and gameplay. In B. Atkins, T. Krzywinska and H. Kennedy (Eds) *Proceedings of the Digital Games Research Association international conference (DiGRA) 2009.* London: DiGRA.

Zaner, R.M. (1981). *The context of self.* Athens, OH: Ohio University Press.

Želvys, V.I. (1990). Obscene humor: what the hell? *International Journal of Humor Research, 3,* 323–332.

Zillmann, D. (1971). Excitation transfer in communication-mediated aggressive behavior. *Journal of Experimental Social Psychology, 7,* 419–434.

Zjawinski, S. (2007). Second Life's version of My Little Pony is NSFW. *Wired*, 18 September. Retrieved 12 June 2009 from: http://www.wired.com/underwire/2007/09/second-lifes-ve/

Zornick, G. (2005). The porn of war. *The Nation*, 22 September. Retrieved 24 February 2010 from: http://www.thenation.com/doc/0051010/the_porn_of_war

Notes

2 Virtual immediacy

1 Attempts have been made to police the communication traffic. It is possible, for example, to block a user for a short period if three or more complaints are made within the space of five minutes. Slattery (2010) even mentions the possible use of a scanner that can detect an exposed penis!

3 Disgust

1 They also recognize that the categories they identify are inter-related (i.e. incest fits into both the sexual and moral categories).
2 This is not to say that this is the only reason, or that another reason could not be found articulating why it is wrong.

4 Obscenity

1 F3d 572 (7th Cir 2001).
2 What is judged to be depraved and corrupting must also be weighed against expert opinion regarding the extent to which the material 'is justified as being for the public good on the ground that it is in the interests of science, literature, art or learning, or of other objects of general concern' (Obscene Publications Act 1959, Section 4:1).
3 In fact, Stone cites the case of Paris *Adult Theatre v Staton* in which the court ruled that obscene material be regulated in part because it is harmful.
4 Under US and UK legislation, in the case of material depicting minors engaged in sexual activity, whilst it may be regarded as obscene there is no need to prove obscenity in order to prosecute (Dooley, 1995).
5 The ruling was made in the case of *Ashcroft v Free Speech Coalition*, 525 U.S. 234 (2002), which set out to challenge the Child Pornography Prevention Act 1996, 18 U.S.C. § 2251 (see Kosse, 2004, for an updated discussion).
6 At the time of writing, the Tokyo Metropolitan Government had postponed discussion of the proposal.
7 Bowing to police pressure, the artwork was removed from the exhibition before it opened to the general public.
8 Virtual images are legal in the US irrespective of community standards regarding offence because they are protected under the First Amendment.

5 The passive voyeur

1 Poole (1982) originally discussed this in the context of pornography. However, we consider it a point that merits a broader context.

6 Virtually real emotions

1 Griffiths does distinguish affect program emotional responses from other, 'higher', cognitive-based emotions such as love and grief. These he accepts do require integration with one's consciously held beliefs.

2 Mellman (2002, p. 8) talks of *aesthetic emotions* that are 'not strictly tied to our conviction that these occurrences are of any pragmatic relevance'.

3 Of course, not all virtual interactions, whether immersive or non-immersive, involve *gameplay*. Nevertheless, many do offer increased personal involvement compared to more traditional fiction; and, certainly, many afford the potential for emotional involvement that requires, as a pre-requisite, such involvement. Perhaps the most common form of this currently available is the video game.

4 The study consisted of two conditions. In one, the learner was visible to the participants. In this condition, 12/23 participants had thought about stopping. In the other, the learner was hidden from view and communicated via text only. One out of 11 participants thought about stopping in this condition.

5 Slater *et al.* report such reflective comments in the form of anecdotal evidence.

7 On the nature of play

1 Chatroulette is also likely to provide opportunities for users to engage in what Suler (2004, p. 321) refers to as *benign disinhibition*, in which 'people share very personal things about themselves . . . [such as] secret emotions, fears, wishes'.

2 In certain countries, even a purely virtual genesis would be considered illegal in the case of child images and paedophilia, for example (see Chapter 4).

8 Single-player games

1 After conducting a large-scale content analysis on the race, gender and age of characters in video games, Williams, *et al.* (2009b p. 831) concluded that 'the world of game characters is highly unrepresentative of the actual population and even of game players'. Because of this, they consider the extent to which such bias in character representation may be influencing player impressions of various social group identities.

2 Galloway (2004) draws an interesting distinction between the realisticness of game representation and social realism in games.

3 This change may have beneficial effects, of course, but in the context of STAs, the danger is that it will have the reverse.

9 Multiplayer games

1 *Naughty America: The game* is similarly based on promoting sexual activity as a main (sole?) theme (see also *Red Light World*).

2 A slightly milder version of what we are suggesting here, involving holographic aliens, can be seen in the film *Star Wars*, Episode IV. More recently, *wizard chess* (*Harry Potter and the Philosopher's Stone*) can be seen to convey this idea (again, in a milder form). See also the computer game *Battle Chess* or *Love Chess* (for a more sexual take on the game).

3 Of course, gamers are also members of the offline 'society', so the two groups are not mutually exclusive. In fact, 'through gaming performances, gamers create spectacles, to which they are also an audience' (Crawford and Gosling, 2009, p. 56). However, certain concerns fit within one group more than the other, so a person may flit between the two groups in terms of the perspective from which the concerns are drawn.

4 *Seeking permission* to rape from the soon-to-be-victim raises the question as to whether the act is even virtual rape (as rape is *non-consensual*, except in the case of a minor).

10 Disembodiment

1 Descartes (1997b [1647]): Sixth Meditation, 76.
2 Descartes (1997a [1637]): Discourse on Method, 32.
3 Descartes (1997b [1647]): Sixth Meditation, 78.
4 Descartes (1997b [1647]): Second Meditation, 25.
5 Ibid., 27.
6 Ibid., 81.
7 Ibid.
8 Ibid., 76.
9 Merleau-Ponty (1968 [1964], p. 107) likewise refers to the cogito as an absurd abstraction.
10 Strictly speaking, Descartes conceived of the body as alive, and therefore as animate (and objective).
11 We say this whilst acknowledging Gallagher's (2005a, p. 29) point that certain aspects of my body, as revealed to me by the anatomist, are excluded from my experience – 'certain internal organs, adrenal glands, or the reticular activating system', for example.
12 See Lakoff and Johnson (1999) for a detailed exploration of the 'embodiment issue'.
13 For a different take on embodiment, based on the notion of 'intuitive dualism', see Bloom (2004).
14 Used originally by Zaner (1981).
15 'Cotardian' refers to the Cotard delusion, a form of delusional misidentification in which the subject believes that he/she (his/her body) is dead.
16 It is worth noting, also, that CMC occurs publicly. To explain: one form of CMC – Internet Relay Chat (IRC) – involves real-time communication between the subject and at least one other person. Hence, the disembodied self is a public self and not a private one in the strict Cartesian sense. As Ryle (1949, p. 11) notes: The workings of the Cartesian mind are 'not witnessable by other observers; its career is private'. This is clearly not the case here.
17 Switzer (1997) asks a similar question.
18 We acknowledge that since its peak in the 1990s, discussion on the cyborg body and feminist theorizing around the issue of cyberculture has become much more fragmented; nevertheless, remnants remain – as is evident in the more recent research cited here.
19 The methods employed in the research on online relating predominantly draw on the participant's own experiences as recalled during offline interviews and/or as gleaned from questionnaires. Analysis of the online communication (the text itself) is also undertaken. The research findings are used, here, to offer insight into the user's own *experience* of (dis)embodiment and/or how (dis)embodiment is featured within online discourse.
20 Adapted from Boler (2007, pp. 154–155).

11 Embodiment

1 The body one's consciousness is directed towards should be understood as more than a mere biological entity, or what Gallagher (2005b), following Metzinger (2004), refers to as *Körper*; rather it constitutes the self embodied, or *Leib*.

12 Progressive embodiment

1 It is worth noting that *Second Life*, at the same time as providing individuals with disabilities the opportunity to 'escape' this aspect of their body-image, also provides the opportunity for wheelchairs users (or even more physically able individuals) to create an avatar wheelchair user – called 'Wheelies'.

2 Here 'ideal' should be understood as representing a cultural ideal, and therefore, on our reading, constitutes *idealized*.

3 For an interesting discussion on how virtual technology can inform the perennial problem of the brain-in-the-vat hypothesis, by constituting a complex *physical* source for the production of embodied experience, see Gallagher (2005b).

4 It could be that the VE is a more suitable environment for the realization of one's embodied potential than a non-VE because, by fighting virtual opponents, one is able to engage in a higher level of combat, with a more skilled opponent, than would be practically possible, or even available, in the offline world.

5 We recognize that we are running somewhat roughshod over the quite serious issue of accurately (authentically) simulating the sensory experience of impact and resistance, as well as the equally problematic issue of pain. This brings us back to Fairweather's (2002) point about 'safe' sport being inauthentic sport.

13 Violent games

1 We accept that some changes that occur during the game are going to be a direct result of the content – increased arousal owing to the scenarios depicted, for example, or the success or failure of the character in relation to a particular task, or ultimately the game.

2 Barely legal pornography uses models who are over 18 years of age, but who are depicted as being under or just over the legal age of consent.

3 P300s are event-related potentials that are understood to be a measure of an individual's reaction to a (perceived to be) meaningful/significant stimulus.

14 Psychological parity

1 Smahel *et al.* (2008) speculate that this is because those aged 27 and younger have not yet developed a strong (or as strong) sense of identity.

2 Davis (2001) uses the term *pathological Internet use*; however, in more recent years, the word 'problematic' has typically replaced 'pathological' within the literature discussing his original model and suggested amendments to it (see Caplan, 2002). This convention will be adhered to here. In addition, Davis distinguishes between *specific* problematic Internet use and *generalized* problematic Internet use. Most discussion on PIU has tended to focus on generalized problematic Internet use; only occasionally is this referred to as GPIU (see, for example, Caplan, 2010). Here, PIU refers to what Davis understood to be generalized problematic Internet use.

3 Smahel *et al.* (2008) reported that gamers spend more time playing MMORPGs than other games (see also Peters and Malesky, 2008).

15 Identity and interpretation

1 For further research on gender-related issues, see Greenberg *et al.* (2010), Jenson and de Castell (2010) and Williams *et al.* (2009a).

2 The example of *Second Life* applies to both aspects of one's body-image – namely the self-as-object and the phenomenal self. However, we recognise that *Second Life*, as yet, does not incorporate full immersion technology. Nevertheless, users do experience a certain degree of *presence* within the VE.

Index